Decolonizing Development and Religion

This book was supported by the Council for World Mission (CWM) through its DARE Programme (Discernment and Radical Engagement).

Decolonizing Development and Religion

Theoretical Frameworks, Case Studies and Theological Models

Co-edited by Joerg Rieger and Sanjana Das

scm press

© Council for World Mission 2025

Published in 2025 by SCM Press

Editorial office
3rd Floor, Invicta House,
110 Golden Lane,
London EC1Y 0TG, UK
www.scmpress.co.uk

SCM Press is an imprint of Hymns Ancient & Modern Ltd
(a registered charity)

Hymns Ancient & Modern® is a registered trademark of
Hymns Ancient & Modern Ltd
13A Hellesdon Park Road, Norwich,
Norfolk NR6 5DR, UK

All rights reserved. No part of this publication may be reproduced,
stored in a retrieval system, or transmitted,
in any form or by any means, electronic, mechanical,
photocopying or otherwise, without the prior permission of
the publisher, SCM Press.

The Authors have asserted their right under the Copyright, Designs
and Patents Act 1988 to be identified as the Authors of this Work

British Library Cataloguing in Publication data

A catalogue record for this book is available
from the British Library

ISBN: 978-0-334-06631-6

EU GPSR Authorised Representative
LOGOS EUROPE, 9 rue Nicolas Poussin, 17000, LA ROCHELLE, France
E-mail: Contact@logoseurope.eu

Typeset by Regent Typesetting

Contents

Contributors   vii

Preface   xi
Jooseop Keum

Introduction: Decolonizing Development and Religion for Good   xiii
Joerg Rieger (United States and Germany)

Part 1: Frameworks

1. Cooperatives and Decolonization: Exploring a Key Source of Economic Stability, Solidarity and Survival   3
   Jamin Andreas Hübner (United States)

2. Decolonizing Knowledge Systems in Development and Theology   28
   Sanjana Das (India and Singapore)

Part 2: Case Studies

3. The Liberative Potentials of Philippine *Itneg* Women's Ministry in Reconstructing a Theology of Development   57
   Ma. Glovedi Joy L. Bigornia (Philippines)

4. Motugā'afa: Timely Reflections on Colonial Developments in the Pacific   74
   Faafetai Aiava (Fiji)

5. De-imperializing 'Development as Happiness' by Re-Appropriating *Atepzung*: A Southeast Asian Massif Experience   87
   Shiluinla Jamir (India)

6 The Resilience of Indigenous Women in the Midst of
   Development   103
   Moakumla Longkumer (India)

Part 3: Theological Models

7 'Sola' Mining, 'Sola' Profit, 'Sola' Development Gloria:
   Extractivist Theology and Heretical Spiritualities   127
   Nancy Cardoso (Brazil) (translated by Francis McDonagh)

8 The Brazilian Favelas: Territories that Challenges Us to
   Think about the Meaning of Liberation in Contemporary
   Latin American Neoliberal Society   144
   Priscila Silva (Brazil)

9 Land, Labour and Liberation: Conversion, *Theosis* and
   Material Pneumatology in the Capitalocene   158
   Luke Larner (Great Britain)

Part 4: Specific Challenges

10 Postcolonial Reparation: Reading Fanon with Aquinas for
   Postcolonial Nations' New Humanity   185
   Hendrawan Wijoyo (United States and Indonesia)

11 Freedom of Religion and Expression of Faith for
   Incarcerated LGBTI+ People in Brazil   211
   Heloisa Melino and Fernando Lannes Fernandes (Brazil)

12 Can the Subaltern Code? AI Ethics and Liberation
   Theology   229
   Matthew Elmore (United States)

Contributors

Faafetai Aiava is a Samoan theologian and currently serves as associate professor and Head of the Theology and Ethics Discipline at the Pacific Theological College in Fiji. He has written, presented at international forums, and continues to teach on the intersections of theology, Pasifika hermeneutics and the ethical issues affecting human and other-than-human life.

Ma. Glovedi Joy L. Bigornia is pursuing her PhD in Philosophy of Religion at United Graduate School of Theology (UGST), Yonsei University, South Korea. She is a member of UGST BrainKorea21 (BK21) Four team project entitled 'Reimagining the Future of Religious Education in the Context of Hyperconnectivity' at Yonsei University. She is an indigenous scholar of Itneg-Ilocano descent from Abra, Philippines, whose research works include themes on indigenous spirituality/philosophy, decoloniality, indigenous women studies, post/decolonial feminist theology/philosophy, and feminist phenomenology.

Nancy Cardoso is advisor on theology and popular education in the Pastoral Land Commission (CPT), advisor and activist at the Ecumenical Center for Biblical Studies (CEBI) in the Zona da Mata region of Minas Gerais, Brazil, visiting professor at the Faculty of Theology of the Methodist University of Angola, member of the editorial committee of the *Journal of Biblical Interpretation of Latin America and the Caribbean* (RIBLA), author of *Everyday Prophecy and the Nameless Religion: Popular Religiosity in the Bible* (2015), and collective editor and author in *When My Words Were Stones: Hermeneutics in Solidarity with Palestine* (RIBLA 93(2), 2024).

Sanjana Das is a research scholar, activist and social development practitioner with a deep commitment to work towards promoting transformative praxis to address systemic and structural factors that contribute to an unjust and unequal world for the poor, oppressed and marginalized. Sanjana has worked for over two and a half decades on women's empowerment, human trafficking, child protection, participation, education and livelihood programmes with international development agencies like Catholic Relief Services, ChildFund International, Habitat for Humanity India, Church of North India and Prayas Institute of Juvenile Justice and World Vision India. Sanjana's mission is to work towards advocating and promoting solutions for a just society affirming the dignity and personhood of the vulnerable, trafficked and migrant working women from the Global South.

Matthew Elmore is an ethicist at Duke Health and Duke University School of Medicine, where he works with the AI Evaluation and Governance team. He has led initiatives to engage underrepresented patient communities in AI-related projects and collaborated with partners across institutions to help define national standards for health AI. His research draws from multiple fields and methods, with publications in clinical and translational science, ethics, philosophy and theology.

Jamin Andreas Hübner is a scholar of ethics, religion and economic history, as well as an activist and organizational leader. He is the former Chair of Christian Studies at John Witherspoon College, and currently teaches organizational behaviour at the University of the People, serves as Research Professor of Philosophy, Religion and Economics at LCC International University (Klaipėda, Lithuania), and as a board member of several non-profits and cooperatives.

Shiluinla Jamir is a feminist theologian from India working in the area of decoloniality, everyday ethics and resistance studies. She was previously teaching at the Masters College of Theology, India. She was also a Polin Monograph Fellow at the Inez and Julius Polin Institute for Theological Research, Abo Akademi University, Finland. She is currently working on a book titled *Feminist Ethics in the Northeast India Borderlands*.

Luke Larner, a bricklayer for ten years, is now part-time priest-in-charge of the diverse parish of St Andrew in Luton, England, and is studying for a doctorate in practical theology at the University of Roehampton, researching the Holy Spirit, mission and community organizing in the Church of England. Influenced by the radical Anglo-Catholic and liberation theology traditions, Luke's faith and ministry are shaped by a weaving of sacraments and social justice. Luke's first book was the edited volume *Confounding the Mighty: Stories of Church, Social Class and Solidarity* (2023).

Moakumla Longkumer is an associate professor at Allahabad Bible Seminary (India) in the Christian Ministry and Psychology Department. She is the author of *Loneliness and Anxiety: A Psycho-Pastoral Analysis* (2023), *Bridging Pastoral Functions with Psychological Therapies: Client-Centred Therapy, Transactional Analysis, REBT, and Logotherapy*, which is under publication. Her latest article is 'Hope in Times of Uncertainty: Pastoral Initiative for Transformation' in *Journey in Faith, Hope and Unity: Indian Christian Conversation* (2024).

Heloisa Melino is an Independent Consultant on gender and decolonial studies and holds a PhD. Her co-author, **Fernando Lannes Fernandes**, is a Reader in Youth and Community Work at the University of Dundee, Scotland.

Joerg Rieger is Distinguished Professor of Theology, Cal Turner Chancellor's Chair of Wesleyan Studies, and Director of the Wendland-Cook Program in Religion and Justice at Vanderbilt University. He is author and editor of 27 books, including *Theology in the Capitalocene: Ecology, Identity, Class, and Solidarity* (2022) and *Jesus vs. Caesar: For People Tired of Serving the Wrong God* (2018). His works have been translated into Portuguese, Spanish, Italian, Croatian, German, Malayalam, Korean and Chinese.

Priscila Silva recently completed her PhD at the Methodist University of São Paulo. She is author and editor of books that seek to identify the role of religion in society, including *Religion and Violence in the Favela* (2020) and *New Dictionary of Protestantism in Brazil* (2024). Priscila works as editor-in-chief for an academical publisher, focused on religion, ecumenism and interreligious dialogue.

Hendrawan Wijoyo is a recent graduate of Duke Divinity School's Master of Theological Studies programme. Before coming to Duke, he earned his BTh in his home country of Indonesia and served as associate pastor for seven years there. His research interests include the intersections of Christian ethics with Christian political economy, political theology and theological anthropology, and virtue ethics.

Preface

This book is fruit of the work of the Council for World Mission (CWM). From its very beginning, the mission of CWM has extended beyond the confines of worship and faith communities, into public arenas where services relating to education, health, welfare and ecology are provided, assessed and re-envisioned. Since the 1970s, CWM has wrestled with how to decolonize mission globally and locally – its praxis, pedagogy and theory – and how to proclaim fullness of life at a time when all of life is threatened.

CWM is committed to radical discipleship and prophetic spirituality. Through the Discernment and Radical Engagement (DARE) Programme, CWM conveys its prophetic role in the present socio-political, economic, ecological and global landscapes. DARE is inspired by liberation theologies that have emerged from the diverse context of struggles, its praxis, pedagogies and theories; and it explores, shares, transforms and tries to make sense of divinities, scriptures, traditions, responsibilities, destinies, practices, experiences, biases. DARE is open to the signs of the times and committed to the mission from the margins. Engagement with the margins is the first step for mission, theology and the ecumenical movement to manifest their radical, liberating, decolonizing spirits.

DARE and liberation theologies are radically interdisciplinary, interreligious and intersectional in their approach. This accompanies the shifts in academic trends, but transcends those trends to root DARE in praxis, pedagogies and theories of struggles for liberation, decolonization and counter-imperial testimonies. As DARE is one of the key priorities of CWM's missiological discernment, I hope this series of publications out of Global DARE Conferences will inspire, encourage and empower mission, theology and movements towards liberation and reconciliation!

Revd Dr Jooseop Keum
CWM General Secretary

Introduction: Decolonizing Development and Religion for Good

JOERG RIEGER

Discourses of development have been part of the modern world, for good or for ill. In the past, various colonialisms have been justified by the notion of development, but so have efforts to provide alternatives to colonization. Historically, a complex picture emerges. During the heydays of the Spanish Conquest in the sixteenth century, the Spanish friar Bartolomé de las Casas argued against conquistadorial violence and for what he considered the development of advanced Native capacities. In the early nineteenth century in Prussia (which did not have colonies yet), the liberal theologian Friedrich Schleiermacher followed the colonial fantasy of his age that dreamed of developing and educating humanity, in contrast to colonial violence, greed and callousness, which he saw at work in the colonial projects of other nations, including Spain, Britain and Holland.[1] And in the mid-twentieth century, self-styled international theologies of development proceeded under the assumption that the flourishing of so-called 'underdeveloped' countries was just around the corner.

While postcolonial and decolonial critiques of development are as old as the idea of development itself, critiques deepened and came into their own during anti-colonial struggles that emerged at different times in various parts of the world. Nineteenth-century movements in Latin America and twentieth-century movements in Africa, for instance, ended various forms of colonialism, accompanied by multiple decolonial critiques that continue to be valuable today. And while theological critique was never completely absent, starting in the 1960s and 1970s, theologians joined postcolonial and decolonial critiques with greater resolve and clarity. Latin American liberation theology, for instance, emerged as a full-blown critique of the theology of development, and today various decolonial and postcolonial theologies continue to challenge and transform the theological landscape.[2]

JOERG RIEGER

The underside of development and the role of religion

Perhaps the most basic question that needs to be raised in any discourse of development is: Who developed the so-called 'developed world' that seeks to present itself as the model of development? Postcolonial and decolonial perspectives remind us of the role colonized peoples played and continue to play in the development of the fortunes of the colonizers. Enslavement of indigenous people around the world produced wealth and power for the slave masters, with various outcomes. Recall that African slaves were brought to the Latin Americas because they were considered to be more productive and resilient in harsh working conditions than the Native Americans. In addition, raw materials extracted from the so-called 'peripheries' in the Global South were used in the 'development' of what are still considered the 'centres' of the Global North. This includes not just metals, rare earths, fossil fuel, agricultural products but also cultural raw materials, including faith. Even today, many Christians in the North visiting the Global South keep reporting about how much they have been 'enriched' by the seemingly genuine and simple expressions of faith they find there. The economic metaphor is no accident.

Add to this that even within the so-called 'developed world' most people are contributing to the development of others more than to their own. Construction workers, for instance, are building the architectural monuments of our time that bear the names of others who also siphon off most of the profit – most famously perhaps the various Trump towers in major cities of the United States, but then there also various 'World Trade Centres' that conveniently erase all traces of the fact that at the heart of everything is always labour. Not even religions or their sacred texts ever fell from the sky but were produced in various contexts and conditions, often without crediting those who worked the hardest in producing and transmitting them – just think of the thousands of scribes who kept copying the texts of the Bible before the invention of the printing press. Service workers of all trades can tell similar stories about contributing to the development of others, often at the expense of their own development.

Under the conditions of capitalism, it is the role of the working majority in both the Global South and the North, whether they are employed formally or informally or whether they are performing productive or reproductive labour, to produce profits that accrue to small minorities at the very top. This does not, of course, mean that the 99 per cent who have to work for a living are all alike, and we should not forget the growing number of those who are excluded from capitalist production altogether, especially in the Global South. The point is, however, that even those who enjoy certain comforts in the so-called 'middle class' are not the ones for whom the lion's share of the profit of development is produced. As I have argued elsewhere, there are various levels of privilege among the working majority, but what ties this majority together is an odd lack of power to change things, which is often obscured by the confusion of privilege and power (Rieger, 2022, ch. 4).

In these developments, religion is not a sideshow but feeds back into maintaining and expanding the structures of the status quo. While it is not necessary to claim, with Max Weber, that the 'Spirit of Protestantism' created capitalism – a classical argument that betrays a certain idealism and lacks a more profound analysis of power – there is an interdependence between capitalism and religious developments that is increasingly the subject of study by scholars of theology and religion (Sung, 2011; Cox, 2016; Tran, 2021; Rieger, 2022).

Emerging resistance and alternatives

From these initial reflections three points emerge that deserve further investigation and reflection, each linked to deepened understandings of religion.

First, those who work for the development of others are never in the minority but always in the majority, providing a new sense of what religion might be. This is perhaps the most fervently guarded secret of the dominant powers as it presents the most dangerous threat do dominant interests. Consequently, the dominant powers fight any emerging solidarity of the working majority at every turn. The most well-known method for defeating broad-based solidarities are so-called divide-and-conquer strategies. In the United States, this meant dividing black sharecroppers and white sharecroppers early on, in seventeenth-century Virginia before the onset of chattel slavery, and it continues by playing off against each other white workers and black and brown workers today, as well as male and female workers. This strategy is further expanded by playing off workers in the Global North and workers in the Global South, and finally workers in the South from other workers in the South. The mechanisms of divide-and-conquer are well known: racism, ethnocentrism, sexism, nationalism and so on. Religion too has come in handy for cutting down to size the majority, by dividing people into different factions and denominations and even by making up modern categories of religion that are drawing lines where none existed.[3]

The mechanism operating in the background is what I have come to call 'unite and conquer' (Rieger, 2022, pp. 156–8). Take the example of religion: in a context where Christianity is dominant, Christian workers are supposed to have more in common with their Christian bosses than their non-Christian co-workers. As a result, the non-Christian co-workers are conquered, but so are the Christian workers as well, as their envisioned affinity to the boss does not stop the boss from being the boss and exploiting their work. To be sure: this is not because the boss is somehow a bad person but because this is the nature of capitalism. The same can be shown for race and gender. White supremacy, for instance, unites white people not only in order to conquer all non-white people but also in order to conquer most white people who (mistakenly) identify with their white bosses rather than with fellow non-white workers. In this context, any identity politics that takes these false identities for granted and fights back directly without looking at the bigger picture will feed into the problem, as it now pits workers against workers according to their assumed identities without considering the role of the bosses and the structures of capitalism. In sum, without addressing the coloniality of capitalist development and its efforts to unite and conquer, no real liberation can take place, and religion gets stuck even more.

Unfortunately, even seemingly progressive identity politics and theologies can play into this dominant scheme by reducing anti-colonial struggles to concerns of minorities rather than majorities or to concerns of specific identity groups over other identity groups.

Second, the various forms of labour that go into development (productive, reproductive, reserve and even excluded/informal labour) are systematically exploited, but this is also the place of potential resistance and solidarity among the many who are condemned to serving the development of the few. Consider that there has never been a more diverse population in the history of the world than the working majority, and there may be no more inspiring place from which to rethink religion, both interreligiously and intrareligiously.

Before talking about resistance and solidarity that emerge here, let's take a quick look at the varieties of labour and the tremendous diversity of the working majority. It would be a grave mistake to think about working people primarily in terms of men working in factories or offices. The definition of the proverbial '99 per cent', which came out of the Occupy Wall Street movement in the United States in 2011, was built on the understanding that 99 per cent of the population have to work for a living. This ranges from regularly compensated productive labour that includes some benefits to informal labour that tends to be struggling, to totally uncompensated reproductive labour that is typically performed by women, enslaved people and other-than-human nature. In Latin America in the 1990s the term 'the excluded' was coined to give expression to the fact that large numbers of people were totally excluded from the formal economy, and this trend is still on the rise today. This phenomenon is linked to Marx's notion of the 'reserve army of labour', which is useful to the capitalist economy because it keeps pressure on those who are currently employed, reminding them that they can always be replaced.

As a result of these developments, labour and working people are fragmented. At the same time, working people are also held together by the demands of capitalism: reproductive labour, although often uncompensated, is the absolute foundation on which everything rests and which undergirds any form of 'development', typically without being accounted for (an 'externality', just like environmental resources). Note that there would no productive labour and no development without reproductive labour, but this is exactly what accounts for the connection of all who work, a fact that the ruling class would prefer to keep quiet. Even the informal labour of the so-called 'reserve army' is needed to maintain pressure on the productive workforce and to provide cheap support from the informal economy whenever convenient. To be sure, there are various levels of privilege involved here, which can be substantial: the most privileged workers are better off than those with the least privileges, workers in the Global North tend to be better off than workers in the Global South (even within the north and south of the United States), but none of this privilege translates directly into power. In the capitalist system, all who work for a living were never meant to acquire the power of those who control the system. This insight is what can help build solidarity among the 99 per cent, which, as already noted, is the most diverse conglomerate of humans the planet has ever seen, including any imaginable difference along the lines of gender, sexuality, race, skin colour, ethnicity, geographical location and so on. Unlike the solidarity of capitalists that is built at the top and closely restricted by gated neighbourhoods and country clubs, the solidarity of the working majority is built from the bottom and open ended, starting with the experiences of the excluded and those most exploited, which accounts for a very different feel.[4] Effective resistance is rooted and can become real in this solidarity only from below, and here religion is fundamentally reshaped, preparing the way for ecumenical and interreligious solidarity that is now no longer a luxury for those who have leisure and interest but absolutely necessary if progress is to be made.

Third, the alternative energy that emerges here from people and the planet is too often overlooked, mistaken for the energy of the dominant powers rather than the energy of the working majority. As a result, the stories of great leaders are told as if they were the main actors. Caesar supposedly launched the Roman Empire and built up Rome, Columbus discovered and explored America and so on; this myth persists even in the world of social movements, as if Martin Luther King Jr was single-handedly responsible for the Civil Rights Movement or Nelson Mandela somehow launched the post-Apartheid South Africa. But none of these social movements emerged and unfolded without the agency of thousands of active participants, often women instead of men, who have remained nameless for the longest time, until recently. And regarding the empires: they were all built on the shoulders of the masses and on their productivity, without exception. This is true for the churches as well: for every landmark church or basilica, ancient or modern, ask who were the people who built it and notice the contrast to the names it bears and to whose statues it proudly displays.

What we want to know, then, is whose energy emerges in developmental and colonial projects, and how this energy can be harnessed differently from the transformation of colonial and neocolonial domination and redirected. The chapters of this book present substantial examples that witness to this energy. But we need to ask ourselves three fundamental questions:

1 How does this alternative energy manifest itself and make a difference? This is the question of an actual assessment of how resistance emerges and how alternatives emerge, not as utopias or figments of the imagination but as embodied realities, however small and insignificant they might seem at first sight.
2 How can this alternative energy organize itself and how can it be harnessed for the transformation of colonial and neocolonial domination? In other words, how can relationships of actual solidarity be formed among these various examples? Without solidarity, the old divide-and-conquer methods will make sure that the system is rarely threatened. Today, this can happen even when certain forms of identity politics promote microresistances and small-scale projects that are celebrated and lifted up ('I hear you, I see you') but not organized.
3 How does this alternative energy redefine religion? If we're agreed that this energy is bigger than any one person or group, might it point to divine energy in a way that the dominant energy does not?

This would lead to radical reversals of everything, for divine energy is commonly identified with dominant rather than subaltern energies.

The structure of the project

In this volume, present-day development and decolonial discourses are engaged together from a plurality of perspectives from various continents around the globe by a variety of authors. In the chapters that follow, the work of younger scholars enters into conversation around specific communities that exist in the interstices and tensions of traditional and capitalist economies and religions, providing models of flourishing that produce alternatives to the prevalent neoliberal capitalist models of development that are wedded to neocolonial economic, political and religious structures. The diversity of voices and approaches in this volume is inspiring not merely for the sake of demonstrating the multiplicity of alternatives and active forms of resistance; this kind of diversity points towards synergies and possible solidarities yet to be explored and deepened.

The case studies presented in this book come to fruition in light of the theoretical frameworks presented in some of the other chapters, which include new assessments of generative places on the underside of development, cooperative developments, resistance to extraction, and knowledge production. The case studies also raise new questions and produce new insights for theological models in Part 3. In the final part, the book presents specific challenges for the present and future that range from intersectional concerns, including the lives of LGBTQIA+ communities in specific contexts, the urgency and dangers of the exponential growth of artificial intelligence (AI), and questions for the future of theology and the life of faith.

Yet in many ways this work is only beginning. Solidarity is on the horizon, but the various examples need to be connected and organized in the light of deeper understandings of what we are up against. Mere celebrations of diversity, so common in many theological and religious enterprises at present, are not sufficient if we face both exploitation and extraction, which together make up the reality of life in the Capitalocene that endangers both people and planet.[5] Merely living in alternative communities is not sufficient if these ways of life are not connected to other ways of life, both locally and globally. Don't forget that the dominant system has always found ways to assimilate small groups, whether by romanticizing or by devouring them.

The chapters of the book

Jamin Andreas Hübner, in Chapter 1, explores the role of cooperatives in decolonial forms of development. In the process, he points out that worker cooperatives in particular provide real alternatives to the dominant economy of capitalism, exchanging the motive of personal profit for the holistic flourishing of all. Cooperative development in Indonesia, Central America and Palestine shows the powerful reality of cooperatives, in conjunction with Islam (Indonesia) and liberation theology (Central America), as well as interreligious solidarity (Palestine). Returning to two examples from the United States, Hübner demonstrates the value of what he calls a 'gradual revolution'.

In chapter 2, Sanjana Das draws attention to the need for decolonization of knowledge systems by critiquing the dominant anti-trafficking campaign and presenting her research that has given epistemic privilege to trafficked and migrant working women in India. She draws attention to the indecent marginalization of women in the informal economy within the structures of global capitalism where the workers of the world are exploited and their voices for justice unheard. Das identifies an epistemic advantage of subaltern women and examines their implications for discourses of theology and development in a context where it is still mostly taken for granted that primarily western 'experts' decide the course of action. The result of engaging the struggles together is what she calls 'just solidarity'. Her notion of just solidarity includes building epistemological relationships with subalterns, to be aware of their context and realities from their standpoint and to look for long-term sustainable economic and justice-orientated solutions together.

Glovedi Joy L. Bigornia in Chapter 3 presents the case study of a mother-based economy found among Christian indigenous women from the *Itneg* group in the Philippines who strive for economic development of their communities through collaborative indigenous practices. She argues that the existence of such liberative decolonial feminist spaces redefines the ontologies and epistemologies of the colonized and protects the indigenous communities from the total annihilation of being and thinking, despite being victims of development aggressions such as encroachment of ancestral lands, exploitation of natural resources, and displacements. By sharing *Itneg* women's engagements within the church and beyond, she shares crucial contributions towards a life-giving theology of development for all.

Chapter 4 by Faafetai Aiava introduces alternative ways of life that have proved themselves for hundreds of years. Slowing down time and frugality in Pacific cultures, for instance, provide viable ways of life that have the potential to challenge the current economic system at its very core. Not only is the focus not the neoliberal capitalist maximization of profit at all costs, the focus is also not primarily individual schemes of well-being and salvation that are so endemic in globalized ways of life. Agency, in this model, accrues to communities, both human and other-than-human, for the benefit of the many rather than the few.

Shiluinla Jamir takes us to Northeast India in Chapter 5, engaging women in the Southeast Asian Massif and their skills in dealing with the forces of neoliberal capitalism. In the hands of women weavers, crafts and hand looms become tools of resistance against well-meaning efforts at development both from the state and religious communities. Making use of new markets in urban centres serving city-dwellers and tourists, these women revitalized an ancient craft that was almost abandoned, working collaboratively rather than in competition, reclaiming their homegrown and gendered skills and a creative spirit.

The lives of Ao-Naga women are the focus of Moakumla Longkumer in Chapter 6. Their resilience and agency present another perspective of alternative development. In the process, Naga women made the educational system once introduced by American Baptist missionaries work for themselves, and empower themselves by engaging in agriculture, crafts and running small businesses. What makes these women succeed is their adaptability in the challenges of male-dominated communities and the modern economy, maintaining the kinds of communities and networks that provide real alternatives.

In Chapter 7, Nancy Cardoso engages extractive projects, with specific reference to mining and usurpation of land in Latin America, where corporations produce sacred narratives along with technological solutions to legitimize their strategies of controlling nature, communities and territories. With capitalism as a religion and intensive mining as the main colonial business that exploits ecosystems and disrupts the conditions of life, theologies of liberation are faced with challenges of opposing the gods of patriarchy and racist capitalism. Cardoso emphasizes the need to understand forms of resistance and 'embodied' living that can bring together dimensions of the spiritualities of women engaged in the struggle.

In Chapter 8, Priscila Silva is rethinking liberation theology from the perspectives of Brazilian favelas in the context of neoliberal capitalism, where exploitation and domination are taken to the extreme. The pressures of this context affect not only the economic and political but also the mental well-being of the residents, which is where liberation theology can make a difference, increasingly picking up and engaging Pentecostal and Evangelical positions rather than the traditional Roman Catholic ones. What emerges is a new sense of dignity and self-worth among the poorest of the poor and a sense that God is with them.

Luke Larner, in Chapter 9, presents the case of the Church of England, its illicit enclosure of common lands and labour in England, and the colonization and exploitation of land and labour in the majority world, which includes the enslavement of indigenous people. Larner argues that the rise of neocolonial capitalism leads to further liberation and decolonial struggles, particularly around class and labour, along with efforts to preserve our mother earth. He invites the larger human family to join the ongoing transformative work of the Spirit of conversion and *theosis* and thereby to enter into the deep solidarity of working for the liberation of land and labour together.

Hendrawan Wijoyo develops an argument putting in conversation Frantz Fanon and Thomas Aquinas in Chapter 10, addressing reparations as one of the major challenges of postcolonial development. In the process, Wijoyo engages complex questions of Fanon's notions of a new humanity as well as his endorsement of violent processes of decolonization, while denouncing indiscriminate violence. What emerges are conversations about reparations that are not primarily backward looking but orientated towards the future, pulling together Aquinas' dual emphases on justice and charity with a radical edge. The result is a decolonial approach that demands the redistribution of wealth because 'undistributed inequality is iniquity'.

Heloisa Melino and Fernando Lannes Fernandes, in Chapter 11, present findings of a research project focusing on LGBTQIA+ persons in detention in Brazil with the purpose of understanding their human rights concerns and the development of national and international policy frameworks. The study notes that religion can be a space of comfort inside prisons, as visiting religious leaders are the only human contact to the outside. However, religious teachings that demonize homosexuality and push conversions leave many inmates feeling violated. By sharing testimonies and lived experiences of incarcerated LGBTQIA+ populations, the authors highlight domestic, structural and institutional violence and propose alternate models of care with progressive religious groups, human rights defenders and formerly incarcerated LGBTQIA+ people. The conclusion calls for a different theological approach that engages solidarity, humanity, love, affection and faith with an appreciation for diversity.

In Chapter 12, Matthew Elmore approaches AI from a subaltern perspective, offering a critical view of the ways AI can overlook or exploit marginalized communities. Focusing on the agricultural sector in India and the exploitation of data workers in Kenya, he explores how AI development risks reinforcing systems of power that alienate local labour from traditional knowledge. Elmore argues for new incentive structures that empower developers in low-income countries to work with their communities on AI projects, while cautioning against imposing codable frameworks on non-codifiable knowledge, drawing from Spivak's concept of 'learning to learn from below'.

In conclusion, as these authors work their ways through specific issues, exploring sociological, political, economic, religious and theological aspects of alternative developments, a deeper sense emerges of the fact that another world is indeed possible, as the World Social Forums have been proclaiming for many years. Reading through these contributions it should be clearer that religion, theology and the praxis of faith have essential roles to play and that much is happening already that points to viable alternatives.

In conversation with these chapters, new questions will have to be raised, for instance about the relation of the stunning productivity of people and planet to the stark inequality of distribution, the relation of alternative developments in religion to political and economic developments, the relation of micro and macro levels, the relation of reforms and revolutions, the relations of minorities and majorities (with the ultimate majority being people and planet who experience exploitation and extraction), and so on. The first and last question is what we are ultimately up against. Is it merely exclusion that could be fixed by inclusion, inhospitality that could be fixed by hospitality, unwillingness to recognize difference versus willingness to recognize it? Or are we up against something more systemic and sinister that has the potential to kill at least 99 per cent of us while fewer than 1 per cent escape to their respective safe havens? Answers are not as elusive as some make it seem, but we will only find them if we dare to pursue and deepen the questions. *Per aspera ad astra.*

Notes

1 For Las Casas and Schleiermacher, see Rieger, 2007, chapters 3 and 5.
2 While postcolonial critiques began earlier in the field of biblical studies, often identified with the work of pioneers like R. S. Sugirtharajah and Fernando

Segovia, the volume that inaugurated this work in theological studies was not published until 2004: see Keller, Nausner and Rivera, 2004.

3 Tomoko Masuzawa, 2005. Hinduism is often referenced as an example, but talk about 'world religions' in general is a modern invention.

4 See my notion of deep solidarity in Rieger, 2022, chapter 4.

5 See Joerg Rieger, 2024, 'Extraction, Exploitation, and Religious Surplus in the Capitalocene', forthcoming in *Religions* 15(1233), pp. 1–13, https://doi.org/10.3390/rel15101233.

References

Cox, H., 2016, *The Market as God*, Cambridge, MA: Harvard University Press.
Keller, C., Nausner, M. and Rivera, M., 2004, *Postcolonial Theologies: Divinity and Empire*, St Louis, MO: Chalice Press.
Masuzawa, T., 2005, *Invention of the World Religions: Or, How European Universalism was Preserved in the Language of Pluralism*, Chicago, IL: University of Chicago Press.
Rieger, J., 2007, *Christ and Empire: From Paul to Postcolonial Times*, Minneapolis, MN: Fortress Press.
Rieger, J., 2022, *Theology in the Capitalocene: Ecology, Identity, Class, and Solidarity*, Minneapolis, MN: Fortress Press.
Sung, J. M., 2011, *The Subject, Capitalism, and Religion: Horizon of Hope in Complex Societies*, New York: Palgrave Macmillan.
Tran, J., 2021, *Asian Americans and the Spirit of Racial Capitalism*, London: Oxford University Press.

PART I

Frameworks

I

Cooperatives and Decolonization: Exploring a Key Source of Economic Stability, Solidarity and Survival

JAMIN ANDREAS HÜBNER

Introduction

This article originated from a brief talk at the 'Development and Decoloniality' portion of the 2023 DARE Forum in Bangkok, Thailand. As it turned out, it was this simple section title that prompted me to explore the subject of cooperative economics. 'Development' and 'Decoloniality', however, would not normally bring cooperatives and cooperative economics to many minds. This paper will explain why it should.

The cooperative movement means different things to different people and is largely contingent on local experiences. For some, 'cooperative' means niche, local shops run by hippies. For others, 'cooperative' means the local grain elevator in rural farmland. For others, 'cooperative' means a particular economic and social model that contrasts with capitalist competition. Still for others, 'cooperative' means a local housing unit down the street, or a group of parents who share homeschooling responsibilities.

From a global and historical perspective, however, it might be portrayed as at least a two-century success story of how ordinary workers and community members can work together to develop more ethical, sustainable and locally helpful alternatives to both industrial capitalism and revolutionary communism. This is not to say the cooperative movement is disconnected from either or is diametrically opposed to either. On the contrary, what makes the cooperative movement particularly interesting is its ability to work within various socio-political forms, and its interconnectedness with countless other movements – whether revolutionary, reformational, religious, financial development,

development of education, anarchism, Marxism, communism, colonialism and decolonialism, class solidarity and so on.

Cooperatives nevertheless suffer from stereotypes. They are, for example, often thought of as small self-help organizations and considered aloof from the 'higher' or more risky endeavours of liberation, decolonialization and global change. But as we will see, this is not the case. Cooperatives have functioned in a variety of ways in relation to development and decolonization and, indeed, served as a platform or interface for developing effective ways of liberation. The purpose of cooperatives has always been liberation of some kind – most immediately, from the dehumanizing conditions of industrialism and life under the control of employers and investors. But because of the inherently intersectional nature of such economic conditions, cooperatives immediately connect with political and religious liberative movements as well.

To demonstrate this thesis, I'll first begin with some remarks about cooperatives and their economic and social roles before looking at three case studies, which reveal important relationships between cooperatives, religion and liberation, and therefore the complex and creative role that cooperatives play in social change.

Capitalism and cooperative economics

There are broader and narrower definitions to 'cooperative economics' and 'cooperatives'. In its broadest sense, cooperative economics might be conceived as the default arrangement for much (though not all) of our species: tribes and indigenous communities cooperating to survive – such as joint hunting and gathering efforts, pooling resources and redistributing them according to need, and respecting life in general (insofar as material conditions allow). Special attention is often given to the elderly and needy; absolute private property is not a legal or socially enforced institution; land and nature is conceived as something given to a people, or given to all peoples of the earth from a deity or higher power.

A more formal and recent understanding of cooperative economics centres on organizations that are owned and run by their members – whether consumers, producers or workers. This means profits are shared by members and decisions that affect members are generally made as a group and by the assembly. Resources are pooled and redistributed within each firm (that is, productive unit or 'business'). This stands in direct contrast to ordinary capitalist firms that are owned by business owners/employers/capitalists, which is where profits and decision-making power are located. A still more specific – and yet still global and historically grounded – understanding of cooperatives are those firms that abide by the International Cooperative Alliance's Seven Principles (1995).[1]

Cooperatives can be found in virtually any political and social environment – and, indeed, have been found throughout the globe in the last two centuries. It is notable that they coexist within capitalist and market-based societies because of their utilization of such things as (1) contract law, (2) principles of accounting and (3) markets. For this reason (appearing too 'soft'), some progressives and Marxists see limited value in cooperatives for changing anything systemic and economy-wide. However, as mentioned above, cooperatives do clash with capitalist economies and their most basic form of business (see the figure below), and do so on a scale that depends on their adoption throughout society.

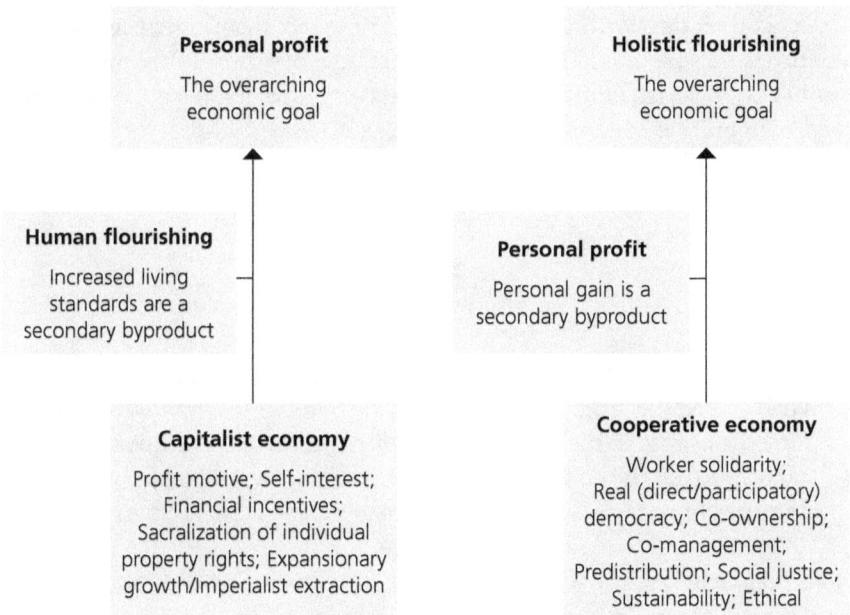

Capitalist vs cooperative

Perhaps more importantly, cooperative economics is not simply a theory but a historical reality. In the late 1700s and early 1800s, there were a handful of consumer and worker cooperatives in France and Britain. Today, 12 per cent of the human population are members of a cooperative – about one billion people in over a hundred different countries. After the Great Recession in 2007–08, the United Nations was so impressed by what cooperatives could accomplish that they named 2012 the International Year of Cooperatives, specifically for their success in poverty reduction and social integration. Cooperative economics can apparently accomplish things that purely capitalist (that is, private-profit driven) systems cannot.

The cooperative mode of labour also invites an ethos of recovery, community building and ethical practice. For many, it is a place of rest and recovery from the rat race of corporate capitalism and from shocking neoliberal changes that lead to local collapse of business (see Klein, 2007, in conjunction with Ranis, 2016). People sometimes choose to work at cooperatives simply because they are a better place to work with a more friendly environment, progressive orientation or better work benefits – in a word, a more humane economy (see Restakis, 2010; and Kelly and Howard, 2019).

The cooperative movement rose in parallel and, as I will argue, in direct connection with colonialism and decolonialism over the past two centuries. It's been said that 'crisis creates cooperation'. Whether in economic downturns, climate disaster or slavery and genocide, cooperation and cooperative organizations emerge as an essential way of surviving, and also exhibit intersections with economic development and religious activism.

Indonesia

> It is no coincidence that the first major joint-stock corporations in the world were the English and Dutch East India companies, ones that pursed the very same combination of exploration, conquest, and extraction as did the conquistadors. It is a structure designed to eliminate all moral imperatives but profit. (Graeber, 2011, p. 320)

The first case study I want to examine is cooperative economics, Islam and the independence movement of Indonesia. The Dutch East India Company was established in 1602 and began to force itself on what we now call Indonesia as early as 1623 (Veracini, 2022, p. 28). But it wasn't until the 1800s that the Dutch established total rule. Throughout the Dutch War of 1873–1913, they eventually gained control. As expected, there was indigenous and local resistance to this colonial rule, and this resistance advocated different forms from the capitalism of the colonizer.

The 'father of the cooperative movement in Indonesia', Mohammed Hatta, was the son of a respected *ulama* and a highly devout Muslim (Hatta, 1957). Similar to cooperators in India under British colonialism, Hatta saw cooperative economics as an essential alternative to Dutch colonialism and European capitalism (capitalism and colonialism often go hand in hand; Veracini, 2022). He organized against the Dutch colonizers, who tried him at the Hague after six months in prison (only to be released in 1928). In 1934, the Dutch again arrested him without trial and sent him to an isolated concentration camp in New Guinea, and then exiled him to a tiny island (Banda Neira) for spreading 'dangerous thoughts' (Kahin in Hatta, 1957, p. vii). The Japanese invaded Indonesia, which ended his exile in 1941. Hatta and others declared independence from the Dutch in August of 1945, and Hatta became the country's first vice president.

Hatta and his colleagues ensured that the country would be different from the kind of industrial capitalism that was spreading around the world. And for him, that wasn't a totalitarian communist state but rather cooperative economics. Article 33 of the 1945 constitution states that 'the economy is organized as a joint business based on the principle of kindship.' The first Cooperative Congress in 1947 led to the Indonesia Cooperative Council. And Article 38 of the 1950 Indonesian Constitution stated that 'The national economy shall be organized on a co-operative basis.' In commenting on this declaration, Hatta specifically grounds this principle in the nationalist, theological ideology of the country's leader (*Pantjasila*), Sukarno:

> In realizing our national ideal that 'the economy should be organized on a co-operative basis,' we should not forget that our state is based on moral principles, which are embodied in the *Pantjasila*, the five principles: Divine Omnipotence [belief in one God], humanity, national consciousness, democracy and social justice. (Higgins, 1958, p. 52)

Here, one can clearly see the intersection where ethical values, political values and theological beliefs all converge into cooperative economics.

After straightening the country out and largely resigning from the political world in the 1950s, Hatta could finally get to work in fulfilling the cooperative mandate of the constitution – but not without the help of others. This help included Roesli Rahim, the Head of the Co-Operative Service Ministry of Economic Affairs. Writing in 1956, Rahim argued:

In order to raise the economic level of the population many problems have to be faced and overcome: (a) limited knowledge of economics, (b) limited knowledge of organizational problems, (c) limited technical knowledge, (d) shortage of land or fragmentation of individual holdings, (e) psychological effects of 350 years of colonial rule. (Rahim in Hatta, 1957, p. xvi)

It was clear that capitalism turned people into cogs and tools in a large machine – specialization and subordination that rendered workers dependent on others for both knowledge and capital for their own economic development. Furthermore, farms were losing profits in the global economy because they were not rewarded for anything but their exports, and they weren't in control of those prices, or the conditions that gave rise to such prices: 'The farmers bring in foreign exchange, but they do not gather the fruits of their productive activity' (Rahim in Hatta, 1957, p. xvi). The lack of (or unavailability) of education and capital/credit on the ground level, as well as the problem of exploiting workers, was something that cooperatives were known (and are known) for effectively fixing.

Before the Second World War, there were 574 cooperatives in Indonesia, but the movement was devasted after the war, and 'the blockade of the Dutch following their military actions resulted in an over-all scarcity of goods' (Rahim in Hatta, 1957, p. xvi). Cooperatives were initially popularized in Jakarta by the Sarekat Dagang Islam (later Sarekat Islam), or society of Muslim traders. People joined because it was associated with Islam.

Although the relationship of Islam to cooperative economics is something that hasn't been explored very deeply (see Hübner, 2025), this connection between the two is not difficult to make. On the one hand, Islam was born out of merchant trade and significant economic consciousness. One anthropologist remarks that 'The veneration of the merchant was matched by what can only be called the world's first popular free-market ideology' (Graeber, 2011, p. 278). Arab poets made jokes about bouncing cheques, venture capitalists financed various investments regulated by commercial law, and others debated 'over the question of whether reputation could (like land, labor, money, and other resources) itself be considered a form of capital' (Graeber, 2011, p. 278). Legal scholars also talked about markets and prices operating by divine direction (pre-empting the 'invisible hand' concept by over half a millennium). Islam, in short, has always been highly economic and consciously developed in response to economic conditions.

Islam exhibited (and exhibits) considerable consciousness towards social justice as well. The phrase 'perform the prayer and gives alms' is found all over the Qur'an (e.g. 5:56, 9:11; 9:18; 22:41; 22:78; 24:37; 24:56; cf. 23:4; 33:33; 73:20). True believers are those 'performing the prayer, giving the alms' (9: 71; 27:3; 31:4; 41:7; 98:6–7). One of the five pillars of Islam (a construction from the hadith of Gabriel) is Zakāt, or 'almsgiving' (9:60). Zakāt is (often) a mandatory procedure of wealth redistribution to ensure a socio-economic safety net for the poorest in the Islamic community.[2] Originally set at 2.5 per cent of an adult Muslim's extra wealth, proceeds from Zakāt 'are earmarked mostly for assistance to specific categories of impoverished and disadvantaged individuals' (Kuran, 2005, p. 19). Other mechanisms that try to address wealth inequality include rules for dividing inheritances: '[a]nd when [other] relatives and orphans and the needy are present at the [time of] division, then provide for them [something] out of the estate and speak to them words of appropriate kindness' (4:8; see Iqbal, 1988). 'While the individual's right to own private property is respected in Islam through his lifetime,' writes Syed Naqvi, 'this right terminates on his death, after which the right of disposition is regulated by the Islamic laws of inheritance' (2013, p. 74).[3] The Qur'an also addresses the poor, spending, usury, wealth, contracts of debt in 2:261–283. Allah does not like 'those who commit excess' (6:141). The 'Qur'an requires moderation even in donations (17:28–29). A key word that would capture the preoccupation while avoiding the extremes is *wasat*. Translated as the "middle" or "midway", the word is typically taken as implying moderation and temperance, but also understood more simply as "justice"' (Arat, 2020, p. 109). Similarly, when it comes to dividing war spoils, wealth must not be concentrated among the wealthiest: 'It is for Allah and for the Messenger and for [his] near relatives and orphans and the [stranded] traveler – so that it will not be a perpetual distribution among the rich from among you' (59:7). Hoarders of resources and wealth will be punished (9:34–5, 4:37; 57:20).

In Islam, a major feature of the Almighty's rules, conveyed in the Qur'an and practised by the Prophet Muhammad, is justice. Thus the Islamic institutional scaffolding and the ideal Islamic economy exude justice. As a result, the promotion of social and human development on this plane of existence is founded on rules that promote justice. The Prophet understood the essential objective of the message to encourage and insert justice in human societies as emphasized in the Qur'an. He particularly emphasized the equality of individuals before the law and that all rules that are incumbent on individuals and the collectivity must be more strictly observed by those in positions of authority, as illustrated by his famous saying: 'Authority may survive disbelief but not injustice.' Insistence on justice became the hallmark of the institutional scaffolding of governance, a structure with full transparency and accountability. Rule compliance that embraces the pursuit of social justice is a requirement of each and every Muslim during every day of his or her life on this earth. Justice is essential in all endeavours, as the pursuit of justice leads to spiritual fulfilment and brings humans closer to their Creator. Rule compliance and justice cannot be compromised. In Islam, social and human development is multidimensional and goes well beyond the highest level of GDP and GDP per capita. Human spiritual pursuits on this earth cannot be compromised for material ends (Askari, Iqbal and Mirakhor, 2015).

But like any theological and economic ethic, the particular context of independent Indonesia faced certain obstacles. For example: 'In some parts of Indonesia the population adheres to the tenets of the Koran in such a way that they are averse to paying any interest, although the interest charged by the co-operatives is far from usury and is aimed merely at combating usurers' (Rahim in Hatta, 1957, p. xxxiii). Worse, the organization was crippled by a revolutionary communist faction, on the one hand, and overexpansion that couldn't sustain itself, on the other. Hatta himself had a doctorate in economics, which (back then) made him sympathetic to Marxism and communism. However, he 'decided that communism was the wrong course for Indonesia' (Higgins, 1958, p. 51) and stuck to the less militant economics of cooperation.

Unfortunately, this course wouldn't last for long. Indonesia had the third-largest communist party in the world at the time and, as Vincent Bevins reveals in his recent book *The Jakarta Method*, the US and anti-communist forces used this as an opportunity to ruthlessly kill over one million people after an organized coup in 1964. Western corporations planted their feet all over the country, and capitalism was officially installed. Article 33 in the constitution was abolished.

Still, even after radical leftist parties were squashed and the constitution was changed, it wasn't the end of cooperatives. In fact, because the neoliberal revolution in Indonesia (like neoliberalism elsewhere) eroded fundamental social supports and the needs of the working class, more and more people turned towards alternatives like cooperative economics. Co-operative Law no. 25/1992 passed in the year 1992 and, while not as bold as the constitutional law of 1950, it retained the legality of cooperatives. Today, there are 212,000 cooperatives and 37.7 million coop members in Indonesia. While cooperatives generate only about 2 per cent of the country's GDP, their impact remains significant for those millions of members that they serve. For example, the 'Muslimat Mandiri cooperative offers a lifeline for women who fall into financial difficulties, providing savings and loans without interest, as well as religious education and a place for community, connection, and support' (Post-Growth Institute, 2021). And the 'Cooperative Business Incubation Program is helping cooperatives to identify and realize their potential, in turn creating platforms for women and jobs for young people.' Recent studies have shown that this cooperative economy facilitates financial liberation for women.

Past studies suggest that organizing into groups like cooperatives can give informal workers greater voice and visibility, and increase prospects for artisans to expand their businesses, improve the quality of their products, and enable them to compete in external markets. Andrew Walker et al. examine whether this is the case in Jakarta:

> [We found that] ... Female cooperative members in Indonesia appear to prefer saving and borrowing with cooperatives to banks for a variety of reasons, including the desire for smaller-scale finance, as well as the administrative simplicity, lower fees, lower interest rates, and flexibility associated with cooperatives' financial facilities. A number of cooperatives have a mechanism through which cooperative representatives go door-to-door daily to collect individual members' savings, which enables easy access for home-based workers. Saving at cooperatives can allow women to accumulate assets under their own name, contributing to their own collateral. Some cooperatives do not require collateral when members borrow, and some offer loans in which only one member provides collateral so that a group of members can also access credit. Cooperatives' saving and borrowing mechanisms may prepare women artisans for future participation in more formalized banking systems. (Walker, 2017)

Cooperative economics was never that revolutionary in Indonesia, but it was a constituent part of a decolonizing independence movement that continues to offset areas of socio-economic weakness and neglect in Indonesia society.

Cooperatives and liberation theology in Central America

Cooperatives, combined with liberation theology in Central and Latin America, had the decolonialist and counter-capitalist overtones of Indonesia, but leaned harder into the resistance factor. The US Empire invaded, intervened and/or assassinated leaders of over a dozen countries in Latin America and Central America, beginning with Guatemala in 1954 and continuing into the present day (McPherson, 2016).[4] The primary purpose of such interventions was to occupy land and/or control governments for resource extraction by American corporations (for example, coffee, silver, palm oil, bananas).

In the case of Guatemala, western powers were exploring for oil and securing land and cashflow for the United Fruit Company. The democratically elected government of President Jacobo Árbenz initiated agrarian reforms that included the expropriation of unused land held by the United Fruit Company for redistribution to landless peasants. The aim was 'meant to redress the injustice of 2 percent of the people owning 72 percent of the land' (McPherson, 2016, p. 140). Because this benefited indigenous people, it upset many of the settlers so much that 'Anti-reform violence began in the countryside before any U.S.-led invasion' (McPherson, 2016, p. 142). Árbenz also legalized a communist party in the country, though the party had little influence and few members. In response, the American CIA, in Operation PBSUCCESS, orchestrated a coup (arming and funding militants) that led to Árbenz's resignation in 1954. 'Except for President Dwight Eisenhower,' writes Coatsworth in the *ReVista: Harvard Review of Latin America*, 'every significant decision maker in this case had a family, business or professional tie to the United Fruit Company, whose interests were adversely affected by an agrarian reform and other policies of the incumbent government' (Coatsworth, 2005). Furthermore, the CIA Director and Secretary of State were brothers who worked for the United Fruit Company (Chiquita today), and 'the Dulles brothers believed that the United States had a duty to overthrow even democratic governments if those governments threatened the independence of corporations' (McPherson, 2016, p. 141). The US propagated lies from Florida on Guatemalan radio that Árbenz 'was about to ban the revered Catholic Holy Week, exile the archbishop, and force children into re-education centers' (McPherson, 2016, p. 144). Members of Árbenz's own military turned on him, and the military dictator Castilla Armas was eventually installed, who rolled back reforms, persecuted dissenters and led with an iron fist. All of this was legitimized by the western public in the political context of anti-communism.

During this entire period, the indigenous populations were facing a threat of total extinction. The rainforest and highland Ixil region in particular 'become the epicenter of both guerrilla organizing and the genocide against Guatemala's Mayan population' (Chomsky, 2021, p. 90). In this region and others, there were a variety of resistance groups, including those who were simply trying to end the bloodbath from the American-sponsored military dictatorship, but also those who facilitated more direct resistance. Among them were Catholic Action and various embodiments of liberation theology – both of which created and maintained cooperatives.

Liberation theology in Latin America is centred on real liberation. As Gustavo Gutiérrez summarized in his seminal 1971 work, *A Theology of Liberation*:

> *liberation* is a term which expresses a new posture of Latin Americans. The failure of reformist efforts has strengthened this attitude. Among more alert groups today, what we have called a new awareness of Latin American reality is making headway. They believe that there can be authentic development for Latin America only if there is liberation from the domination exercised by the great capitalist countries, and especially by the most powerful, the United States of America. This liberation also implies a confrontation with these groups' natural allies, their compatriots who control the national power structure. It is becoming more evident that the Latin American peoples will not emerge from their present status except by means of a profound transformation, *a social revolution*, which will radically and qualitatively change the conditions in which they now live. The oppressed sectors within each country are becoming aware – slowly, it is true – of their class interests and of the painful road which must be followed ... In Latin America we are in the midst of a full-blown process of revolutionary ferment ... socialism, moreover, represents the most fruitful and far-reaching approach. There is, however, no monolithic orientation. (Gutiérrez, 1988, pp. 54–5; emphases original)

Liberation theologians in Guatemala organized study groups and raised consciousness about social injustice within religious frameworks, and this inevitably had immediate political and social implications. This awareness included the injustice of indigenous, patriarchal power structures and community hierarchies. Liberation theologians also raised awareness of more cooperative and socialist forms of economy, such as credit unions and 'other cooperatives to free campesinos from the control of local principals, landlords, and moneylenders. They established hospitals, health clinics, and barefoot doctors' training programs' (Chomsky, 2021, p. 83). This was a social movement 'from below' and appealed most to 'the poorest and most land-deprived area that supplied most of the migrant labor for cotton plantations' (Chomsky, 2021, p. 83). It was popular among the Ixil people in the highlands.

> Guerrilla leader Mario Payeras described how a few survivors of the 1960s guerrilla uprising and its repression regrouped in Mexico and decided to return to Guatemala and 'do things right' this time by building a strong base of support before relaunching an armed struggle. The small group crossed into Guatemala in early 1972, in the Ixcán rainforest region where the first colonizers had only recently established settlements.
>
> The cooperatives proved fertile ground for organizing. 'The insurgents spoke in terms similar to those of the priests, the nuns, the students, the social promoters, and the political activists back in the highlands. Those experiences could be uplifting, hopeful and inspiring.' ...
>
> Slowly, at the end of 1973, the group approached the older highland Ixil villages. As in so many villages in the highlands, Catholic Action and peasant organizations had brought new ideas and new economic prospects to the villages, which engaged many of the youth. (Chomsky, 2021, p. 90)

As Aviva Chomsky notes: 'Traditional village institutions and authorities were profoundly threatened by the new religious activism through Catholic Action and the cooperative movement' (Chomsky, 2021, p. 83). Some traditional leaders even called on the army to intervene and claimed that 'there is now among us a bad seed, the communists, who are fighting against us with cooperatives and other idiocies' (Chomsky, 2021, p. 83). In 1976, the army then began to target leaders of cooperatives, Catholic Action, and thus 'the Ixil soon became the epicenter of the country's genocide' (Chomsky, 2021, p. 83). Everyone who didn't directly and explicitly endorse the western-supported authoritarian regime were considered threats.

The civil war continued and by 1982, with the support of Ronald Reagan, General Efraín Rios Montt took power of Guatemala in another military coup. He was a proud Evangelical Christian, which meant being anti-communist, and so targeted the Revolutionary Organization of Armed People (ORPA), the Guerrilla Army of the Poor (EGP) and continued the genocide against the Ixil and the cooperators. Montt's campaigns involved widespread human rights abuses, including massacres, forced displacement and scorched-earth tactics in indigenous communities suspected of supporting or sympathizing with the guerrillas. Less than two years later, Óscar Humberto Mejía Victores took over in another coup, who continued the same violence. The military ultimately killed over 200,000 people from 1978 to 1983 (Bevins, 2021, p. 228).

Something similar to Guatemala happened in El Salvador during the 1960s. When the country implemented the first rural minimum wage in 1965, coffee planters responded by simply expelling peasants from their plantations. The cotton, sugar and cattle revolutions after the Second World War concentrated more fertile land in the hands of the oligarchy and further squeezed El Salvador's peasants (Chomsky, 2021, p. 125).

The country suffered decades of civil war, regime change and constant US intervention. The Catholic Church and the Jesuits of the Central American University became a source of support for exploited peasants and coffee farmers. The masses began to learn about God's concern for the oppressed and social justice in the teachings of Jesus. This liberation theology translated into demands for sugar mills to pay the wages they promised. However, landlords and the military began to take notice and began various attacks. One Jesuit organizer, Rutilio Grande, assassinated in 1977, deeply influenced Óscar Romero, the new Archbishop of San Salvador. Reaching a state of siege, the Jesuits 'received a threat that if they did not all abandon the country within thirty days, they would be systematically executed' (Chomsky, 2021, p. 133).

All in all, in the context of neocolonialism, a theology that dignified workers was apparently one of the most terrifying things to the economic and political ruling class, and it was certain to earn a death sentence.

Cooperation in Palestine

We've briefly looked at the role of cooperatives and Islam in Indonesian independence and of cooperatives and liberation theology in Central America's struggle with neocolonialism. Now I want briefly to turn to the role of cooperation in Palestine during and after the British occupation.

After the First World War, the British Empire occupied Palestine under what is called the 'British Mandate' (1918–45). Palestine was inhabited by Palestinians, who were primarily Muslims but also included Jews and

Christians. Palestine has a rich history both culturally and politically, being occupied by a variety of different entities and regimes since the second millennium BCE, and functioning as a holy site for the Abrahamic religions. Most of the Jewish and Christian story centred on Palestine, and it later became a holy place for Muslims as well.

While there has always been conflict in Palestine (like every region of the world), it is a common, racist stereotype (largely of the West) to say, 'Those two peoples [Muslim Arabs and Jewish Jews] never got along and never will.' In fact, Jews, Muslims and Christians found a variety of ways to get along before and during the British colonization of Palestine – with and without shared enemies. These Palestinians also found ways to welcome the waves of settler Jews pouring in from Europe before and after the Jewish Holocaust.

The historian Ilan Pappé highlights the role of economic and social cooperation of the Palestinians during the British Mandate in his renowned work *A History of Modern Palestine*. Similar to how the American empire drove a wedge between white and black workers so that they wouldn't cooperate to challenge capitalists (Foner, 2018), the British drove a wedge between Jews, Arabs and Muslims so that they would not cooperate to challenge British colonial power (Marcus, 2007; Khalidi, 2009). The Zionists were an exception, 'who regarded segregation as a prerequisite for the creation of an independent Jewish state in Palestine' (Pappé, 2006, p. 110).

> The entire history of Mandate Palestine is dotted with instances of cooperation between workers ... At every escalation of violence – 1920, 1929, 1936, or 1948 – I can find a case study of economic or social cooperation that was strongly opposed and destroyed by the national leaderships, especially the Zionist one. In many of these instances, courageous people tried to prevent the clash between the Jewish proletariat (which was turning into a lower middle and working class) and the impoverished indigenous rural and unskilled town dwellers (who were slowly becoming a proletariat in their own country). The political elites on both sides, who did not share the miserable conditions of their communities, found it easy to depict the poor as a 'national mass' that could be exploited during the successive waves of violence and bloodshed. In other cases, the elites themselves were engaged in cohabitation practices that defeated the claims made in their fiery speeches and sermons. (Pappé, 2006, p. 11)

COOPERATIVES AND DECOLONIZATION

Haifa in the 1920s exhibited all kinds of businesses co-run and organized between (settler) Jews, Arabs and Christians. In 1920:

> Palestinians, Jews, and Arabs from Syria and Egypt established the first trade union in Palestine in the yards of workshops of the railway, telegraphic, and postal services. Faced with long working hours, underpayment, inhumane living conditions and, above all, cruel treatment by their employers (the British government), they united in demanding a fundamental improvement in their conditions. (Pappé, 2006, p. 111)

One leader of Haifa 'rebuked Jewish workers who joined forces with Palestinians' (Pappé, 2006, p. 111). Eventually, as critics 'put national interest above class solidarity', an exclusively Jewish union was formed. The Palestinian workers then formed their own union in 1930 (in a building that today serves as the headquarters of the Israeli Communist Party (Pappé, 2006, p. 112)).

Nevertheless, cooperation was persistent. Jewish and Palestinian truck drivers organized an effective strike in 1931 and 'for eight days in November 1931, Palestinian and Jewish drivers stood shoulder to shoulder in a strike that paralysed the country' (Pappé, 2006, p. 112). Similarly, the 'municipality of Haifa was jointly run by Jewish and Arab clerks. Throughout the revolt, islands of cohabitation also existed in the labour and land markets' (Pappé, 2006, p. 113; Newsinger, 2013, 'The Palestine Revolt'). Even Zionist leftists advocated cohabitation and cooperation. Generally, however:

> the Zionist elite tried more than its Palestinian counterpart to kill the instinct for cooperation ... It moved beyond the labour market into the state and private sectors. It even penetrated areas crucial for national triumphalism, such as industry. A high level of cooperation was maintained during the Mandate in the citrus industry ... Similarly, Jews and Palestinians co-ran the salt plant of Atlit, a profitable business then and today. (Pappé, 2006, p. 114)

Eighteen months before the Mandate ended, when politicians from each side of the divide, as well as those in London and in the Arab capitals, seemed to be preparing for a Greek tragedy on Palestine's soil, several groups of workers and employees across the divide decided to put occupational expediency above national solidarity. For two weeks a strike by government clerks paralysed official business. Their success was so overwhelming that the two segregated national unions, the Histadrut and the Arab Union of Workers, were obliged to join in. In April 1946, postal services were brought to a halt by a joint Arab–Jewish strike. Even in May 1947, when the drums of war could be heard once Britain relinquished its obligation to rule the country, Palestinian and Jewish workers in a telegraph service embarked on a joint strike (Pappé, 2006, p. 114).

Pappé documents a number of other joint Arab–Jewish strikes in the 1940s, and also notes the emergence of agricultural cooperatives in the countryside, which 'sprang up in the Marg Ibn 'Amr in the 1940s between kibbutzim and villages, and in the city new joint commercial boards were established' (Pappé, 2006, p. 115). The Palestine Communist Party and 'a socialist discourse within the Palestinian community' validated and promoted such economic and social cooperation. The British government documented that during its colonial rule, '1,400 commercial partnerships between Jews and Arabs were forged on what the government defined as an "Inter Racial Basis"' (Pappé, 2006, p. 116). As with liberation cooperatives in Central America, cooperatives and cooperation in Palestine threatened colonial forces because they broke cultural barriers, created class solidarity and built an economic system that wasn't orientated towards their own exploitation.

Obviously, all of this paints a very different picture from what is typically imagined when it comes to the 'Palestinian–Israeli Conflict' or an eternal 'war between Abraham's siblings'. But the main point to underscore is that even in the most violent periods of Palestine's modern history, people organized and created cooperative relationships and institutions to combat colonial exploitation, bypass religious fundamentalism, and survive.

As history turned out, the Zionists would score victories in establishing the ethno-state of Israel, which then carried out its ('inherently violent' (Veracini, 2022)) settler colonial project by force over the next half-century and into the present day.[5] Besides violating international law with illegal settlements, many major human rights organization have declared Israel a state of 'apartheid' (for example, Human Rights Watch, Amnesty International, B'Tselem, Al-Haq, PCHR, SAHRC). On 19 July 2024, the International Court of Justice finally declared Israel an apartheid state and said it must tear down its settlements and pay reparations to Palestinians. Those who survived apartheid in South Africa are actually far more critical of Israel, as one Muslim theologian, Farid Esack, reflects:

> If anything, I think the apartheid analogy is often a weak analogy in relation to how the Palestinians are experiencing Zionism. In apartheid South Africa we never had the walls that we see in Israel. We never had separate roads for black people and white people as we see in Israel and in Palestine. We didn't have separate number plates for Arab cars. No, our courts never sanctioned collective punishment. Our courts never sanctioned torture, as the Israeli courts have. No, the apartheid regime never singled out for particular abuse the land, the destruction of olive groves and their fruits … Our engagement in solidarity with the Palestinians is not for the Palestinians. We are really doing this for ourselves. (Esack, in Ateek, 2009, pp. 158–9)

Given Israel's military support for apartheid South Africa's government throughout the twentieth century, it is not surprising that it was South Africa that sued Israel for committing genocide in December 2023 at the International Court of Justice (a case that is still open at the time of writing).

Despite massive violence and uprisings in the twentieth century, a brutal regime of military occupation and billions of dollars in annual aid from the United States, economic cooperation continued to provide for Palestinians. The International Cooperative in 2019 recorded 342 active cooperatives in the West Bank alone, with 39,370 members. This may not seem significant given the millions living there, but these pockets of cooperation are resilient and provide support for an intentionally impoverished society (the Israeli government explicitly put Palestinians on a 'diet' and cut off all food and water to Gaza in what has been called the Second Nakba in the autumn of 2023 (Institute for Middle East Understanding, 2014)).

> The cooperative movement in Palestine began under the British colonial administration in the 1920s. After independence from British rule, while the movement witnessed growth in diverse sectors with the support from Jordan and Egypt, the continuing conflict between Palestine and Israel resulted in weakening of the movement. During difficult war times between 1960s and 1990s, cooperatives were used as a means to organise refugees and promote socio-economic development among them. Post 2000s, with the support from international organisations, the cooperative movement has again seen a positive impetus with focus being on an enabling policy and legal environment for cooperatives, peace and development, agriculture, housing, women and youth as key areas. (ICA, 2021)

One of the most interesting projects is The Land of Despair Sprouts with Hope, or *Ard el-Ya's* in Arabic, which was initiated by a small group of students in the village of Saffa in the West Bank (Samer, Adham, Nawras and Qasem). Naiq Mari of the Swiss Society for the Middle East and Islamic Cultures describes the situation:

> Saffa's land was under threat of Zionist settlers while their professional prospects vacillated between the Scylla of unemployment and the Charybdis of underpaid wage labor. With Ard el-Ya's they not only hoped to protect the land and its ecology, but to establish a 'resistance economy' – an economy of self-reliance as the basis of a viable Palestinian liberation struggle, and one that offers dignified work opportunities.
>
> Today, Ard el-Ya's has grown into one of the most successful youth cooperatives and is a catalyst for over twenty similar ones. Its story reflects young people's recognition of the role of capitalism in the colonization and the economic destruction of Palestine as well as their pursuit of alternative economic models. Its perseverance is one of the best examples of what resistance economy in Palestine can accomplish but also highlights its shortcomings. Understanding the potential and limitations of those agricultural experiments is important, not only for the future of Palestine, but also for a world that is suffering from a grave ecological crisis and in need of a path beyond unfettered capitalist growth. (Mari, 2023)

A patient ferment, a gradual revolution

One of the most insightful histories of early Christianity is entitled *The Patient Ferment of the Early Church*. In the book, Alan Kreider describes the early Christian community as a kind of slow-growing, organic life that creatively embodied the Spirit of Christ in continually changing political and social circumstances (Kreider, 2016). Given what has briefly been surveyed here, I think this is also a fair analogy for the role of cooperatives and cooperative social and economic practice throughout the last several centuries.

There are two other contemporary examples that embody this practice that are worth mentioning. The first is The Southeastern Center for Cooperative Development, which is a Nashville-based programme for creating worker cooperatives. The Center, which has connections to Vanderbilt Divinity School, also offers education primarily for those within the Christian tradition, showing the tight bond between economic justice and cooperative economics – in contrast to exploitative capitalism. In the Center's own words:

> Working for a more just economy is not an optional charity project: it is at the heart of many faith traditions. But even faith itself can be distorted as the hallmarks of our current economic system find their way into our faith communities and theology. There are biblical traditions that counter these distortions and point toward a cooperative, bottom-up alternative. (Southeast Center for Cooperative Development, 2024)

The Center has developed a ready-made toolkit for those in churches who want to explore alternative ways of labour that are both more ethical and more empowering to the ordinary person. The Center furthermore provides steps towards conversions – which is a practical and extremely beneficial solution to ageing businesses that have no future strategic plan of ownership. Converting ordinary businesses into cooperatives changes the ownership structure (making it democratic), and also changes profit-redistribution (at the very least), which sets up workers on a more stable financial footing.

Another goal of the Center is building networks of solidarity within the working class – across cultures, traditions and demographics. Society changes through mass movements, and bringing together those within faith communities with those workers with the same struggles outside faith communities can build significant momentum, which is necessary for larger societal change.

This particular aspect of social change is more pronounced in the second example, Cooperative Jackson. Cooperative Jackson's 'Jackson-Kush Plan' is a comprehensive, long-term plan for the social and economic transformation of the city and community of Jackson, Mississippi, USA. The devastating effects of racism, slavery and settler colonialism are felt in communities like Jackson (see also Nembhard, 2014). Cooperative economics and 'ecosocialism' is, in the view of the founders and participants, the best answer to many of these problems (Akuno and Nangwaya, 2023). The plan (currently being implemented in varying degrees) includes a federal of mutual aid networks, land trusts, cooperative incubators and training schools, credit unions and banks, eco-villages, activism for local political change (including the adoption of human rights by the city council), and support for progressive candidates. The common dispute between 'top-down' versus 'bottom-up' approaches to social change does not apply here, since the approach is multi-directional. There is no reason to put all of one's eggs in the same basket (for example, voting and political reform versus grass-roots activism and civil disobedience), since both are important.

Cooperative economics is not a supplementary form of capitalism or an ethical form of capitalism in the view of its founders and activists. 'Reproducing capitalism, either in its market-oriented or state-dictated forms,' write Akuno and Meyer,

> will only replicate the inequities and inequalities that have plagued humanity since the dawn of the agricultural revolution. We believe that the participatory, bottom-up democratic route to economic democracy and ecosocialist transformation will best be secured through the anchor of worker self-organization, the guiding structures of cooperatives and systems of mutual aid and communal solidarity. (Akuno and Meyer, 2023, p. 17)

The goal is to reconfigure economic and social relations within existing economies – which thereby undermine the system bit by bit:

> Non-reformist reforms seem to create new logic, new relations, and new imperatives that create a new equilibrium and balance of forces that weaken capitalism and enable the development of an anti-capitalist alternative ... The formulation centers on waging struggle for demands and reforms that improve conditions in people's immediate lives in ways that don't strengthen the capitalist system but subvert its logic, upend its social relations, and dilute its strength. (Akuno and Meyer, 2023, pp. 4, 28)

In a chapter entitled 'Seek Ye First the Worker Self-Management Kingdom', Ajamu Nangwaya contends that worker cooperatives 'ought to see [themselves] as part of the broader class struggle movement that seeks to give control to the laboring classes over how their labor is used and the surplus or profit from collective work is shared' (Nangwaya, 2023, p. 144). Capitalism centres on capitalist ownership of the means of production and profit-making at all costs. Cooperative economics centres on worker and member ownership, and on service to the needs of its members, and any profits go to those workers and members. Each cooperative firm therefore stands as a challenge to the great corporate giants. Every dollar consumers pay at a cooperative is one dollar taken away from shareholding investors who are pillaging the earth and enslaving bodies via capitalist extraction.

Revolution is in many ways, therefore, the point of Cooperative Jackson – not the storming-the-capitol-and-beheading-politicians kind of revolution, but building networks of worker solidarity and overwhelming the existing system with a mass movement and strategic planning that results in both short- and long-term socio-economic results.[6]

Conclusion

While we have only scratched the surface of three primary case studies and two other case studies (among thousands), we've seen how cooperatives facilitate decolonization and resistance to oppression, work within several religious frameworks, and provide both indirect and direct paths to the liberation of subjugated peoples. Furthermore, the worker/class solidarity forged by cooperation and cooperatives can build meaningful relationships across cultural and religious boundaries that facilitate survival and much more. We also learn that the relationship of cooperatives to colonization can be a somewhat complex one, because cooperatives can take different shapes and flavours, sometimes peacefully building community wealth while bombs are being dropped, while in other cases the cooperatives themselves are training grounds of anti-colonial resistance. Cooperative movements – like the Palestinian organizer and revolutionary, Jesus of Nazareth[7] – have much to teach us in this regard, and probably have much to teach us in continuing decolonial efforts in the twenty-first century.

Notes

1 See International Cooperative Alliance, ica.coop.

2 For example, the 1979 programme in Pakistan ended interest-bearing savings accounts and made Zakāt on wealth and income mandatory. It has been made mandatory 'for certain groups in Malaysia, Saudi Arabia, and the Sudan'. Kuran, 2005, p. 1.

3 This quote comes in the context of a contrast between Islamic economics and socialism.

4 For a more complete history, see also Eduardo Galeano, 1973, *Open Veins of Latin America: Five Centuries of the Pillage of a Continent*, New York: Monthly Review Press.

5 In addition to Pappé, see Rashid Khalidi, 2021, *The One-Hundred Years' War on Palestine*, New York: Picador. On the use of 'holy land theology' to justify Israel's settler colonialism, see Mitri Raheb, 2022, 'The Occupation of Theological Minds', in Miguel A. De La Torre and Mitri Raheb (eds), *Resisting Occupation*,

Minneapolis, MN: Fortress Press; Gary Burge, 2010, *Jesus and the Land*, Grand Rapids, MI: Baker Academic.

6 An important essay on this subject is David Calnitsky, 2022, 'The Policy Road to Socialism', *Critical Sociology* 48(3), pp. 397–422, https://doi.org/10.1177/08969205211031624.

7 See Joerg Rieger and Kwok Pui-Lan, 2012, *Occupy Religion*, Lanham, MD: Rowman & Littlefield; Richard Horsley, 2003, *Jesus and Empire*, Minneapolis, MN: Fortress Press; John Dominic Crossan, 1994, *Jesus*, New York: HarperOne; Marcus Borg, 2015, *Jesus*, New York: HarperOne; Joerg Rieger, 2007, *Christ and Empire*, Minneapolis, MN: Fortress Press.

Further reading

On cooperatives and cooperative economics

Lovie, Dovev, 2023, *A Cooperative Economy: A Solution to Societal Grand Challenges*, London: Routledge.

Schneider, Nathan, 2018, *Everything for Everyone: The Radical Tradition that is Shaping the Next Economy*, New York: Nation Books.

Williams, Richard C., 2007, *The Cooperative Movement*, Burlington, VT: Ashgate.

Wolff, Richard, 2013, *Democracy at Work: A Cure for Capitalism*, Chicago, IL: Haymarket Books.

On religion, socialism, labour and cooperatives

Dorrien, Gary, 2019, *Social Democracy in the Making: The Political and Religious Roots of European Socialism*, New Haven, CT: Yale University Press.

Rieger, Joerg, 2009, *No Rising Tide: Theology, Economics, and the Future*, Minneapolis, MN: Fortress Press.

Rieger, Joerg and Henkel-Rieger, Rosemarie, 2016, *Unified We Are a Force: How Faith and Labor Can Overcome America's Inequalities*, St Louis, MO: Chalice Press.

Rieger, Joerg and Choi, Jin Young (eds), 2020, *Faith, Class, and Labor: Intersectional Approaches in a Global Context*, Eugene, OR: Pickwick.

Ruether, Rosemary Radford, 2005, *Integrating Ecofeminism, Globalization, and World Religions*, Lanham, MD: Rowman & Littlefield.

On colonialism, western imperialism and economic history

Bevins, Vincent, 2021, *The Jakarta Method*, New York: Public Affairs.

Blaut, James, 1994, *The Colonizer's Model of the World*, New York: The Guilford Press.

Bown, Stephen, 2009, *Merchant Kings*, New York: St Martin's Press.

Chomsky, Aviva, 2021, *Central America's Forgotten History: Revolution, Violence, and the Roots of Migration*, Boston, MA: Beacon Press.

Chomsky, Noam, 2003, *Hegemony or Survival: America's Quest for Global Dominance*, New York: Henry & Holt.
Dunbar-Ortiz, Roxanne, 2014, *An Indigenous People's History of the United States*, Boston, MA: Beacon Press.
Horne, Gerald, 2018, *The Apocalypse of Settler Colonialism*, New York: Monthly Review Press.
——, 2020, *The Dawning of the Apocalypse*, New York: Monthly Review Press.
Katz, Jonathan, 2022, *Gangsters of Capitalism*, New York: Saint Martin's Press.
Khalidi, Rashid, 2009, *Palestinian Identity*, New York: Columbia University Press.
Lockard, Craig, 2021, *Societies, Networks, and Transitions*, 4th edn, Boston, MA: Cengage.
Parenti, Michael, 1997, *Blackshirts and Reds*, San Francisco, CA: City Light Books.
——, 2011, *The Face of Imperialism*, London: Routledge.
Rodney, Walter, 2018 (1972), *How Europe Underdeveloped Africa*, London: Verso.
Stannard, David E., 1992, *American Holocaust: The Conquest of the New World*, New York: Oxford University Press.
Streets-Salter, Heather and Getz, Trevor, 2016, *Empires and Colonies in the Modern World*, New York: Oxford University Press.
Veracini, Lorenzo, 2022, *Colonialism: A Global History*, London: Routledge.

References

Akuno, Kali and Nangwaya, Ajamu, 2023, 'Toward Economic Democracy, Labor Self-management, and Self-Determination', in Kali Akuno and Matt Meyer (eds), *Jackson Rising Redux*, Oakland, CA: PM Press.
Akuno, Kali and Meyer, Matt (eds), 2023, *Jackson Rising Redux*, Oakland, CA: PM Press.
Arat, Zehra F. Kabasakal, 2020, 'Economic Rights and Justice in the Qur'an', *Human Rights Quarterly* 42(1), pp. 85–118.
Askari, Hossein, Iqbal, Zamir and Mirakhor, Abbas, 2015, *Introduction to Islamic Economics: Theory and Practice*, Singapore: Wiley.
Ateek, Naim Stifan, 2009, *A Palestinian Cry for Reconciliation*, Maryknoll, NY: Orbis Books.
Bevins, Vincent, 2021, *The Jakarta Method*, New York: Public Affairs.
Chomsky, Aviva, 2021, *Central America's Forgotten History: Revolution, Violence, and the Roots of Migration*, Boston, MA: Beacon Press.
Coatsworth, John, 'United States Interventions: What For?' *ReVista* 4(2) (Spring/Summer 2005).
Foner, Philip, 2018, *Organized Labor and the Black Worker*, Chicago, IL: Haymarket Books.
Graeber, David, 2011, *Debt*, New York: Melville.
Gutiérrez, Gustavo, 1988 (1971), *A Theology of Liberation*, Maryknoll, NY: Orbis Books.
Hatta, Mohammad, 1957, *The Co-Operative Movement in Indonesia*, George McT. Kahin (ed.), Ithaca, NY: Cornell University Press.

Higgins, Benjamin, 1958, 'Hatta and Co-Operatives: The Middle Way for Indonesia?', *The Annals of the American Academy of Political and Social Science* 318, pp. 49–57, p. 52.

Hübner, Jamin, 2025, *Religion and Cooperative Economics*, London: Palgrave Macmillan.

ICA, 2021, 'Palestine', *Coops4Dev*, https://coops4dev.coop/en/4devasia/palestine (accessed 8.01.2025).

Iqbal, Munawar (ed.), 1988, *Distributive Justice and Need Fulfilment in an Islamic Economy*, Leicester: Islamic Foundation.

Institute for Middle East Understanding, 2014, 'Putting Palestinians "On a Diet": Israel's Siege & Blockade of Gaza', 14 August, https://imeu.org/article/putting-palestinians-on-a-diet-israels-siege-blockade-of-gaza (accessed 8.01.2025).

Kelly, Marjorie and Howard, Ted, 2019, *The Making of a Democratic Economy*, Oakland, CA: Berrett-Koehler.

Khalidi, R., 2009, *Palestinian Identity*, New York: Columbia University Press.

Klein, Naomi, 2007, *Shock Doctrine*, New York: Picador.

Kreider, Alan, 2016, *The Patient Ferment of the Early Church: The Improbable Rise of Christianity in the Roman Empire*, Grand Rapids, MI: Baker Academic.

Kuran, Timur, 2005, *Islam and Mammon: The Economic Predicaments of Islamism*, Princeton, NJ: Princeton University Press.

Marcus, Amy Dockser, 2007, *Jerusalem 1913*, New York: Viking.

Mari, Faiq, 2023, 'Youth Cooperatives: An Emergent Model for a Palestinian Resistance Economy', *Swiss Society for the Middle East and Islamic Cultures*, https://www.sagw.ch/sgmoik/news/details/news/youth-cooperatives-an-emergent-model-for-a-palestinian-resistance-economy (accessed 8.01.2025).

McPherson, Alan, 2016, *A Short History of U.S. Interventions in Latin America and the Caribbean*, Chichester: Wiley Blackwell.

Nangwaya, Ajamu, 2023, 'Seek Ye First the Worker Self-Management Kingdom', in Kali Akuno and Matt Meyer (eds), *Jackson Rising Redux*, Oakland, CA: PM Press.

Naqvi, Syed Nawab Haider, 2013 (1994), *Islam, Economics, and Society*, London: Routledge.

Nembhard, Jessica Gordon, 2014, *Collective Courage: A History of African American Cooperative Economic Thought*, University Park, PA: The Pennsylvania State University Press.

Newsinger, John, 2013, *The Blood Never Dried: A People's History of the British Empire*, 2nd edn, London: Bookmarks.

Pappé, Ilan, 2006, *A History of Modern Palestine*, 2nd edn, Cambridge: Cambridge University Press.

Post-Growth Institute, 2021, 'How Cooperatives are Building Solidarity and Resilience in Indonesia', *Medium*, 5 October, https://medium.com/postgrowth/how-cooperatives-are-building-solidarity-and-resilience-in-indonesia-3a9fc2a761a3 (accessed 7.01.2025).

Ranis, Peter, 2016, *Cooperatives Confront Capitalism*, London: ZED.

Restakis, John, 2010, *Humanizing the Economy: Cooperatives in an Age of Capital*, Gabriola, British Columbia: New Society Publishers.

Southeast Center for Cooperative Development, 2024, 'Faith and Co-Ops', *Southeast Center for Cooperative Development*, https://www.co-opsnow.org/tool-kit (accessed 8.01.2025).

Veracini, Lorenzo, 2022, *Colonialism: A Global History*, London: Routledge.

Walker, Andrew and the Georgetown Institute for Women, Peace, and Security, 2017, 'Cooperative Connections: Connecting Female Artisan Home-Based Workers through Women's Cooperatives in Jakarta, Indonesia', *Georgetown Institute for Women, Peace and Security*, https://giwps.georgetown.edu/resource/cooperative-connections/ (accessed 7.01.2025).

2

Decolonizing Knowledge Systems in Development and Theology

SANJANA DAS

Introduction

I want to begin by sharing about three reasons that motivated me to bring the subject to the forefront of discussion in this book. First, over two decades back when I started working in the development sector, I worked on the issue of human trafficking in India. During this time I got invited to speak in advocacy forums in the Global North, where people expected me to talk about the plight of women in Indian brothels. In the first decade of this century, around the time when there was panic around sex trafficking globally soon after the Cold War, the campaign on violence against women became fierce. The anti-trafficking campaign picked up momentum focusing on the vices of female sexual slavery while another small group of lobbyists focused on the rights of sex workers. Therefore, the audiences I engaged with were familiar with sex trafficking. Human trafficking, as depicted in campaigns and mass media, is conceived as being synonymous with women forced into sexual slavery who need to be rescued from the existing conditions of exploitation. The personal and not the political continues to be at the centre of discourse even today, with individual victims showcased in the forefront instead of the structural violence that puts people, including women and children, at risk of trafficking. The recognition of labour trafficking as a significant issue within the broader context of neocolonialism and globalization, and its place in the modern-day slavery discourse, is a relatively recent development.[1]

Labour trafficking takes multiple forms, ranging from traditional settings in agriculture, brick-making, the garment industry, leather-making, mining, quarrying, gem work, jewellery-making, cloth- and carpet-making, domestic servitude, prostitution, to forced labour in construction, fishing, manufacturing, the adult entertainment industry and in spas and massage parlours (Das, 2024, p. 50). Though much of the consumption of these services and products used to be at local level, neoliberal economic globalization has opened avenues for bringing slave-made goods and services from the Global South to the doorsteps of consumers in the Global North (Bales, 1999; Quirk, 2007; Kara, 2009). The cost of slaves in the Global South is much less than in the Global North. The corporations in our global economy therefore move to countries where the cost of production is cheap but yields high profits (Kara, 2009). Most of this labour trafficking takes place in informal settings. Women constitute a majority group in sex trafficking, sexual labour and other forms of labour, some of which are in highly regulated industries such as nursing, while many are in prostitution, which can be illicit and illegal.

Saskia Sassen, in her article 'Women's Burden: Counter-Geographies of Globalization and the Feminization of Survival', mentions that 'households and whole communities are increasingly dependent on women for their survival. Governments are too dependent on their earnings, as well as enterprises where profit-making exists at the margins of the "licit" economy' (2002, p. 255). Sassen mentions that in the context of the broader structural conditions, women's presence in the cross-border circuits has been increasing in the past few decades. These circuits are diverse; they are a source of livelihood for women themselves and a source of profit-making and accrual of foreign currency. These are places where illegal trafficking for sex work and other forms of work take place. These sites are also used for cross-border migrations, documented or not. The key actors in these circuits are illegal traffickers, contractors, governments of home countries and disadvantaged women, who are a source of convertible currency for the governments in home countries (Das, 2024, p. 41).

Sassen (2002) conceptualizes this as counter-geographies of globalization, which overlap with some of the major dynamics that compose globalization: the formation of global markets, the intensification of transnational and translocal networks, and the development of communication technologies, which easily escape conventional surveillance practices. The strengthening and, in some cases, formation of new global circuits is made possible by the existence of a global economic system and the associated development of various institutional supports for cross-border money flows and markets. The counter-geographies are dynamic; to some extent they are part of the shadow economy, but they also use some of the institutional infrastructure of the formal economy.

Joerg Rieger (2022, p. 23), citing the works of Raj Patel and Jason W. Moore, mentions that 'Nature and labor are among the "seven cheap things" on which the history of the present-day world rests, along with cheap money, care, food, energy, and lives.' He further points out:

> The labor of enslaved people – both past and present – and the reproductive labor of women (including gestational labor) provide the most severe examples of these dynamics, as these forms of labor have often been more closely identified with nonhuman nature than with productive labor and therefore have mostly been unpaid and treated as externalities!

My second motivation for discussing this subject is that the systems and structures that perpetuate people at risk of being trafficked are minimally deliberated upon in conferences, policy circles and theological discussions. I have heard several speakers in conferences who have highlighted their roles as saviours of naive and helpless victims who are portrayed as women lacking wisdom and agency with regard to their lives. Therefore, a single-lens focus on the rescue of trafficked victims has gained importance in the anti-trafficking paradigm, which is then followed by women's rehabilitation and reintegration back into their homes. I noticed that the inter-linkages between labour migration, human smuggling and human trafficking are not issues that the very aware, knowledgeable and well-read audiences are interested in listening to.

Third, when I worked with trafficked women, they shared experiences of how their personhood, dignity and agency were at stake even after they were rescued from situations of domination and oppression. The shame and stigma of trafficked survivors further pushes women out of the active labour force. It excludes women from living a life of dignity in their communities and deprives them of their right to decent work. Therefore, policies that are shaped not by collaborative work with survivors but by a system that perpetuates racism and colonialism within development research and praxis fail to meet the needs of the trafficked and migrant women workers in the informal economy.

The International Labour Organization (ILO) defines decent work as 'productive work for women and men in conditions of freedom, equity, security and human dignity'.[2] The European Commission's website notes that, generally, work is considered decent when it pays a fair income, it guarantees a secure form of employment and safe working conditions, it ensures equal opportunities and treatment for all, it includes social protection for the workers and their families, it offers prospects for personal development, it encourages social integration where workers are free to express their concerns and to organize.³ The Commission's website further mentions that informal work represents more than 50% of non-agricultural employment in most regions of the developing world: 82% in South Asia, 66% in Sub-Saharan Africa, 65% in East and Southeast Asia and 51% in Latin America. Female labour-force participation is low in Asia and the Pacific. South Asia holds the highest rates of informal employment in the world. With precarious and informal employment remaining high, along with a high youth unemployment rate, the income disparities are getting worse. Further, the region is faced with the challenge of absorbing a lot of migrant workers. Women's economic empowerment is fundamental to gender equality; for most women, a job is the most important source of economic empowerment and dignity. Closing gender gaps in employment, ensuring decent work for all women and equal pay for work of equal value is thus key to achieving gender equality, fair income, security in the workplace and social protection for individuals and families. However, this dream is far from reality, with the lack of opportunities for decent work available specifically in the Global South. People accept jobs that are available for them, despite unfair income, unsafe working conditions, lack of social protection, lack of decency and dignity in the workplace. Women and young people are vulnerable in the informal economy. They accept indecent work to survive. Society in-dignifies them for engaging in work that is supposedly 'indecent', while employers make profit out of their labour and consumers benefit from the low-cost services or products they receive. Women are shamed and stigmatized for choosing the work opportunities that are available for them, despite, for example, unsafe working conditions and unfair wages; they are categorized as indecent women having given in to indecent work. People-centred, gender-focused and micro- and macro-economic policies in the globalized economy are not only necessary, but in my opinion it is the right of every woman to have access to and opportunities for decent work. Inclusion of social protection policies, fair-wage policies and inclusive approaches to female labour participation is necessary (Das, 2024, pp. 58–60).

This chapter is premised upon my doctoral research, titled 'Towards a Feminist Theology of (In)-Decent Work in the Context of Human Trafficking and Migration: Journeying with Economic Migrant Women in India in their Struggle for a Life of Dignity' (Das, 2024). I have emphasized the importance of having the knowledge of women on the margins as critical to research that contributes to influencing public policy, praxis and public theology. With feminist standpoint theory, intersectional feminism and liberation theology as the core theoretical and theological foundations, the research engaged the academic work of postcolonial feminist scholars, theologians and biblical scholars on human trafficking, migration, labour, neoliberal economic globalization, body, human dignity and solidarity. The methodological foundations are within the discipline of qualitative critical feminist research and have engaged in feminist interviews, informal encounters, focus-group discussions and contextual Bible studies. Therefore, the research was designed to listen to the lived experiences of trafficked and migrant working women as a starting point of inquiry. Women's standpoint and voices that come from their knowledge as the 'outsider within' are critical in shaping a theology for the human dignity of the trafficked and migrant working women. A creative, interactive and participatory engagement was therefore conceived to have women in the margins contribute to the body of knowledge and to doing theology as the best agents of knowledge about their context, challenges and strategies for empowerment. I believe that the complexities of the intersecting experiences of the vulnerable, trafficked and migrant people cannot be understood without listening to and understanding their lived experiences from a human rights perspective, not just the dehumanizing experiences but also the agentive, empowering and life-affirming lived experiences. This was done by using empowering participatory processes that uphold the dignity and agency of the participants, who became my research collaborators contributing immensely to the process and outcome of this research. By giving an epistemic privilege and advantage to migrant working women who are in the margins of knowledge production systems – both in sociology and theology – I attempted to develop a feminist theology of (in)decent work in the context of human trafficking and migration.

I now draw attention to the development field and anti-trafficking campaign and praxis and argue that the voices and knowledge of people in margins be utilized to produce knowledge that is essential to influence development policy, praxis and theology. I contend that the systemic racism and exclusion of the marginalized knowledge systems, rhetorics and epistemologies, reflects the biases and politics of those in power of decision-making.

I begin here by asking a basic question: Who produces knowledge and why in academic research, development and theology? The Latin aphorism *Scientia potentia est* means 'Knowledge is power'. While the transformative power of knowledge has been emphasized by several key philosophers, such as Althusser, Foucault and Bourdieu, it is important to ask: Who controls, manipulates or facilitates knowledge production;

for whom is knowledge produced and who will benefit from it? And most importantly, whose knowledge matters (Das, 2024, p. 137)? The politics of knowledge production is critical to the design and process of research and is dependent on whose interest it is meant to serve (Jenkins et al., 2019). With different actors in research – namely, the producer, controller and consumer – it is critical to be aware of the political interest/s of the producer/s of research (for example, the researcher, research team or research centre), controller/s (for example, political systems, research grant committees, interest groups, review committees of professional journals and publishing houses) and consumer/s (for example, business organizations, government departments and interest groups) of the outcome of the research, as they play an important role in the design of the research paradigm (Das, 2024, pp. 137, 138).

Development for transformative change

Development is a complex term. The idea of development varies from people living in diverse realities, locations and contexts, with different experiences and therefore varied perspectives. However, the notion of development is universally understood as a process that involves working towards bringing transformative changes from the present situation towards a desired one. It involves stages of transformative action and praxis that lead to positive outcomes for people and communities living in unjust and inequal socio-economic and political conditions. The strategies required for bringing developmental changes for people with different needs may differ across people living in different socio-economic and geopolitical contexts. For example, in the underdeveloped and developing countries, the dropout rate of children after primary school is higher for girls than boys due to lack of toilet and sanitation, unsafe travel to long-distance schools for children living in rural areas, or for the simple reason of taking care of siblings at home, and so on. Boys in the same places may have different reasons for dropping out, from the prevailing practice of caning and strict disciplinary actions in schools to working on the farms or engaging in other forms of child labour. Similarly, the development needs of starving children in a conflict zone, or children and families on the move, or the homeless populations, will differ from the needs of people living with adequate resources required for their well-being.

Economic growth has long been understood to be an important indicator for development. This position is limited if 'economic growth [is] measured solely in terms of annual increases in per-capita income or gross national product, regardless of its distribution and the degree of people's participation in effective growth' (Mahmoud, 1991). Though GDP (Gross Domestic Product) remains one of the main indicators to assess economic growth in almost every country, there are varied opinions whether GDP is enough to measure a country's progress and development as it does not take into consideration important aspects such as the overall well-being of all inhabitants and citizens of a country, the social inequalities and existing oppressive systems and degrading environmental factors that affect the daily lives and health of people.

In 1984, David Korten, a former regional advisor to USAID, introduced the concept of people-centred development, which centres the values of justice, sustainability and inclusiveness. It promotes the self-reliance of local communities, social justice and participatory decision-making processes. With a call to action in social, political and environmental values and practices, the people-centred development approach proposed human development beyond economic growth. Pearson (1992, cited in Abuiyada, 2018) argued for development that adapts diverse strategies for socio-economic and environment transformation from current states to desired ones. He posited that development requires an improvement in either or both qualitative and quantitative use of the resources available (Abuiyada, 2018). The Pakistani economist and international development theorist Mahbub ul-Haq devised and launched the Human Development Index (HDI) in 1990. The HDI, which was devised to evaluate development not just on national income, was meant to shift focus from development economics to people-centred policies that encompass the well-being of people. The new method of measuring HDI, which was first published in 2010, combined three dimensions: (1) a long and healthy life: life expectancy and birth; (2) education: mean years of schooling and expected years of schooling; and (3) a decent standard of living: GNI (Gross National Income) per capita. However, critics of the HDI have pointed out that it not only has data errors, which are a work in progress within the UN system (UNDP in particular) along with economists, but the excessive focus on national performance and ranking keeps several aspects out of focus. Several gaps have been addressed, yet people's participation in their qualitative and sustainable development process still needs to be incorporated. The main argument here is that people's voice and active participation in the making of the policies that are designed to help them is often missing from the development agenda and practices. I argue that people are the best knowers of their lived realities and contexts; therefore their knowledge and aspirations for the improvement in their quality of life and protection of their resources is incomplete without their active engagement. In my opinion, the protection, transformational development and dignity of the living conditions of humans and all of creation is critical for coexistence and harmonious living, where conditions of dominance, oppression, socio-economic and geopolitical inequality and imbalances are minimized or ideally eliminated.

International policies, which are built on decades of work on this issue, from the Earth Summit in 1992, Millenium Summit in 2000, World Summit on Sustainable Development in 2002 to the UN Sustainable Development Summit in 2015, are currently driven and guided by the adoption of several major agreements in 2015, such as the Sendai Framework for Disaster Risk Reduction, Addis Ababa Action Agenda on Financing for Development, Transforming our World: The 2030 Agenda for Sustainable Development and the Paris Agreement on Climate Change. With the aim to transform our world, 17 SDGs (Sustainable Development Goals) were adopted at the UN Sustainable Development Summit in New York in September 2015. The SDGs are a call to action to end poverty and inequality, leaving no one behind. They aim to protect the planet and ensure that all people enjoy health, justice and prosperity.[4]

Joerg Rieger (2013) draws attention to the world of economic inequality that exists even in the Global North, with income inequality in the United States being greater than it has ever been, greater than that of most other wealthy countries. Rieger mentions that:

> While many lament the existence of economic inequality, others welcome it. Christians who follow the teachings of the so-called gospel of prosperity, for instance, are rarely bothered by economic inequality because they see economic success as a result of faithfulness to God, while stagnation or even poverty is the result of lack of faith. Among economists, one of the dominant perspectives on economic inequality is that it is necessary and beneficial. More specifically, one current economic theory that is widely agreed upon holds that cutting taxes for the wealthy and providing subsidies for large corporations is the only way to maintain economic growth as well as job growth. This theory is maintained despite mounting empirical evidence to the contrary.
> (Rieger, 2013, p. 153)

However, despite the challenges faced by the poor and working class in the Global North, this chapter is concerned with the developmental concerns of the Global South. While the Global North represents that part of the economic world which is wealthy, politically stable and technologically advanced and constitutes developed societies, the Global South represents economically backward countries and agrarian societies lacking in their standard and quality of lives, with high levels of poverty, growing income inequality, lack of or limited opportunities of educational and feasible vocational and skills trainings, unemployment, broken health systems and inadequate health infrastructures. These countries are burdened with high population growth rates, gender disparity, violence against children and women and larger concerns of rising sea levels, land degradation, biodiversity loss and displacement.

The health and economic repercussions of climate change are among the most pressing challenges faced by the Global South, particularly in regions with limited resources, weak economic systems and inadequate health infrastructures. Even though the industrialized nations have been at the forefront of greenhouse gas (GHG) emissions owing to their long-standing industrialization and economic growth, the Global South with a lower rate of greenhouse gas emission is often the most exposed to the effects of climate change. The Global South disproportionately bears the health and economic consequences of climate change, with degradation of biodiversity, lack of financial and technological resources to implement adaptation and mitigation measures, and limited access to renewable energy sources (Suri, 2023). Coastal regions with low-income populations that are impacted by sea levels rising are deeply affected by lack of clean water, water-borne diseases, flooding, erosion and saltwater infiltration. With the disruption of natural resources, indigenous communities are impacted by land degradation and loss of biodiversity on which they are historically dependent. Women and girls from traditional societies face the challenges of climate change that come with their traditional socio-economic roles (Suri, 2023).

Balgis Osman-Elasha (2009), citing the findings of the Intergovernmental Panel on Climate Change (IPCC), mentions that the existing poor, vulnerable and marginalized women, primarily in developing countries, who are disproportionately affected by climate change, are increasingly being seen as more vulnerable than men because they represent the majority of the world's poor and are proportionally more dependent on threatened natural resources. She mentions that:

> The difference between men and women can be seen in their differential roles, responsibilities, decision making, access to land and natural resources, opportunities and needs, which are held by both

sexes. Worldwide, women have less access than men to resources such as land, credit, agricultural inputs, decision-making structures, technology, training and extension services that would enhance their capacity to adapt to climate change. (Osman-Elasha, 2009)

Women tend to work more in extreme weather conditions such as droughts and floods, which leaves them with insufficient time to access education, skill training or participation in income-generating activities. Osman-Elasha (2009) further adds that women, in many developing countries, suffer gender inequalities with respect to human rights, political and economic status, land ownership, housing conditions, exposure to violence, education and health. Climate change will be an added stressor that will aggravate women's vulnerability. It is widely known that during conflict, women face heightened domestic violence, sexual intimidation, human trafficking and rape.

The experiences of western economic history, together with the Industrial Revolution and the emergence of capitalism, have contributed to a typical form of western thinking that has further influenced the shaping of development theory until recently. Abuiyada (2018) points out that development in the third world was expected to be an imitative process in which the less-developed countries gradually assumed the qualities of the industrial nations, by increasing gross levels of savings and investments (both internal and external, private and state) until the economy reached a take-off point into self-sustaining development. Therefore, an appropriate combination of domestic savings, international investment and international aid would provide the fuel to drive the process through stages of growth that would ultimately bring the benefits of modernization to the entire population.

However, while economic growth is an important aspect of civilization, it cannot by itself fix the developmental problems specifically in the Global South, which have to deal with rising poverty, inequality, unemployment, human rights violations, gender inequality, climate disasters, conflicts, wars and colonization. The insidiousness of coloniality and white supremacy is embedded in development work, with policies designed and framed in the Global North, most of which are imposed upon the Global South to abide by to meet those standards. In particular, the wisdom and knowledge of subaltern women, people of colour and indigenous communities do not have a place at the centre of these development policy circles. At most there is tokenism in representation of people in the margins from the Global South, while the real voice of the Global South is alienated. They are represented by the development elites who speak and seem to know on behalf of the poor and excluded about what is good for the poor, marginalized and excluded to live a better life.

In his book *Black Skin, White Masks* (1952), Frantz Fanon argued that both white and black people trapped in their racial identities because of colonization behave differently and have different experiences. Citing the example of black Antilleans who travel to France, he shares how the black person becomes whiter and superior back in his homeland because he assimilates with the white person's culture and language. In contemporary times, the development policy and praxis circles are dominated by people belonging to development elite circles, whose colour, race, gender, ethnicity, caste may be similar to that of the poor and exploited people from the Global South, yet they become the allies of the North by wearing white masks while supposedly representing people of the Global South. They carry the North's message to the South and inform how the South should work to overcome the barriers that keep the poor in margins. With a western lens, the development efforts do not always meet the expectations and aspirations of the poor and do not necessarily achieve impact-driven long-term sustainable goals. A flawed perception of the needs of the poor with a paternalistic lens itself becomes a barrier in designing transformative policies, strategies and praxis. The knowledge and voice of the excluded, exploited, marginalized and poor communities, I argue, would best be generated and brought to the centre through participatory processes of learning and development. Development programmes will then not be thrust upon but built and owned by the poor and marginalized themselves.

As most developmental programmes are designed and implemented without understanding the needs of the grass roots (Abuiyada, 2018), I contend for decoloniality in academic research not just as an epistemic critique but to align decolonial praxis in anti-imperial struggles of the subaltern. I insist that the development of a robust theory and practice of decolonizing knowledge systems in development research and academia is necessary. Within the structures of global capitalism that is dominated by neoliberal economic policies and economic imperialism, the workers of the world's labour are exploited. I posit that to understand the impact of capitalism and imperialism on the power relations between the capitalists, corporations, governments and their allies, and the workers of the world, it is pertinent to understand the aspirations and the intersectional experiences of the vulnerable, dominated, exploited, oppressed and the marginalized. Bringing people's voices and knowledge from their lived experiences to the centre of research is fundamental to adding value to the policies that are meant to improve their quality of life and to ensure the justice, peace and dignity of people in the margins of development, academic and theological research. Furthermore, the dimensions of class, race, caste, ethnicity, gender, sexuality and ability are essential for research scholars, activists, educators, lobbyists and theologians who work against multiple structures and systems of domination, oppressions, exploitations and marginalization.

Demystifying the anti-trafficking paradigm

This section brings to attention the dominant model of knowledge production that informs policy and praxis in the anti-trafficking paradigm. By citing the example of the dominant campaign and praxis on human trafficking in India, I critique contemporary western ideology with neocolonial and neoliberal interests that influences aid, development research and development work. It further highlights the strong anti-prostitution and anti-migration foundations in anti-trafficking work and draws attention to its impact on the migrant female labour force working in the informal and shadow economy in the globalized world.

Human trafficking involves movement of people from one place to the other, from rural to semi-urban and urban cities, within countries and across international borders. Trafficking in persons, especially of women and children, has been understood to be done primarily for 'sexual slavery' with phenomenal profits estimated to be as high as the clandestine gains made from the underground trade in arms and narcotics (Sanghera, 2005, p. 6). The notion of human trafficking has been evolving with time. In recent times, it is understood as not necessarily involving movement of people from one place to the other.[5] People in a state of servitude, or victims of exploitation at the home state or destination places, including those who consented to work but experience exploitation and enslavement by traffickers, are all included in the ambit of trafficked persons. This is what is called 'modern slavery'.[6] However, the dominant discourse and anti-trafficking paradigm assume and project that most trafficking takes place for the purpose of prostitution. Therefore, policy, action and advocacy lean heavily in this direction (Kempadoo et al., 2012). Most anti-trafficking response is centred on raid, rescue, rehabilitation and reintegration or repatriation of girls and women from brothel-based prostitution (Sanghera, 2005, p. 16), which thereby excludes or limits assistance to other trafficked victims (Das, 2024, pp. 26, 27).

The anti-trafficking interventions, with specific reference to South Asia and India, focus on rescue, rehabilitation and reintegration/repatriation (Sanghera, 2005, p. 13). Raids and rescue operations of brothels make the operation of traffickers clandestine, thereby housing women in extremely repressive conditions, making them invisible and inaccessible. Despite their good intentions, these models of rescue operations often curb and deprive women of their freedom to exercise their agency. Women's agency in the rescue, rehabilitation and reintegration in the anti-trafficking praxis gets overshadowed in the presence of a paternalistic and protectionist approach (Das, 2024, p. 61). The sexualized image of a trafficked woman makes her vulnerable to stigma and shame in her home after return. Studies indicate 'secondary victimization' of returnees (Cojocaru, 2016, pp. 12–38). Most often, those reintegrated back to their homes return to the very places that were detrimental to their existence and survival (Poudel, 2011; Simkhada, 2008; Sanghera, 2005). They are doubly re-victimized because of their trafficking status and the stigma attached to it, whether sex trafficked or not. Reintegration of rescued girls and women from the sex industry has been the most difficult one (Das, 2024, p. 25).

Stella (name changed), a former trafficked woman, shared her experiences of living with stigma and shame both in the shelter she was housed in and when reintegrated back to her village:

> If you have been in the brothel, it means you asked for it then and deserve to be a prostitute always. When I returned to my village, it was impossible for me to visit a neighbour, to attend church or go to the market. People not only gossiped about me, but men thought I must be available for them too.

She further shared:

> No one asked me how I was treated in the shelter or back in my home and village. I had no choice then as to where I must live and what work I can do. Life was more hellish outside the brothel. I had no value or respect in my own society. Today, living and working in the city, I feel confident and cared for by my friends here.

Hostility towards trafficked women and migrant working women has become a norm even though they now send remittances back home. However, their male counterparts, migrant working men, are cheered and acknowledged because of their labour and thereby financial contributions to their families (Das, 2004, p. 2).

Women contribute to the economies of the host and home countries. The home countries benefit from the accrual of remittances that are sent. The receiving of foreign currency is beneficial for the home country. Similarly, the host country enterprise benefits from the labour of migrants. The labour of women working in the margins of what Sassen describes as 'licit' economy (2002) profits the economy of the host country as well as the enterprises that recruit and profit from their labour. None defend women's rights for decent work. While migrants contribute to these profit-making industries, the recruiters do not take responsibility for fair wages and decent workplaces. This makes women vulnerable to indecent housing, indecent sanitation, indecent healthcare and indecent work. These cross-border circuits, while being a source of livelihood for women and their families, are sites where exploitation of women's labour and trafficking takes place. These hidden populations most often are unreached by assistance because of the legal–illegal construct within the migration framework. Undocumented migrants and women in forced labour are further pushed out of assistance. Therefore, I recommend developing a broader perspective and analysis on the interconnectedness of human trafficking with migration, decent work, fair wages and dignity in labour (Das, 2024, pp. 294, 295).

In the trafficking discourse especially in the Indian context, agency is a very contentious and neglected term, where decisions for the 'rescue', 'rehabilitation' or 'reintegration' of women are mostly taken by the NGOs or government agencies following the stipulated guidelines, without the full participation or informed consent of women in the decision-making process. The police in India, under the Immoral Trafficking (Prevention) Act, carry out raid and rescue operations along with NGOs. The notion of a female 'victim' of trafficking in need of 'rescue' and 'return' is a pervasive image that conjures their agency to make informed choices regarding their own lives (Kempadoo, 2015; Sleightholme and Sinha, 1997). Critics argue that such raids and rescue operations not only lead to arbitrary arrests, detention, confiscation of property and valuables, but to forced rehabilitations and deportation of undocumented migrant sex workers, trafficked or not (Wijers, 2015, p. 67). This approach has been critiqued for being insensitive towards women, further damaging the social image of returned women. It has been argued that the process of reintegration of returned women excludes their voice, participation and agency in the process of return. Existing literatures on the experiences of women focus on the exploitation of women, which includes deception, violations, violence, subjugation, exclusion, isolation and living and working in 'slavery'-like conditions as a trafficked victim.

However, there is a gap in the post-trafficking narratives of women's experiences post rescue, including women's strategies of empowerment and women's own understanding of their identities, subjectivities and agency in the context of trafficking, migration and work, which it is necessary to fill to inform public policy and action (Das, 2024, p. 4).

With the notion of trafficking deeply entrenched in strong anti-prostitution and anti-migration foundations (Kempadoo, 2015, pp. 12, 16), the conflation between sexual slavery and sex work, with abolitionist feminists demanding an end to prostitution, is stronger than the lobby of rights-based feminist groups demanding rights of women to sex work, safe workplaces and social security like any other workers (Kempadoo, 2015, p. xiii; Kempadoo et al., 2012, pp. 9–12; O'Connell, 2006). The anti-migration foundation within a protectionist approach curbs the right of mobility and agency of female economic migrants (Pattanaik, 2008). Women's agency to work, mobility and resourcefulness gets sidelined in the dominant anti-trafficking discourse. This gender bias is further established by a protectionist and paternalist approach that re-enforces the gender norm that women need constant male and state protection (Pattanaik, 2008). In the past few decades, women have been migrating from one place to the other in search of a better life, better opportunities for work to support their families back home or to move out to escape from domestic violence. In a globalized economy, the role of gender is a distinctive pattern in the case of female migration, which puts women at high risk of trafficking (Russell, 2014, p. 536). The feminization of migration has heightened the global attention towards the issue of human trafficking (Russell, 2014, p. 532). However, the systemic and structural causal factors of women's economic migration get less attention in the presence of sensationalized stories and images of women's oppression in the sex trade (Das, 2024, pp. 5, 6). The gendered narratives silence and suppress the voices of trafficked women with their victim status or as sexualized others (Russell, 2014, pp. 532–48). It is, therefore, important to examine and understand how women view themselves and construct their identities and subjectivities, and how they negotiate the decision-making process that concerns their lives and dignity.

In my doctoral research I explored the challenges that trafficked and migrant women workers face in their journey towards a better life in the host cities. I explored how they utilize their agency and collective solidarity to liberate themselves from situations of subjugation and exploitation. Further, I examined how they affirm their dignity and rights in their empowerment process as trafficked women and as migrant workers. Women who participated in this research identified themselves as Christian migrant working women, with some having experiences of trafficking and hostility in the host cities. They shared their initial experiences of vulnerabilities in the host city, which ranged from not having skills for work, to not knowing the spoken language of the city, or not being able to negotiate wages or work ethics. They emphasized the importance of collective solidarity as it helped them to support one another in times of crisis. Achui (pseudonym) shared about how she was not given her salary in one of the spas where she worked and wanted to leave. She was new to the city but managed to contact a student union from her ethnic tribe that helped her in this desperate situation. The leaders of the union approached Achui's employer and got her salaries and dues without her having the need to face the terror of the employer. The employer, incidentally, happened to be from Achui's home state but lacked work ethics. For Stella, Achui and others who contributed to this research, economic independence and self-reliance is the key indicator for their confidence, sense of self-worth and dignity. The spirit of solidarity and community for them in the host city is greater than being part of a typical conservative, alienating and discriminatory church or community back home. Most of them found that community through a church, church group or a student workers network in the host city (Das, 2024, pp. 238, 239).

To further the argument on the need to decolonize knowledge systems in development research and theology, I refer to Kamala Kempadoo's article, 'The Modern-Day White (Wo)Man's Burden' (2015), where she critiques the role of white supremacy in the anti-trafficking paradigm. White supremacy, Kempadoo (2015, p. 13) notes, operates to maintain and defend a system of white wealth, power and privilege – an ideology and not a skin colour – that also takes for granted the role of those who adhere to the ideology as national and global leaders, thinkers, creators, authorities and decision-makers. Persons of racialized minorities and the Global South are not always in opposition to white supremacy, but indeed may be complicit with it, where the racialized oppressed become 'honorary whites' who 'assimilate to succeed' (hooks, 1995, p. 189; Macedo and Gounari, 2006). Moreover, white supremacy does not always require a distancing, exclusion or hatred of the racial other. When steeped in neoliberalism, it can express a longing for the presence of, or a desire to help, the other, neither of which unsettle unequal racialized relations of power (hooks, 1995, p. 185).

White supremacy is present in the dominant anti-trafficking campaigns, which, being developed from within the racialized circles of the

Global North, serve the immediate interests of 'victims' in the Global South, with the 'saviours' in the South implementing these programmes to rescue the suffering bodies of women from Indian brothels for rehabilitation and return them to their homes, to the very conditions that they had fled from, in search of a better life. Abolitionist feminism imbibes humanitarian fantasies and lacks the ideologies required to challenge oppressive systems and structures that demonize the labour of the poor, sex work or not.

Transformative developmental changes, in policy and praxis, are required to protect the interests and dignity of the workers in the informal economy in the neoliberal globalized world. The inclusion of the knowledge of the racialized other in contemporary development policies and praxis, including the anti-trafficking campaigns, must be able to challenge the economic institutions that instead of promoting the well-being of the poor promote and protect the interests of the capitalist economies. This complex web of racism and neoliberalism broadens the gap not just between the Global North and Global South, but also between the richest of the rich, the poor and the middle class in the North.

Kempadoo (2015, p. 17) prompts how 'several centuries of globalizing capitalism and (neo) liberal agendas have produced the problems that underpin the concentration of wealth in the hands of a few and the dire circumstances for the world's majority'. She further shares David McNally's (2012, p. 115) views on the vampire-like qualities of capitalism as 'the essence of capitalist monstrosity is its transformation of human flesh and blood into raw materials for the manic machinery of accumulation'. The Credit Suisse Global Wealth Report 2021 reports that:

> Wealth creation in 2020 was largely immune to the challenges facing the world due to the actions taken by governments and central banks to mitigate the economic impact of COVID-19. Total global wealth grew by 7.4% and wealth per adult rose by 6% to reach another record high of USD 79,952. Overall, the countries most affected by the pandemic have not fared worse in terms of wealth creation.

Worldwide, the report estimated that there were 56.1 million millionaires at the end of 2020, up 5.2 million from a year earlier. In 2020, the year after Covid-19 hit the globe, for the first time, more than 1% of all global adults are dollar millionaires. The report further mentions that 'Wealth differences between adults widened in 2020 for the world as a whole and also in most countries. The ultra-high net worth (UHNW) group added 24% more members, the highest rate of increase since 2003.' The report states that female workers initially suffered disproportionately from the pandemic, partly because of their high representation in businesses and industries badly affected by the pandemic, such as restaurants, hotels, personal service and retail. The International Labour Office reports that, before the pandemic, 40% of female workers globally were employed in industries destined to be worst affected, while 36.6% of men were in those industries. The results were evident in labour force statistics at the start of the pandemic (Credit Suisse, 2021, pp. 5, 13, 17, 18, 20). This working of capitalism, as many scholars have pointed out, creates an apartheid between the haves in the economic systems and the have-nots, with the gap widening in the social and economic participation of the included ruling class and the excluded. Critical labour studies need deep reflection to investigate the corelation between the strength and growth of the power structures and economic institutions and the growing violence and exploitation of the workers, specifically female economic migrants. While the lives of poor workers are dependent on neoliberal capitalism, the lack of systems to address the structural violence of the workers further excludes the participation and voice of the workers.

A preferential option for the poor: practising solidarity by centring the voice and knowledge of communities in margins

Gustavo Gutiérrez (1988, p. 174) mentions that the purpose of doing liberation theology is not for 'intellectual self-satisfaction' but to 'build a true human fellowship, in our historical initiatives to subvert an order of injustice – with the fullness with which Christ loved us'. With this theological foundation, I contend for utilizing communities in the margin as a theology-generating agency. Giving epistemic advantage to people in margins of knowledge production and centring people's voice and standpoint is in fact practising solidarity and working towards bringing transformative changes to change the conditions of those whose lives we seek to improve. With liberation as the central theme in the Bible, it is important to develop strategies to establish a relationship between theology and praxis. How can we develop a relationship with the oppressed to design methodological frameworks that can contribute to liberative scholarship, praxis and advocacy (Das, 2024, pp. 12, 13)?

A preferential option for the poor means working towards economic justice. Gutiérrez (1988, p. 163) elucidates and clarifies the term 'poverty': the term *poverty* designates in the first place *material poverty*; that is, the lack of economic goods necessary for a human life worthy of a name. In this sense, poverty is considered degrading and is rejected by the conscience of contemporary humanity. Even those who are not, and do not wish to be, aware of this root cause of poverty believe that this should be struggled against.

Gutiérrez (1988, pp. 163, 164) further argues that when Christians tend to give material poverty a positive value, considering it to be a religious ideal, it actually means to be indifferent to the plights of the contemporary poor who aspire to freedom from exploitation and oppression. The theology of liberation, Gutiérrez describes, is a process of reflection and active participation of the oppressed who raise voices against their oppressor to attain a form of freedom from all forms of exploitation. They aspire to a life of dignity. Gutiérrez elaborates thus:

> The theology of liberation attempts to reflect on the experience and meaning of the faith based on the commitment to abolish injustice and to build a new society; this theology must be verified by the practice of that commitment, by active effective participation in the struggle which the exploited social classes have undertaken against their oppressors. Liberation from every form of exploitation, the possibility of a more humane and dignified life, the creation of a new man – all pass through this struggle ... we will have an authentic theology of liberation only when the oppressed can freely raise their voice and express themselves directly and creatively in society and in the heart of the People of God, when they themselves 'account for the hope,' which they bear, when they are the protagonist of their own liberation. For now, we must limit ourselves to efforts which ought to deepen and support that process, which has barely begun. (Gutiérrez, 1988, p. 174)

In a world that exhibits deep and widespread oppression of the poor both within the workforce and outside, how do feminist liberation theologies address the issue of the dehumanization of women that has accepted androcentric injustice and undervaluation of women's work as a norm? In the context of highly insensitive feminized jobs worldwide and sexist work environments that exhibit and breed misogyny and sexism, how can women from the Global South be protected by law while working in the informal labour sector? How can feminist liberation theology dismantle patriarchy and address the structural and systemic injustices towards vulnerable women to protect and empower them from being trafficked? How can we discern and work towards a transformative and liberative praxis and establish egalitarian relationships with the dominated and oppressed? How can a dialectic of communal experience and solidarity create an organic movement and social order that transcends class, caste, race, ethnicity, gender and sexuality? How can theology challenge those who profit from the undervalued work of women from the Global South? How can the church be in solidarity with women and ensure that they be enablers and active advocates of peace and social and economic justice for women worldwide, especially those whose bodies and labour are dehumanized, impersonalized and in-dignified? Importantly, how can the unjust systems within theology create spaces for women's contribution to knowledge production and in doing theology (Das, 2024, p. 119)?

In their article 'Deep Solidarity: Broadening the Basis of Transformation' (2017, p. 2), Joerg Rieger and Rosemarie Henkel-Rieger share how solidarity, a concept that is often used in progressive circles, pushes us a step beyond advocacy. They argue that rather than merely helping others in need and thus engaging in acts of charity, advocates speak out about the problems that affect others, challenging the powers that be. Yet while advocacy seeks to address the causes of the problems overlooked by charity, advocacy reaches its limits when advocates fail to understand their deeper connections with those for whom they are advocating. Too many advocates assume that they are somehow above or unaffected by the problems they are addressing, speaking for others out of the goodness of their own hearts.

The anti-trafficking advocates and saviours believe that they know best about what must be done with the 'fallen sisters', the naive trafficked and prostituted women, who are in dire need of rescue and rehabilitation and lack the agency to contribute to the decision-making processes concerning their lives. With the dominant anti-trafficking rhetoric conceptualizing women as passive victims, they marginalize the voice of the very women they intend to care for. For instance, trafficked and rescued women shared their concerns for not being able to send money home since they were unable to earn during the time they lived in shelters. In the absence of utilizing the resourceful agency and autonomy of women in the anti-trafficking paradigm, the advocates lack being in true solidarity with women despite the goodness in their intent. Such a paternalistic approach can render women to secondary victimization, and hence the need to reflect on ethical approaches to address the concerns of the vulnerable and trafficked women (Das, 2024, pp. 57, 61).

If the oppressed as individuals or as peoples must fight for the restoration of humanity, what would be their praxis amid the oppressors' acts of systemic violence and lovelessness, and also when the fear of freedom afflicts the oppressed? What would generate and give voice to the critical consciousness of the oppressed to liberate themselves? Most importantly, what would be our role as a society and as a church partaking in this process of liberation, in the reimagination of a world liberated from the vices and depravities of exploitation and injustice (Das, 2024, p. 125)? To break an unjust social order, Freire (2000, p. 45) advocates for true generosity that works towards transforming the world.

True generosity consists precisely in fighting to destroy the causes that nourish false charity. False charity constrains the fearful subdued, the 'rejects of life', to extend their trembling hands. True generosity lies in striving so that these hands – whether of individuals or entire peoples – need be extended less and less in supplication, so that more and more they become human hands that work and, working, transform the world.

Rieger and Henkel-Rieger further mention:

In the past, solidarity has sometimes been misunderstood as the privileged supporting the underprivileged. Well-meaning people in the countries of the global North, for instance, have at times declared their solidarity with people in the countries of the global South, without understanding what they might share in common ... One-sided forms of advocacy and solidarity create several problems. One is that those who consider themselves privileged are calling the shots, acting as if they had the ability to fix the problems by themselves. This rarely works, because the problems are usually too big and because the privileged group is not able to understand what is going on without those who are most immediately affected. Moreover, advocates often assume that they are speaking for those who have no voice, without realising that others may have a voice and are using it in their own ways. Another problem has to do with the fact that those who consider themselves privileged might feel like they can walk away from solidarity whenever they had enough because they fail to understand the deeper connections that link them to the struggle. (2017, p. 2)

They propose the term 'deep solidarity' to address these problems and to suggest a better way forward. They describe deep solidarity as:

a situation where the 99% of us who have to work for a living develop some understanding that we are in the same boat ... The question is how faith communities can begin to understand that they are mostly made up of working people, that most of us are workers now and that even what is considered divine appears to be joining us in deep solidarity. Other communities, including the unions and their supporters, can benefit from this perspective as well. To be sure, understanding our deep connections and relationships does not mean that our differences have to be covered up. Just the opposite: deep solidarity allows us to respect our differences and to put them to productive use. (2017, p. 2)

I truly believe in a liberative praxis that not only frees those who are oppressed but also those who live disentangled, unbothered and insensitive to the impact of unjust social, economic and theological systems and practices that oppress and exploit our sisters and brothers without whom we are not one humankind. To be in solidarity with our fellow human beings means to be conscious of their realities, to understand the need for just action and work towards just solidarity. Liberation of the other would mean liberation for all. Our understanding and strategy for just solidarity must begin with creating a ground of common interest, moving from one-sided charity to mutuality. To make solidarity a reality, we must look at ways of creating a praxis of mutuality with and for the oppressed. The moment of insight, even 'from a "naive awareness" to "critical awareness" will take shape from dialogue' (Isasi-Díaz, 1996, p. 94).

Conclusion

A saviour complex distorts the gospel of love and does not assert the rights and dignity of the marginalized. A protectionist agenda in the neocolonial and free-market capitalist context draws the attention of the moral majority that work tirelessly towards the redemption of the 'fallen sisters' while distracting the real political and policy goals of working towards a just economy. The politicization of religion to fulfil the goals of the neoconservatives, nationalists and fascists who focus on the protection of borders from the influx of immigrants promotes violence against 'neighbours' (Matthew 22.36–40) instead of just love for communities and people in margins (Matthew 25.35–40). Religious teachings that endorse a culture of moral hegemony is anti-people and unabashedly promotes oppressive systems of work. Women are further harmed by exploitative work ethics that are defined by patriarchal and chauvinistic values. Lack of safety nets and unions further harms migrant women working in unorganized sectors. The neocolonial exploitation of the vulnerable, poor and migrant working women from the Global South is dangerously becoming an accepted norm with fascist regimes. Fascist ideologies, by bringing religion into politics, have given rise to white supremacy, Christian nationalism and white heteropatriarchal systems of domination and oppression. Such hostile, racist and sexist violence against women must be called out and addressed from within religious institutions and theological circles.

With this in the background, this chapter has argued for decolonization of knowledge systems and the acknowledgement of communities in the margins as resourceful agents of their liberation and empowerment, both in development research and in theology. Creating transformative pathways for a just world requires our collective action and solidarity with vulnerable and marginalized populations. It further asserts women's rights to decent work and invites the wider community to be in just solidarity with female economic migrants.

Women do form circles and networks of solidarity to support one another. Despite their experiences of vulnerability, exploitation and subjugation in their experiences with trafficking and in their migration pathways, they evolve as women who affirm their dignity and assert their rights in society, in their families and communities and in their workplaces. Women expect the wider community to participate and contribute to address the socio-economic marginalization and discrimination that they face in their everyday struggles for a life and work with dignity. So how can we be in just solidarity with trafficked and migrant working women? The notion of just solidarity is an aspect that emerged as a recommendation from this research, which encapsulates all recommendations within one framework (Das, 2024, pp. 295, 296).

My notion of just solidarity is political and invites the larger community to engage with and work for a just transformation of people and communities in margins, for social and economic justice. To be in just solidarity with the oppressed and marginalized means to be aware of their context and realities and understand it through their lens. It calls for just action and just peace. Just solidarity is not a top-down charity nor a short-term relief service; it is looking for long-term, sustainable social and economic solutions for the poor and marginalized. Just solidarity means understanding the concerns of poor and marginalized people and communities from their perspectives. It means building epistemological relationships with the poor and marginalized. It means building collaborative relationships with them to work together for a mutually empowering and transformative praxis. A just solidarity, in my opinion, is a long-term commitment and yields accountability for establishing justice, peace and a new social order (Das, 2024, p. 313). I recommend more research on how people, communities, church and other faith groups can be in tangible and just solidarity with the poor and marginalized communities, grounding the production of knowledge and doing theology with the poor and marginalized.

Notes

1 The United States Department of State Office to Monitor and Combat Trafficking in Persons, June 2023, reports: 'The growing awareness of boys exploited in human trafficking is fairly recent. While male trafficking victims are receiving more attention than in years past, social and health services as well as legal and advocacy frameworks still predominantly focus on female victims of sexual exploitation', according to the UNODC report. Media and civil society groups alike consistently refer to boys and adolescent male human trafficking victims as 'unseen and unhelped', a 'silenced minority', 'invisible' or 'secret victims', https://www.state.gov/wp-content/uploads/2023/12/Overlooked-for-Too-Long-Boys-and-Human-Trafficking.pdf (accessed 27.01.2025).

2 International Labour Organization, https://www.ilo.org/global/lang--en/index.htm (accessed 27.01.2025)

3 European Commission, 'Employment and Decent Work', https://international-partnerships.ec.europa.eu/policies/sustainable-growth-and-jobs/employment-and-decent-work_en (accessed 8.01.2025).

4 See UN Department of Economic Affairs, 2023, 'The 17 Goals', https://sdgs.un.org/goals (accessed 8.01.2025).

5 Human trafficking can include, but does not require, movement. People may be considered trafficking victims regardless of whether they were born into a state of servitude, were exploited in their hometown, were transported to the exploitative situation, previously consented to work for a trafficker or participated in a crime as a direct result of being trafficked. At the heart of this phenomenon is the traffickers' aim to exploit and enslave their victims and the myriad coercive and deceptive practices they use to do so. See https://www.state.gov/what-is-modern-slavery/.

6 'Trafficking in persons', 'human trafficking' and 'modern slavery' are used as umbrella terms to refer to both sex trafficking and compelled labour. 'The Protocol to Prevent, Suppress and Punish Trafficking in Persons, Especially Women and Children, supplementing the United Nations Convention against Transnational Organized Crime (the Palermo Protocol) describes this compelled service using a number of different terms, including involuntary servitude, slavery or practices similar to slavery, debt bondage, and forced labour.' See 2009-2017.state.gov/j/tip/what/index.htm (accessed 27.01.2025).

References

Abuiyada, R., 2018, 'Traditional Development Theories have Failed to Address the Needs of the Majority of People at Grassroots Levels with Reference to GAD', *International Journal of Business and Social Science* 9, doi: 10.30845/ijbss.v9n9p12.

Bales, K., 1999, *Disposable People: New Slavery in the Global Economy*, Oakland, CA: University of California Press.

Cojocaru, C., 2016, 'My Experience is Mine to Tell: Challenging the Abolitionist Victimhood Framework', *Anti-Trafficking Review* 7, pp. 12–38, www.antitraffickingreview.org (accessed 27.01.2025).

Das, S., 2024, 'Towards a Feminist Theology of (In)-Decent Work in the Context of Human Trafficking and Migration: Journeying with Economic Migrant Women in India in their Struggle for a Life of Dignity', PhD thesis, University of KwaZulu-Natal.

Fanon, F., 1952, *Black Skin, White Masks*, New York: Grove Press.

Freire, P., 2000, *Pedagogy of the Oppressed*, New York: Continuum.

Gutiérrez, G., 1988, *A Theology of Liberation: History, Politics, and Salvation*, Maryknoll, NY: Orbis Books.

hooks, b., 1995, 'Overcoming White Supremacy: A Comment', in *Killing Rage, Ending Racism*, New York: Henry Holt and Company.

Isasi Díaz, A. M., 1996, *Mujerista Theology: A Theology for the Twenty-First Century*, Maryknoll, NY: Orbis Books.

Jenkins, K., Narayanaswamy, L. and Sweetman, C., 2019, 'Introduction: Feminist Values in Research', *Gender & Development* 27(3), pp. 415–25, doi: 10.1080/13552074.2019.1682311.

Kara, S., 2009, *Sex Trafficking: Inside the Business of Modern Slavery*, New York: Columbia University Press.

Kempadoo, K., Sanghera, J. and Pattanaik, B., 2012, *Trafficking and Prostitution Reconsidered: New Perspectives on Migration, Sex Work, and Human Rights* (2nd edn), New York: Routledge.

Kempadoo, K., 2015, 'The Modern-Day White (Wo)Man's Burden: Trends in Anti-Trafficking and Anti-Slavery Campaigns', *Journal of Human Trafficking* 1(1), pp. 8–20, doi: 10.1080/23322705.2015.1006120.

Macedo, D. and Gounari, P., 2006, 'Globalization and the Unleashing of New Racism: An Introduction', in D. Macedo and P. Gounari (eds), *The Globalization of Racism*, Boulder, CO: Paradigm.

Mahmoud, F., 1991, 'African Women and Feminist Schools of Thought', in M. Suliman (ed.), *Alternative Development Strategies for Africa, Vol. 2: Environment, Women*, London: Institute for African Alternatives, pp. 141–7.

McNally, D., 2012, *Monsters of the Market: Zombies, Vampires and Global Capitalism*, Chicago, IL: Haymarket Books.

Observer Research Foundation, https://www.orfonline.org/research/a-global-south-perspective-on-the-fight-against-the-climate-crisis (accessed 25.02.2025).

O'Connell Davidson, J., 2006, 'Will the Real Sex Slave Please Stand Up?', *Feminist Review* 83, pp. 4–22, http://www.jstor.org/stable/3874380 (accessed 25.02.2025).

Osman-Elasha, B., 2009, 'Women ... In The Shadow of Climate Change', *UN Chronicle, Special Climate Change Issue: To Protect Succeeding Generations* 46(3–4).
Pattanaik, B., 2008, Anti-Trafficking and a Rights-Based Approach: Are they Compatible?', *Gender-Migration-Labour-Trafficking Roundtable: Exploring Conceptual Linkages and Moving Forward*, Bangkok (6–9 August), p. 18. Bangkok: GAATW.
Poudel, M., 2011, *Dealing with Hidden Issues: Social Rejection Experienced by Trafficked Women in Nepal*, Saarbrucken: Lambert Academic Publishing.
Quirk, J., 2007, 'Trafficked into Slavery', *Journal of Human Rights* 6(2), pp. 181–207.
Rieger, J., 2013, 'The Ethics of Wealth in a World of Economic Inequality: A Christian Perspective in a Buddhist–Christian Dialogue', *Buddhist-Christian Studies* 33(1), pp. 153–62.
Rieger, J., 2022, *Theology in the Capitalocene: Ecology, Identity, Class, and Solidarity*, Minneapolis, MN: Fortress Press.
Rieger, J. and Henkel-Rieger, R., 2017, 'Deep Solidarity: Broadening the Basis of Transformation', *HTS Teologiese Studies/Theological Studies* 73(3), a4578, doi: 10.4102/hts.v73i3.4578.
Russell, A. M., 2014, 'Victims of Trafficking: The Feminisation of Poverty and Migration in the Gendered Narratives of Human Trafficking', *Societies* 4(4), pp. 532–48, doi: 10.3390/soc4040532.
Sanghera, J., 2005, 'Unpacking the Trafficking Discourse', in K. Kempadoo, B. Pattanaik and J. Sanghera (eds), *Trafficking and Prostitution Reconsidered: New Perspectives on Migration, Sex Work, and Human Rights*, Boulder, CO: Paradigm Publishers, pp. 3–25.
Sassen, S., 2002, 'Women's Burden: Counter-Geographies of Globalization and the Feminization of Survival', *Nordic Journal of International Law* 71(2), pp. 255–74, doi: 10.1163/157181002761931378.
Simkhada, P., 2008, 'Life Histories and Survival Strategies Amongst Sexually Trafficked Girls in Nepal', *Children & Society* 22(3), pp. 234–48, doi.org/10.1111/j.1099-0860.2008.00154.x.
Sleightholme, C. and Sinha, I., 1997, *Guilty Without Trial: Women in the Sex Trade in Calcutta*, New Brunswick, NJ: Rutgers University Press.
Suri, S., 2023, 'It's Time for Climate Justice: A Global South Perspective on the Fight Against the Climate Crisis', *Observer Research Foundation: Commentaries*, https://www.orfonline.org/research/a-global-south-perspective-on-the-fight-against-the-climate-crisis.
Wijers, M., 2015, 'Purity, Victimhood and Agency: Fifteen Years of the UN Trafficking Protocol', *Anti-Trafficking Review* 4.

Reports and documents:

Credit Suisse, 2021, *The Global Wealth Report*.
ILO, 2012, *Global Estimate of Forced Labour: Results and Methodology*, International Labour Organization Special Action Program to Combat Forced Labour (SAP-FL).

International Labour Conference, 2009, *Gender Equality at the Heart of Decent Work*, 98th Session, International Labour Office Geneva, https://www.ohchr.org/sites/default/files/Documents/Issues/Racism/IWG/Session7/GenderEquality.pdf (accessed 27.01.2025).

US Department of State, 2023. *Office to Monitor and Combat Trafficking in Persons*, June.

PART 2

Case Studies

3

The Liberative Potentials of Philippine *Itneg*[1] Women's Ministry in Reconstructing a Theology of Development

MA. GLOVEDI JOY L. BIGORNIA

Introduction

In a highly globalized world, the western colonial and neoliberal definition of development has taken root in every society. In its strategic positioning, it evolved and metamorphosed into a form that is consumable to cultures and traditions that were initially resistant to it. Despite the western colonial power that encroached on and redefined the ontologies and epistemologies of the colonized, I argue that areas and spaces exist that are relatively resilient to the total annihilation of being and thinking. In my view, these locales can be found in indigenous communities.

In the Philippines, I look at the case of the Cordilleran indigenous people in Northern Luzon, particularly a group of Christian women in the *Itneg* community found in the province of Abra, as they operate within a cooperative and sustainable framework that is deeply rooted in their indigenous beliefs and practices. These collaborative indigenous practices are tied to their ontological and epistemological views that inform their perspective on development. These practices are also strongly connected to feminist values, and women, particularly those who are members of the women's ministry in the church, are leveraging them for economic growth. However, the impact of engaging in these activities and practices goes beyond the economic level towards the social, political and public realm. This is not to say that the *Itneg* community, like others in the Cordillera Region, is untouched by any modern colonial and neoliberal progress. Developmental shifts as far as physical infrastructures are concerned can be seen predominantly in the improvements built in the area, from road pavements to bridges, buildings and houses. These changes show the visible side of modern development in the community. However, beyond the physical changes lies an obscure yet darker side. This is the shift in ways of thinking, knowing and doing by the *Itnegs* as well as changes in values and the non-material culture of the community. Undoubtedly, there are benefits of modern development from which the *Itnegs* have enjoyed an improved way of living, such as in education and technological innovations in agriculture or farming. The way the *Itnegs* view modern development also evolved over time and emerged in response to the changes of time. In analysing the *Itnegs*' present conception of development it is crucial to acknowledge the western modern colonial influence, through coloniality configured in neoliberal capitalism among other things, in reconstituting the concept.

Nevertheless, their perspective on development should be understood from a holistic integrative approach. In the next section, I elaborate briefly on the traditional notion of development for the *Itnegs* – one that is largely informed by a world view shaped by their indigenous ontological and epistemological views.

Development in the *Itneg* community

The holistic integrative approach to the *Itnegs*' notion of development begins with an acknowledgement of its mutually inclusive relationship with religion. Their religious and spiritual understanding of the world prefigures their conception of development. The definition and conceptualization of development from the *Itneg* point of view cannot be detached from their indigenous knowledge and understanding of life. Central to their cosmological and ontological view are their spiritual beliefs, the interconnectedness of all creation and the holistic approach to life. Accordingly, religion occupies a major part of their lives (Valera and Valera, 2016; Cole, 2016). Prior to the Christianization of the *Itnegs*, their beliefs were highly animistic, as in other parts of the Philippine Cordillera. The significance of religious beliefs and practices is attached not only to their individual lives but, more importantly, to their communal existence. There is an inseparable link between *Itnegs*' religious rituals and their community life (Weygan, 2009). This is to say that the socio-political and public appearances of the *Itnegs* are influenced by their religious beliefs and experiences. At present, this can be seen by the inseparable connection between the community and the church. This also means that the practical dimension of their lives is intimately linked to their ethical, spiritual and religious realities. This holistic and interconnected mode of looking at the world is applied in all aspects of their lives and covers their view of all creation. For the *Itnegs*, the idea of a good life and well-being is maintaining a balanced relationship between humans, land, nature and all other beings. Well-being or good life, which is *pansayaatan/panpiyaan/pan-amayan*[2] in the *Itneg* vernacular, is their traditional understanding of development. This is similar to the concept of well-being, or *pansigedan*, in another indigenous group in the Philippine Cordillera, the *Igorots* of Benguet province (Adonis, 2018). The *Itneg* indigenous concept of *pansayaatan/panpiyaan/pan-amayan* is achieved and maintained by communal practices and the application of indigenous knowledge and social codes. The communal practices such as *ganap*[3] and *botantes*[4] emphasize the collaborative sense of the *Itnegs*.

Over time, development conceived in its traditional and cultural sense is subordinated to, if not superseded by, the modern colonial and neoliberal definition. It is relevant at this point to look into the impact of colonial history and coloniality – as it is reconfigured in neoliberal capitalism and in ways of being and knowing – on the definition of development in the Philippines. Development was colonially designed and imposed even after the country's independence. This imposed concept of development echoes in the *Itnegs*' mindset and, as I argue later, reshapes their theological view of a good life (*pansayaatan/* development).

Development, colonialism and coloniality in the Philippines

Current development is planned in an attempt to catch up to the global economy and is informed by colonial epistemologies. The colonizers' imposition of their own knowledge production systems subsequently realigned the definition of development. In the Philippine context, the notion of development cannot be divorced from its colonial history.

The entrance of western knowledge occurred during the supposed 'discovery' of the Philippines by Spain. The Spanish colonial rule in the country lasted for 377 years. Within these years, the colonial power was bolstered by the propagation of colonial thinking. It was colonial mentality (Mendoza, 2001) that formed a relation of dependence between the colonizers and the colonized by setting up a ruling elite (Brainard and Litton, 1999). The acceptance, assimilation and revelation of colonial thought in the minds and lives of Filipinos happened when the colonizers established the local ruling elites. The appointment of local elites consolidated the colonial power and made it easier to control different groups from various geographical locations in the Philippines. Working with local leaders was a strategic move that spread the colonization of the mind and the promotion of colonial knowledge. In addition to this, the baptism of the Philippines as a Christian nation (Brainard and Litton, 1999) supplanted local religious traditions, redefined the native world views and made them conform to the European paradigm (Herrera, 2015). This civilizing mission was continued by the Americans when the Philippines was ceded to them.

In addition to Christianity, democratic government and formal education were introduced by the Americans (Lewis and Murphy, 2006) as strategies to achieve the colonial mission. During the American occupation, it was argued that education became a colonial instrument to make Filipinos follow the creation of the ideal American image (Brainard and Litton, 1999). This resulted in an ingrained colonialism among Filipinos, manifested in their love for anything American or western. Both the Spanish and American occupations in the Philippines created a colonial mindset that concedes to colonial knowledge and adheres to a western framework of development. Speaking of American intervention in the Philippines, their successful introduction of development meant the achievement and extension of the colonial interests of the American empire. Accordingly:

> As Walden Bello and his colleagues amply document, McNamara has achieved in the Philippines precisely the kind of 'victory' he earlier sought as Secretary of Defense for American imperial interest in Vietnam, namely the subjugation of a people to priorities and interests set by distant economic and political power centers. (Bello et al., 1982, p. xi)

Beyond colonialism, I argue in reference to the works of Latin American thinkers like Aníbal Quijano, Enrique Dussel, Walter Mignolo, Ramón Grosfoguel, Nelson-Maldonado Torres, Arturo Escobar, Catherine Walsh, Maria Lugones and others, that there is a global structure that continuously and persistently configures the power relations between nations. This structure of power is asymmetrically tipped in favour of the West, the so-called Global North against the rest, especially the former colonies like the Philippines. This power structure is coloniality or coloniality of power, which according to Aníbal Quijano 'is the most general form of domination in the world today, once colonialism as an explicit political order was destroyed' (2007, p. 170). Nelson Maldonado-Torres further explains that coloniality 'refers to long-standing patterns of power that emerged as a result of colonialism, but that define culture, labor, intersubjective relations, and knowledge production well beyond the strict limits of colonial administrations' (2007, p. 243). One specific configuration of coloniality manifests in the control, domination and regulation of labour and markets. This is capitalism, underpinned by the centrality and hegemony of the West, now re-emerging as borderless democratic global markets (neoliberalism), and dictating the form of development undertaken by dependent countries (those underdeveloped or developing countries by western definition). This is coloniality of power in its economic and political dimensions. With this dimension of coloniality at play, I argue that development in the Philippines is modelled from the western development paradigm, and the process of development planning is anchored in neoliberal and colonial epistemologies. For instance, this can be deduced from the country's development goals that overly emphasize the bottom line, evidenced by Philippine Development Plans that were greatly 'informed by the influence of economic growth models' (Jurado, 2003, p. 20). Another example is the numerous cases of violence perpetuated in the name of development that exhibit and affirm the hierarchical, brutal and exploitative character of coloniality. The victims of development aggressions are mostly the indigenous communities and the environment, such as through encroachment on ancestral lands and displacements of indigenous people, and exploitation of natural resources in the Cordillera Region (Molintas, 2004).

On a further note, the neoliberal capitalist dimension of coloniality overlaps and is accompanied by other forms such that the imposition of a westernized definition of development is actualized through ontological[5] and epistemic[6] violence. According to Ndlovu, 'coloniality must be understood as a project-like power structure that affects various aspects of the lives of colonized subjects, including their ways of knowing, seeing and imagining the world' (2018, p. 99). In other words, it is made possible through the subjugation and erasure of subjectivities, histories and knowledge of the colonized by co-opting the academic, religious, political and socio-cultural structures. In the subsequent discussion, I contend that the *Itneg* indigenous group's theological approach to development is formed within a background of colonial continuities found in various structures of society but that this background is also a contested space – a space that allows indigenous world views to contradict and resist coloniality.

Theology of development in the present-day *Itneg* community

It is coloniality, configured in neoliberal capitalism that didactically intersects with other dimensions, and extensively dictates the present form of development in the Philippine society. The imposition of this kind of development on the *Itnegs* happens in different ways. For instance, it occurs through the adoption of colonial, western and global market-centred development goals and neoliberal policies that are translated into national and regional development plans. These are then devolved to the local government units of which the *Itneg* community is a part. The planning and implementation of local development projects happen mostly in a top-down approach with the bare minimum of or no consultation with local recipients such as the *Itneg* indigenous communities. As these projects are detached from grass-roots realities, they do not align with or effectively address the urgent needs of indigenous people.

On a different front, the colonialized version of development has been introduced and integrated through the adoption of modern western material culture that has become the mainstream culture. This also facilitated the acceleration of the effort to catch up with western advancements. Although the invention of computers, and the advent of the internet, social media platforms and emerging technologies can be considered ambivalent, it has contributed to the *Itnegs*' drive to catch up with modern communities around the globe, but mostly centred on the western. Certainly, the contemporary *Itneg* society is not immune to these changes and has had to adapt to survive. But to what extent these transformations lead to the total annihilation of the *Itnegs*' way of being, thinking, knowing, relating and becoming necessitates constant interrogation.

While political and socio-cultural structures are relevant machinery for the remaking of subjectivities and knowledge reprogramming of the *Itnegs* in service to the acceptance of a colonial form of development, education and religion have much to do with this as well. With western-standardized education, from the basic to the tertiary level, students are presented with an advanced and scientific form of knowledge that render subordinate their indigenous knowledge and beliefs. Presently, the *Itnegs*' animistic religiosity has been supplanted by Christian beliefs. The majority of *Itnegs* have converted to Christianity and become Catholics, Protestants or Pentecostals.[7] To a great extent the civilizing mission – that is, the Christianizing mission of the natives in Abra Province of the Philippines – carried with it the ontological and epistemological imposition that negated their world view. It is from this religious milieu, which overlaps with the political, socio-cultural and academic contexts, that much of the *Itneg* church's theological approach to development is formed.

This theology of development echoes the hierarchical, bottom-line focus and western hegemonic characteristics of coloniality. For instance, the *Itneg* church's theologizing subscribes to a good life that is equated with modern progress and keeping up with the present system. In this particular *Itneg* community, the physical church or the building itself, beautified and renovated according to modern architectural standards, seems to symbolize church and community advancement. It became the focal point of their thinking around the idea of a truly blessed church. Another is the economic well-being of the church pastor. These do connote the church's adherence to development as material progress that coheres with a colonial and neoliberal theology. In other words, it is materialistic theology – a theology of wealth with a single-minded goal of accumulating capital and physical assets because it is a manifestation of God's blessing. The focus is to catch up while maintaining the core characteristic of neoliberal capitalism and other configurations of coloniality – the reliance on commodified and materialistic economic practices and the centrality of men as providers of wealth (equated with development) in the family. This kind of development does not genuinely serve the needs of the present *Itneg* indigenous community, and it certainly does not fit into their indigenous way of life.

From another take, the *Itneg* church's improvement of their church building tells the story of church and community members' willingness and voluntariness to come together and cooperatively accomplish this task. It is also a symbol of solidarity. This solidarity springs from both their Christian and indigenous values and world views. The church building stands as a testament to the *Itnegs*' cooperative labours making possible the kind of development to which they aspire. It also speaks of the value and reverence they ascribe to their place of worship – a sacred place of the divine. For the *Itnegs*, to take extra care of the physical appearance of the church is to show love and respect to God. This is one way they grow and develop in their faith. Moreover, the physical well-being of the church and its leader (pastor) also reflects the well-being of all. Like the value of solidarity, the ascription of sanctity to any meeting place or contact point with the divine comes from an inner well of indigenous spirituality and Christian faith. Therefore, although they associate a modernized church structure with a developed church (materialistic and asset-based development), it also signifies the *Itnegs*' holistic and interconnected view of well-being or good life – the intertwined relationship of the physical and spiritual such that development of one means the development of the other. Hence, in my view, the *Itnegs*' belief in God's promise of prosperity is also not totally split from their traditional culture-based understanding of well-being. Their colonial historical context, emergent situations and lived experiences as indigenous people add layers and nuances to the *Itnegs*' theological reflections and practice of development. This way, their theology of development is characterized by ambiguity and liminality – a constant struggle of contraries that are real and present in the very being and becoming of the *Itnegs* as they live, relate and engage with each other in their church, community and wider society.

To complexify their theological stance on development, acknowledgement must be given to the modern ways of living that have been adopted by the *Itnegs*. As a community of faith, they have embraced modern technology and equipment not just in their religious practices but also in their everyday activities. Their access to the virtual world and online resources has opened a plethora of avenues for recolonization and reinforcement of colonial continuities. Recognizing the changes at present and the impossibility of returning to a precolonial past, development for the *Itnegs* integrates their indigenous notion of well-being with their need to adapt to the changing times. However, the integration and adaptation are neither clear-cut nor linear in the context of intersecting realities. The *Itnegs*' realities deal with confrontations between persistent colonialities that are systemically and structurally perpetuated and resilient indigenous values (axiology) and modes of being (ontology), knowing (epistemology), imagining (imaginary) and doing (methodology). This meeting is playing out in a volatile, uncertain, transborder global world. Thus, the *Itnegs*' theological understanding and practice of development is happening against the background of in-between realities as well as the fluidity, tensions and contradictions existing in their community. This is to say that the *Itneg* church and community is a site of tension between colonial and decolonial practices as well as the ongoing negotiation of modern and indigenous ways of life.

This makes essential the exploration and exposition of liberative and decolonial spaces for the negotiation and renegotiation of the *Itneg* place, including their positions for meaning-making and theologizing about their own development, in the contemporary world. The church's role in this project is essential because, in the *Itneg* world view, the church and community are closely interlinked. From the perspective of a Christian *Itneg*, the church's theology is extensively reflected in the community. In this regard, I argue that women's ministry in the church is a creative avenue for the renegotiation not just of the Christian *Itneg* women's place in the world but the *Itnegs*' being and becoming as a community of indigenous people and Christians. With the indigenous sense of well-being as the underlying foundation, women's ministry is a site for liberative and decolonial practices that make way for the reconstruction of a life-giving theology of development. This group's liberative and decolonial potential lies in its active continuous recentring of the *Itneg* women's contribution in building and developing the community through their participation in autochthonous collaborative practices. In what follows, I make an argument that *Itneg* women's ministry is a space that challenges and offers a new way of theologizing about development.

Itneg women's ministry: towards reconstructing a theology of development

In the organizational make-up of the church in this village, the women's ministry is one among other sub-groups (like the men's, youth and children's ministries) that are collectively formed to take charge of certain assigned functions. The interest in this particular church sub-group is sparked by an initial conversation with key collaborators during the conduct of a seed ethnographic research study[8] on mother-based economics. I was primarily interested in exploring *Itneg* mothers' participation or contribution to the well-being of their family, church and community and how their Pentecostal faith informed their participation. The focus of this chapter, that is, *Itneg* women's collaborative participation in women's ministry activities, is one among other things they identified as their development contribution.

Most of the women referenced their participation as members of the women's ministry when asked about their contribution to the development or well-being of the community. The term 'women's ministry', in this context, takes on an expansive meaning that covers all activities collectively done by women members for the church and community. Specifically, most women commonly refer to their cooperative indigenous work, initiated as part of their ministry, as their primary input in community development. For example, much of the improvement of the church building is attributed to the efforts of the women's ministry through *ganap* and *botantes*.[9] According to them, the cleaning of roads and clearing the community's water source were also accomplished through the labours of the women's ministry. However, these collaborative autochthonous practices are not exclusive to women. Rather, these practices allow for the participation of all and any willing member of the community except when they are called for or by specific groups, meaning there are cases when cooperative work is initiated by women for women. However, participation even in exclusive group work is mostly fluid so that any person regardless of age, gender and religion, so long as willing and able, can join.

Presently, though, it is women who frequently participate in these practices, more than any other members of the church or community in this particular *Itneg* group. A particularly interesting observation is that many if not most of the community building and developmental projects in this *Itneg* village involved the active participation of women through collaborative works. Even when cooperative work is called forth for the whole church or community regardless of gender, it is mostly women and mothers who participate, as representatives of their families. Meanwhile, men or/and husbands are working mostly as construction workers (of buildings, houses or roads) and drivers. Although even in construction works (church building and roads), women are there to help within their capacity, such as in carrying stones and gravels. In these instances, *Itneg* women break even the gender stereotypical barrier imposed on physical work as they also do the work of men.[10] This is especially true when *ganap* or *botantes* are called by the women's ministry for the benefit of the church and the community. In this sense, these collaborative indigenous practices have deep feminist liberative and decolonial ties as they are inclusive and resistant to rigid gender roles and norms especially in divisions of labour. They are also aligned with feminist liberation principles and decolonial goals as these indigenous practices allow for *Itneg* women's empowerment in decision-making and their recognition as essential agents of development. The women's ministry, by opening a space for these liberative indigenous practices, also becomes a location for the realization of liberation and decolonial aims.

Through the women's ministry the persistence of the indigenous cooperative communitarian spirit is shown despite the individualistic pull of modern life. It shows that living and working together is still very much alive in the *Itneg* community. This means that the very activation of indigenous practices by women in the church subsequently results in two things – the continuity and sustainability of the *Itneg* indigenous world view and the repositioning of women at the centre of development works. What is revealed further is the symbiotic sustainable relationship that exists between the women's ministry and the indigenous works they engaged with. On the one hand, these practices find their special niche and hope for preservation in the women's ministry. An analysis of the village dynamics reveals the inclusive, non-hierarchical and interconnected nature of these practices, but the role of the church's women's ministry is pivotal in the consistent actualization of these practices, thus assuring their perpetuity. Consequently, the *Itnegs*' ways of being, thinking and doing are revalidated. According to Anacin (2015), this becomes necessary at a time when, similar to other Cordilleran groups, globalization is threatening their culture. In a society where the youth perceive modernity as giving more space for self-actualization (Adonis and Couch, 2017), the *Itnegs*' autochthonous practices are not yet totally abandoned.

However, as they have embraced Christianity and modern lifestyles, the women's ministry also becomes a conduit for the convergence of indigenous *Itneg* practices and modern Christian beliefs. In this context, this ministry makes way for the adoption of the feminist decolonial concept of hybridity (Lugones, 1992) and the recognition of a multiplicitous self (Ortega, 2001) as a means of repositioning oneself in the modern world. Hybridity points to the reality of inhabiting and embodying multiple subjectivities and is deployed as resistance to the essentialist and singular mode of thinking and imagining our self – the purist and fixed notion of being in the world as valorized by western tradition. As an exercise of resistance, hybridity[11] critiques the dichotomizing tendencies and rigid binary categorizations that are placed for western colonial domination and control. The coexistence of multiple and contradicting realities in the women's ministry allows *Itneg* women to form multiple ways of being and inhabit a hybrid status. It is a way to defy the western, colonial and patriarchal gaze that constantly boxes indigenous women into a subordinate position and devalues their contributions. The space for hybridity provided by the women's ministry also reinforces the indigenous framework of a holistic and interconnected world that is a decolonial resource for the recognition of the complex interlocking relationship of worlds and the intersectional nature of injustices. Taking off from Lugones' discussion, Ortega's concept of multiplicitous self is one that is 'caught in between the norms and practices of different cultures, classes, races, or "worlds"' (2001, p. 4). Additionally, the women's ministry as a site of cultural hybridity also corresponds to Homi Bhaba's third space, 'which gives rise to something different, something new and unrecognizable, a new area of negotiation, of meaning and representation' (1990, p. 211). The women's ministry becomes a creative liminal space for a hybrid Christian indigenous way of being, thinking, living and engaging with the present society. With the women's ministry as an in-between space, indigenous collaborative practices can take new forms and shapes that take on transformative meanings. Another pattern of thinking and doing indigenous cooperative works may also arise but nonetheless coheres with the *Itnegs*' values, beliefs and way of life. From this space, a new way of reconstructing theology of development can emerge – one that embraces the life-giving forms of the present context and seeks to dialogue and coexist with the life-giving indigenous ways of life.

On another note, the very act of engaging in these indigenous cooperative practices sustains and solidifies the position of *Itneg* women in their community. As these indigenous practices are also financial activities that ramp up economic development, they highlight the key contribution of *Itneg* women to the economic sustainability of the church and community. With this economic power, they are recognized as conscious agents of their own welfare and the well-being of their family, church and community. As women in the *Itneg* church ministry actively take charge of the development projects for the church and community, the modern-day tendency to relegate them to the periphery is erased. The recentring of *Itneg* women in the development framework goes beyond the recognition of their economic contribution – it is accompanied by a reclamation of their socio-political standing in the community. According to women participants in the study, their insights are solicited and given similar weight to those of men during public assemblies.[12] Some of the members in the women's ministry are also elders and are assigned leadership positions in the church, while some are elected as local government officials. In these ways the women's ministry can become a liberative space that informs and helps usher in a new way of doing a theology of development. However, there remains the task of nuancing the privilege and power afforded to some women especially with the unique social and political context of the *Itneg* community. Also, there is a need to look into the kind of positions given to women in the church as these might end up stereotyping them or perpetuating the same coloniality. Nevertheless, the women's ministry promotes a more comprehensive form of development in contrast to its profit-centred and materialistic orientation. Their ministry also negates the patriarchal character that somehow entered into the theological approach of the church towards development. The women's ministry becomes a model and praxis to liberate the theology of wealth that is economic-orientated and results in the commodification of the gospel.

Instead, it is transformed into a theology of blessing that accounts for the multidimensionality of development and actualizes the overall well-being/common good of communities.

Lastly, with the recognition of women's agency in the well-being of the community, the women's ministry in this *Itneg* Christian church opposes the top-down form of development. For example, the revitalization of the communal water source and the structural improvements of the pastoral house point to the direct involvement of women in their church and community development.[13] These women's ministry-led initiatives are evidence of actively taking ownership of their own development and subsequently sustaining it through their own resources. These are positive indicators of a participative community development that can lead to communal empowerment for the good of all. This is opposed to the empowerment of the few that can lead to participation contributing to the formation of a hegemonic development. It forwards a kind of thinking and doing of development interventions that are not dependent on external agents. As such, it offers an alternative to the preaching of prosperity that is always brought and done by anyone other than the community itself. By actively engaging with indigenous collaborative practices such as *ganap* and *botantes*, the women's ministry creatively reintroduces a grass-roots theology of development.

Conclusion

In this chapter I have argued that the *Itneg* women's ministry is a creative and transformative space for the actualization of a more life-giving theology of development – one that recognizes, in a holistic integrative manner, the contextual and cultural needs of the *Itneg* community. In my discussions I started with a claim that resilient pockets exist to the persistent coloniality, charged by neoliberal capitalism and configured in the ontological and epistemological dimensions, that aims to realign everything into one agenda. This includes colonial realigning of the concept of development to the detriment of indigenous ontology (being), epistemology (knowing), axiology (valuing) and methodology (acting/doing). I claimed that this resilience is exhibited by the *Itnegs*, particularly through their continuous practices of collaboration in order to achieve collective well-being. These collaborative indigenous practices are employed by *Itneg* women's ministry, especially as part of their development initiatives and participation in church and community. The *Itneg* women's ministry, by engaging in these indigenous practices, challenges the church's theology of development that diametrically rejects their indigenous ways of being and relating to the world. I argued that much of the church theologizing about development adheres to the modern colonial and neoliberal capitalist definition that prioritizes catching up with anything modern, accumulating material wealth and recognizing only men's contribution to the well-being of the family, church and community. The autochthonous collaborative practices by *Itneg* women's ministry resist this kind of theology, while the women's ministry itself becomes a creative in-between space that brings to the surface new patterns of thinking and doing cooperative works. The emergence and sustainability of this space is assured through the continuous engagement of women in collaborative works and makes possible as well the recognition of economic, social and political contributions of *Itneg* women. Consequently, the women's ministry is an avenue for the continuation of indigenous practices and all that they represent. On a final note, in order to harness the full potential of the women's ministry as a transformative and inclusive space, it is critical to engage the perspectives of *Itneg* men and other members of the community, specifically their insights on those indigenous collaborative practices as resources for actualizing solidarity in view of more life-giving development and liberation and decolonial possibilities.

Notes

1 The *Itnegs*, also known as Tinguians, are the natives or the indigenous people of Abra Province, located in Northern Luzon Philippines. Their communities can be found in the lowland and in the mountain areas of the province. So geographically they can be classified as lowland and upland Tinguians or valley and mountain groups. Ethno-linguistically they can be classified in 11 groups – Inlaud, Adasen, Maeng, Masadiit, Banao, Binongan, Mabaka, Gabang, Balatok, Belwang and Muyadan. See Elizabeth Valera and Red Marian Antonette Valera, 'Preserving the Tinguian Culture Heritage: Mother Tongue-Based Multi-Lingual Education as Tool', *Sampurasun e-Journal* 2(1) (June 2016), pp. 79–89; Fay-Cooper Cole, 2016, *The Tinguian: Social, Religious, and Economic Life of a Philippine Tribe*, np: anboco.

2 It also refers to their idea of goodness or whatever is good. Sometimes *pansayaatan/panpiyaan/pan-amayan* is also stated as *kinsayaatan/kinpiyaan/kinamayan*.

3 It is a form of collaborative work for mutual aid by members of the community. It is done freely and voluntarily to achieve a communal goal. In the *Itneg* community, at least one family member should participate to represent the family during *ganap*. The absence of a representative is considered shameful (Avelina, *tongtong*, 2023).

4 *Botantes* is a form of *ganap* – cooperative work but with minimal fee/wage. It can be initiated by any group/ministry in the church. Hence, there could be *botantes* of women's ministry, men's ministry, youth ministry or even by the whole church itself. If it is *botantes* for women, all women members (young, old, married, single) will participate and work. It differs from *ganap* in this case because it is no longer one head per family but all women members in the family. The wage earned from the cooperative work will be collected and used for whichever project the work was called for.

5 The ontological dimension of coloniality (of power) is discussed by Nelson Maldonado-Torres as coloniality of being. This is expanded by Maria Lugones in her conceptualization of coloniality of gender. See Nelson Maldonado-Torres, 2007, 'On the Coloniality of Being', *Cultural Studies* 21(2–3), pp. 240–70; Maria Lugones, 2008, 'Coloniality and Gender', *Tabula Rasa* 9, pp. 73–102.

6 The epistemological dimension of coloniality (of power) is coloniality of knowledge, explored by Catherine Walsh. See Catherine Walsh, 2007, 'Shifting the Geopolitics of Critical Knowledge', *Cultural Studies* 21(2–3), pp. 224–39.

7 In this chapter, the *Itneg* women I am referring to here are from a specific *Itneg* sub-group, the Maengs of Supo, Tubo, province of Abra, Philippines. The majority of the community members in this particular group belong to a Pentecostal church, specifically the Assemblies of God Church. Thus, all the women who collaborated in the study are Pentecostals. The use of the term *Itneg* Christian in this study refers to the *Itneg* Pentecostal Christians.

8 The ethnographic study is done within a feminist and indigenous framework. Within the feminist framework, women or mothers were considered to have agency and be valuable contributors to their families and the community. During the data-gathering process, the study adopted the indigenous concept of *tongtong*, *kumkumusta*, *ay-ayam* or *awaw-key*. These concepts refer to the day-to-day conversations and storytelling that occur when two or more people happen to be in one place, usually to keep abreast of each other's experiences. In most cases, it happens when women spontaneously gather, while in some, especially in the case of elderly women (elders), they seek out and intentionally visit each other's houses for conversations.

9 Rodelyn, Vilma and Avelina, *tongtong*, February 2023.

10 The women collaborators all agreed when one of them said, *Uray trabaho ti lalaki, basta kaya* … ('We do the work of men, as long as we are able to do it …'). Rodelyn, *tongtong*, February 2023.

11 Maria Lugones used the term *mestizaje* as a metaphor for impure resistance. See Maria Lugones, 2003, *Pilgrimages/Peregrinajes: Theorizing Coalition Against Multiple Oppressions*, Oxford: Rowman & Littlefield Publishers.

12 Salome and Avelina, *tongtong*, February 2023.

13 In her own voice, one of the research partner states, *Wen, ta kina-agpayso na toy ganganapen mi nga mapan idiay source ti danom mi tatta, babbai ti adadu nga nag-aramid idiay.* ('Yes. The truth is, this *ganganapen* or cooperative work that we are doing right now, that is going to our water source, the majority of those working for that are women.') In a separate statement, she adds, *Isunga ti babbai tatta, dakkel ti project mi, project ti WM dyta pastoral (house) idi. Tapos dita church, adu pay ti kua ti babbai ah, women's.* ('That is why we as women, we have a big project now. The pastoral house improvement was WM's or women's

ministry project. The church (improvement) was also included. There are still more projects by the women's ministry.') Vilma, *tongtong*, February 2023.

References

Adonis, D. L., 2018, 'Ili-based Community Organising: An Igorot Indigenous Peoples' Concept for Grassroots Collaboration', *Journal of Social Inclusion* 9(1), pp. 58–70.

Adonis, D. and Couch, J., 2017, '"The Trails to Get There": Experiences of Attaining Higher Education for Igorot Indigenous Peoples in the Philippines', *Australian Journal of Adult Learning* 57(2), pp. 197–216.

Anacin, C. J., 2015, 'Syncretism in Rituals and Performance in a Culturally Pluralistic Society in the Philippines', *The Social Science Journal* 52(1), pp. 40–5.

Bello, W. F., Kinley, D., Elinson, E. and Institute for Food and Development Policy and Philippine Solidarity Network, 1982, *Development Debacle: The World Bank in the Philippines*, San Francisco, CA: Institute for Food and Development Policy.

Bhaba, H. K., 1990, 'The Third Space: Interview with Homi Bhabha', in J. Rutherford (ed.), *Identity: Community, Culture, Difference*, London: Lawrence & Wishart, pp. 207–21.

Brainard, C. M. and Litton, E. F. (eds), 1999, *Reflections on the Centennial of Philippine Independence*, Pasig City: Anvil Publishing Inc.

Cole, F-C, 2016, *The Tinguian: Social, Religious, and Economic Life of a Philippine Tribe*, np: anboco.

Herrera, D. R., 2015, 'The Philippines: An Overview of the Colonial Era', *Education About ASIA* 20(1), pp. 14–19.

Jurado, G. M., 2003, 'Growth Models, Development Planning, and Implementation in the Philippines', *Philippine Journal of Development* XXX(1), pp. 1–26.

Lewis, J. and Murphy, P., 2006, 'The Old Pal's Protection Society: The Colonial Office and the Media on the Eve of Decolonisation', in Chandrika Kaul (ed.), *Media and the British Empire*, London: Palgrave Macmillan, pp. 55–69.

Lugones, M., 1992, 'On Borderlands/La Frontera: An Interpretive Essay', *Hypatia* 7(4), pp. 31–7, doi: https://doi.org/10.1111/j.1527-2001.1992.tb00715.x.

Maldonado-Torres, N., 2007, 'On the Coloniality of Being: Contributions to the Development of a Concept', *Cultural Studies* 21(2–3), pp. 240–70, doi: 10.1080/09502380601162548.

Mendoza, L. S., 2001, *Between the Home and the Diaspora: The Politics of Theorizing Filipino and Filipino American Identities*, New York: Routledge.

Molintas, J. M., 2004, 'Indigenous People's Struggle for Land and Life: Challenging Legal Texts', *Arizona Journal of International & Comparative Law* 21(1), pp. 269–306.

Ndlovu, M., 2018, 'Coloniality of Knowledge and the Challenge of Creating African Futures', *Ufahamu: A Journal of African Studies* 40(2), pp. 95–112, doi:10.5070/F7402040944.

Ortega, M., 2001, '"New Mestizas," "World Travelers," and "Dasein": Phenomenology and the Multi-Voiced, Multi-Cultural Self', *Hypatia* 16(3), pp. 1–29.

Quijano, A., 2007, 'Coloniality, and Modernity/Rationality', *Cultural Studies* 21(2–3), pp. 168–78, https://doi.org/10.1080/09502380601164353.

Rigney, L. I., 1997, 'Internationalisation of an Indigenous Anti-colonial Culture Critique of Research Methodologies: A Guide to Indigenist Research Methodology and its Principles', *Journal for Native American Studies* 14(12), pp. 109–21.

Weygan, P. L., 2009, 'Tingguian Abra Rituals', in Yvonne Belen (ed.), *Cordillera Rituals as a Way of Life*, The Netherlands: ICBE.

Valera, E. and Valera, R. M. A., 2016, 'Preserving the Tinguian Culture Heritage: Mother Tongue-Based Multi-Lingual Education as Tool', *Sampurasun e-Journal* 2(1), pp. 79–89.

4

Motugā'afa: Timely Reflections on Colonial Developments in the Pacific

FAAFETAI AIAVA

Introduction

This undertaking began as an internal conversation where village communities, educators, theologians, politicians and economists from Fiji and the Pacific region gathered in Suva to discuss indigenous and decolonial alternatives to economic development.[1] I then conveyed some of the synergies created there before a more global audience through the Council for World Mission's DARE forum in Bangkok.[2] Its warm reception in the latter not only encouraged further investigation but also reaffirmed my conviction that many of the indigenous stories and wisdoms from the Pacific have not been wholly appreciated with respect to informing economic development and its environmental impacts. This chapter aims to present some of those conversations through a Samoan rhetoric known as *motugā'afa*.

Literally, *motugā'afa* refers to fragments (*motumotu*) of a sinnet cord (*'afa*) made from the fibres of a coconut husk. Before the days of hammers and nails, the construction of many Pacific dwellings and fishing apparatus relied heavily on sinnet. Sinnet-making in Samoa was a widespread skill found in many families and villages, regularly performed by chiefs and elders known as 'the sinnet braiders' (*o le 'au fili 'afa*). In community discussions and decision-making, seasoned orators or 'the sinnet braiders' would often preface their counsel as *motugā'afa*, denoting them to be mere fragments of a story and not a complete one. This rhetorical device is rooted in the world view that all stories can have multiple versions and that no individual possesses absolute knowledge. Anyone familiar with this etiquette, however, knows that *motugā'afa* is anything but fragmented. They are wisdoms imbued with meaningful experience and pregnant with the potential to form longer and stronger cords.

The following chapter has been structured in accordance with three *motugā'afa* related to time. The first section reflects on indigenous notions of slowness where the iconic 'island time' is interpreted with reference to instant gratification. The second section reflects on some of our traditional views of rest and restraint in contrast to the concept of fast-tracked growth. The third section reflects on the lesser-known virtue of frugality, where hope for a more sustainable future is grounded in life-affirming relationships instead of competition.

Faifai mālie: too slow or timely?

The wisdom of *faifai mālie* originates from a Samoan sporting event known as *tāgā ti'a* or spear throwing. It is an event that has inspired many proverbs in Samoa, with one of them translated as 'The spear that flies well is prepared well.' According to this proverb, *faifai mālie* relates to the timely preparation stage; a phrase often uttered to those who are about to embark on an important journey or event. When used colloquially, however, *faifai mālie* carries negative connotations. It can refer to a task that is excessively slow or to actions viewed largely as time wasting. Today, it is the latter interpretation of *faifai mālie* that remains prominent. Its former traditional sense has been reduced to being nothing more than a relic of a life-world where slowness was a virtue.

It was in primary school where I first heard the legend of how Maui and his brothers made ropes out of flax and lassoed the sun to make the days longer for the people to complete their tasks. As in the wisdom of *faifai mālie*, the story taught us that time is fluid, malleable, and can be yielded to serve and maintain relationships, just as Maui did with the rushing sun (or *Tama-nui-te-rā*). Though nonsensical in terms of our mortality, this has parallels with the common understanding that nobody really *has time* but rather has to *make it*. This view might also bear resonance with Albert Einstein's theory that time itself is not universal but rather relative to a person's 'frame of reference' (DiSalle, 2020).[3]

Benjamin Franklin's catchphrase 'time is money', espoused by billionaire influencers all over the media, suggests that the more appropriate frame of reference in today's world is money. Apparently, money is a language that all nations understand. Joerg Rieger calls this frame of reference the 'economic unconscious' (2011, p. 26), an underlying force so powerful that it dictates how we spend our waking hours. In contexts governed by this 'economic unconscious', keeping time is not only expected of everyone but a necessary survival skill. In shift work, individuals are expected to adhere to start, break and finishing times to ensure that they are paid correctly, retain their jobs and keep a steady income.

This can be seen in formal education where the skills being developed and much of the content delivered are done predominantly with the workplace in mind. John Roughan voiced a similar concern about education in the Solomon Islands. In his view: 'No amount of tinkering with curricula ... will advance unless it is understood that the marketplace is firmly in the driver's seat' (2021, p. 69). This puts into perspective why some of my own teachers would remind us, as strict deadlines were reluctantly extended, that the real (market-driven) world will not be as merciful.

The result, as I saw it, was that adolescents were now imbued with a skewed understanding of time. Time was no longer valuable because of what or who it was spent on. It was a mere means to material wealth; a seemingly small trade-off with economic security becoming the main priority. Jione Havea argued that the opposite is true in the Pacific: 'We spend time, but time does not spend us' (2013, p. 297). This view not only challenges the premise that time can be 'spent' or 'wasted' in the same way money can, but also transcends the view of time as being rigid. I experienced this personally in the village wherein the days felt longer when I stopped obsessing about keeping time. This sensation, in the view of Upolu Vaai, is because island time resonates more with *kairos*, where time is measured in moments and opportunities, than it does with *chronos*, where time is sequential and linear. He elaborates further: 'Island time is not controlled by the Western notion of immutability, because the Pasifika attitude to time is always flexible and indeterminate due to the importance of seasons and the relationships that cluster around those seasons' (2023, pp. 77–8).

At best, the iconic 'island time' celebrated by our peoples has been embraced for its *kairos* dimension, where being in the moment and savouring the memories supersedes any need to hurry things along. At worst, 'island time' is a stereotype used in the chronological sense to belittle islanders for their apparent lack of punctuality or laziness. How island time is perceived, therefore, depends largely on a person's frame of reference. James Bhagwan made a similar observation:

> Expressions such as 'island time' and 'Bula time' are often used to promote tourism in the idyllic Pacific islands, where 'time stands still'

and visitors can relax and enjoy a break from the 'rat race.' At the same time, these terms are used in derogatory fashion when things in so-called developing countries in the Pacific and elsewhere are moving too slowly for development agencies and expatriates. The idyllic timelessness romantically associated with the Pacific is then presaged as *mokusiga* – 'wasting the day' in Fijian. (2020, p. 38)

In addition to the wholesome experience of trying exotic foods and enjoying the tropical scenery, the tourist experiences a majestic sense of timelessness. For these individuals, wasting the day is precisely the goal, as if to be liberated from one's master. As the obligation to make money recedes, time seemingly expands and there is suddenly a newfound space to make memories.

It is an entirely different experience of time from the Fijian resort worker who has to wake up at 4 a.m. to catch two buses for a shift that starts at 7 a.m. For these individuals, time is linear and scarce. Since paying bills and putting food on the table takes precedence, one has to divide the little time that remains between other responsibilities. While those in the former group have the luxury to 'spend time', those in the latter are being 'spent by time'. For many, this is non-negotiable in today's global economy, with some being convinced that the slowing down of time is impossible. This was until our economies were hit by the Covid-19 pandemic, thereby revealing that it is possible. But do we really need another pandemic to reassess our values and frames of reference?

When time is dictated by economic pursuits, needs turn into desires and thus a vicious cycle is formed between desire and instant gratification. It is an invasive sequence because it is constantly validated by a world built on the indulgence of fast foods, faster cars, instant internet speeds, get-rich-quick schemes, and the list goes on. This world has no room for *faifai mālie* or timely preparation. If time is not linked to immediate reward, it is wasted time. This will progress to the point at which we start to spend money that we do not have and then have to sacrifice more time to sustain such a lifestyle. Like a hamster in a wheel, the 'economic unconscious' creates an infinite time-loop ultimately resented by persons on their deathbeds.

Taga'i i le galu: traditional views on rest and growth

The phrase *taga'i i le galu* ('beware of the breakers') is derived from a fishing proverb of Samoa. This proverb serves as a warning to fishers not to get overly distracted in catching sea birds (used for bait) that they miss the waves breaking on the reef. Although it appears pessimistic on the surface, it is ubiquitous in Pacific wisdom for binary opposites to be treated as complementary: for instance, life and death, night and day, sea and land, rest and activity, or in this particular proverb, opportunity and risk.

In the last three or more decades there has been a growing interest within the region and in the global community regarding the mining of our Pacific Ocean. What started covertly as a series of pilot explorations for minerals is now being hailed as the solution to the planet's environmental woes. This has put the leaders of Pacific Island nations in a predicament. On the one hand is the need to capitalize (pun intended) on the opportunity to improve the economic conditions of its citizens. On the other is the ability to do so effectively without accruing further financial and environmental risks often bundled in colonial development strategies. This has unsurprisingly garnered mixed responses, with the call for restraint being one of the most prominent.[4]

In the western industrial world, the practice of restraint is perceived rather negatively as it presumes inactivity. According to the Samoan historian Latu Latai, it was the missionaries of the London Missionary Society (LMS) who introduced Samoans to the Protestant work ethic as well as capitalism. The system was supposedly introduced to ensure that the local LMS mission became self-sufficient and financially independent. However, in adopting this spirit of industriousness, our peoples participated in the exploitation of our natural resources and in creating a relationship of dependency with Britain. As Latai explains:

> [Samoans] were taught to produce coconut oil and arrowroot which were donated to the LMS and sold in Britain for money. The land was seen as a resource and things of nature as commodities. Anything that is commodified can then be bought and sold. [...] Pacific Islanders slowly became consumers of British goods. Missionaries' emphasis on covering up the islanders was in line with the booming cotton industry, one of Britain's biggest exports during the Industrial Revolution of the eighteenth and nineteenth centuries. (2021, p. 163)

The fact that Pacific Island States and Territories remain dependent on foreign funding and aid today demonstrates the deep-seated impacts of this colonial project. Although the colonial agents of yesteryear have left most of our countries, their neoliberal capitalist system remains present through the dependency it created. As Afereti Uili explains:

> We have become dependent on hand-outs in the form of loans that are strictly regulated by the agents of capitalism, namely the World Bank, IMF and ADB. Economic dependence on these outside forces has had a detrimental impact on the social, cultural, educational and religious lives of Pacific peoples. (2023, p. 41)

One of these impacts is the prevailing notion that growth is strictly economic. It has made human productivity the only measure of progress, considering anything less to be counterproductive. This view is negated in Samoan cosmogony, where rest and pause are integral to our becoming. Unlike the Genesis story, where the creative tasks of God each day are followed by rest, the reverse is true in Samoan mythology. As John Fraser reports, Tagaloa, the Samoan progenitor, travelled to and from the great expanse before deciding to rest. It was during this rest that the first cosmic beings were created (1892, pp. 167–8). This account suggests that it was not activity but rather rest that led to our becoming. This is not a new school of thought in Pacific Island cultures, where any big expedition is preceded by rest and meditation, or where community consensus is always sought no matter how painstaking it may be. It is also not new to those whose diets consisted of fermented and slow foods that took longer to prepare and demanded immense levels of restraint.

Similar sentiments were at the heart of Ellen Davis's call for a more agrarian interpretation of the Bible. Davis argued that the lack of human restraint, seen in the first eating violation familiarly known as the First Sin, can be blamed for the ongoing exploitation of our natural resources (2009). This view, with which many Pacific Island Christians would concur, considers restraint as a necessary condition of justice for the earth. I accept that this condition cannot be readily enforced worldwide with the majority of the world's populations struggling with food security, whereby access to a daily meal would be more of a luxury than a violation. It is also why I accept the turn to genetically modified (GM) crops and the headway it has achieved in meeting the short-term needs of certain populations. Regardless, I still see GM foods as an unsustainable workaround in the same way that there is free cheese only in the mouse trap.

In Keith Barber's 2021 study of GM foods and the possibility of integrating the methods of *Mātauranga Māori* ('indigenous knowledge' in Aotearoa), he voices three major concerns. The first had to do with the relationship of dependency it creates between farmers and GM seed suppliers. The second is the manner in which agricultural technologies are being patented and treated as intellectual property; a privatization of knowledge done for the sake of personal gain and not for the benefit of the collective. The third is in relation to the erosion of biodiversity. Since natural pesticides are rather ineffective on GM crops, the reliance on more powerful artificial chemicals also comes with increased risk of disease for farmers and other life-forms (2021). But even with all the signs pointing to the dangers of fast-tracking, there is no telling whether humans will accept that growth takes time or possess the willpower to let nature take its course.

This is not to say that fast-tracked production does not occur in the Pacific. Many families in Samoa today have lamented the quality of our 'fine mats' (*ie toga*) necessary in many of our gifting rituals. The lengthy production process, which used to take up to a year or longer, can now be completed in about a month with inferior results. The silk-like quality of the former mats – achieved through the careful selection of Pandanus leaves and the meticulous curing, splitting and weaving of its strands – is hard to come by nowadays. In trying to keep up with the high demand, or with eyes fixed on increasing revenue, many weaving groups have had to cut corners. Though there are no obvious compromises in size, the main issue with the newer 'fine mat' is its coarse and stiff texture.

Fast-tracking can also be found in childbirth, where expectant first-time mothers are advised to come into the hospital once they go into labour. If, however, they are to arrive before labour they can end up being induced. This induction process puts the expectant mother on a dilation fast-track, where doctors and midwives scurry in and out of the room trying to get 'things' (read: 'life') moving. While I am cognizant that healthcare is a business, which implies busyness, it does not remove patience, emotional connectedness and a mature mitigation of risk from the business of 'wellness'. This is not a personal attack on a specific healthcare system or business sector, but rather to unveil the symptoms of a failed market system and the capitalistic values embedded in them.

This system has ignored the visible hands of peoples and communities and placed its hope in the 'invisible hand of the market' popularized by Adam Smith (1904). It operates on the assumption that this invisible hand would somehow equalize an unfettered market and any wealth amassed at the top would eventually trickle down. That great hope, however, has served only a privileged few. It has failed our healthcare workers, workers in the retail and tourism industry, our farmers and teachers alike. As Rieger observed: 'the economic production of the lower classes has aggregated into a flood of wealth upward' (2011, p. 27). The rich 1 per cent at the top has pulled so far away from the rest of society it has led some to believe that the middle class may be disappearing.

The salvation rhetoric publicized by these systems is just as disastrous. It has all but eternalized the logic and values of colonialism. This rhetoric predestines a handful to an abundant life while simultaneously orchestrating what Achille Mbembe calls 'deathworlds' for the masses (2019). Within these deathworlds, industrial production and consumerism are baptized at the expense of others, including the earth. Meanwhile, rest or restraint has become demonized (or demonetized?) because of its association with the poor or lazy. Tom Beaudoin labels this cult 'theocapitalism', but what he and Brian McLaren were actually referring to was today's 'global suicide machine' (cited in McLaren, 2007, p. 190). Yet irrespective of whether people refer to this machine or the invisible hand as God, it does not change the fact that it has become an object of worship.

Pacific frugality: towards a sustainable future

In Samoa there is a well-known adage, *aua le naunau i le i'a, ae manumanu i le upega*, translated as 'curb the desire for fish, but cherish the net'. This wisdom deliberately juxtaposes the desire (*naunau*) for more fish and the frugal treatment (*manumanu*) of the net as a stern reminder to fishers never to sacrifice the long-term for immediate gain. The advice also conveys a uniquely Pacific understanding of frugality where being frugal is not about being stingy or the individual accumulation of wealth, but rather implies an 'other-orientated' consciousness, where the net is symbolic of the collective. Since the construction of the fishing net is made by and for communities, being thrifty with its safety (implying less fish) is about being in solidarity with the lives that depend on it.

In the neoliberal capitalist economy, the net is disposable and expendable, where individual interest has promoted an infamous 'throwaway' culture. Within this culture, frugality is self-serving and thus resources for the many are seen as wasted resources. This is a far cry from the Christian teachings of John Wesley, who preached that 'wherever true Christianity spreads, it must cause diligence and frugality, which in the natural course of things, must beget riches!' (*Sermon 116*). In today's global economy, this understanding of wealth manifested in communal solidarity is found most wanting. Wealth has been reduced to mean financial profit, while the desire for more is continually inflated by market competitiveness.

Soong-Chan Rah traces this attitude back to the 'unholy trinity of Western philosophy' comprising me, myself and I. In his view, the primacy of the individual has been a driving factor and universal motif from the days of Hellenistic philosophy, the medieval period, the Enlightenment, all the way to postmodernity (2009, p. 29). According to this view, the militant preoccupation to outdo the competition through any means necessary stems from individual pride. It is no coincidence that many of the development policies and practices deemed unsustainable in the Pacific have been based on this human-centric and individualistic philosophy.

In Pacific indigenous societies, the individual is not the centre but rather a mere strand within a cosmic net. Within this network, the moon is the timekeeper of the year and the seasons, while the sun is the timekeeper of the day.[5] When it came to monitoring the climate and predicting oncoming weather systems, our peoples relied on other life-forms for clues. For instance, cockroaches coming indoors at dusk denoting clear skies for the following day; hermit land crabs digging big holes and stacking the mud to indicate the direction of incoming storm winds; the appearance of frigate birds, particularly the females, to indicate cyclones; chickens running for cover during a depression, and finally cloud variations and wind directions – each bearing their own unique names (Lefale, 2010).

This cosmic time-keeping helped former generations decide on what to plant and when. It also informed them that a year beginning with an unusually large yield of breadfruit was not a sign for families to relax, but rather to prepare for an imminent cyclone (Fakasiieiki, 2022, p. 140). These frugal practices where people worked side by side with nature to form a life-sustaining community were the tools that enabled their economies to survive and thrive. It is the reason island communities, like those in the Pacific, continue to fight for the common good of all life.

As seen above, time in subsistence economies is driven by an eco-relational consciousness. These communities harvested enough to sustain their livelihoods using methods that preserved the well-being of human and non-human life. For these generations, efficiency was not about producing as much as possible in the least amount of time. It was about making the little they had last longer. Timeliness, therefore, was about being resourceful or frugal. There are numerous proverbs across the Pacific testifying to this mutually reciprocal rhythm of life. Such wisdoms have brought me to the same conclusion as Vaai, that 'human time is meant to revolve around Earth time, not the other way around' (2023, p. 79).

Summary and challenges

In an age in which indigenous values and cultures are quickly declining, this chapter invites readers to reassess precisely what the world stands to lose. According to K. David Harrison, our societies will lose 'centuries of human thinking about time, seasons, sea creatures, reindeer, flowers, mathematics, landscapes, myths, music, infinity, cyclicity, the unknown, and the everyday' (2007, p. viii). The seriousness of such events, a view in which I concur with Harrison, is like 'dropping a bomb on a museum' (2007, p. 7). To that end, leaders and policy-makers from the Pacific are encouraged to be more assertive in transforming the development trajectories in their respective countries. This entails taking advantage of our unique and resilient philosophies of time, more attuned to the rhythms of ecology than the hands of a clock. It is a worthwhile venture because it preserves *who we are* as opposed to *what we have*, but also because many of these wisdoms are often treated as afterthoughts or as the counterproductive remnants of a bygone era.

Miguel De La Torre reckons this is the usual reality when conversations on ecological justice come up:

> The voices of those on the margins who are most impacted are ignored. The world's disenfranchised are all too often dismissed to the role of object of the conversation. What does it mean to center their voices and explore environmental degradation from the perspective of those on the global margins? (2022, p. 3)

In agreement with this question, I close with three broader challenges to the global community regarding how the *motugā'afa* or wisdom-threads discussed earlier could potentially inform the shaping of economic development frameworks.

First, that our development paradigms reconceive time as fluid, malleable and flexible in the service of relationships. The very notion of *being in time* (*kairos*) is as vital to the future as *being on time* (*chronos*), even if the latter has economic and entrepreneurial value. In the *kairos* of the Pacific, an event that nurtures relationships may take time but never wastes it. Although gratification may be delayed, its outcome cannot be worse than the dehumanizing hamster wheel. The question for those in leadership roles is: Can we forego some of the low-lying fruits for the sake of nurturing more viable economies in the long run? In a metaphoric sense, are we willing to sacrifice a limb to save the body?

Second, that we acknowledge that earth time consists of both growth and rest, a notion vastly different from the economic systems that privilege speed and production. This growth implies restraint, reflexive mitigation and the maturity to let nature take its course. Do our current paradigms of development include these notions? Are there more sustainable alternatives to fast-tracking that could reduce the harm inflicted on human and non-human life?

Third, that the earth and all of its life-forms be treated as having their own systems of time-keeping and frugality. These systems connote that more is not always better; it is the cosmic net of life that determines wealth and not human interests; and that the future is not to be sacrificed for the present. As Marie Alohalani Brown puts it: 'As we look to the past for knowledge and inspiration on how to face the future, we are aware that we are tomorrow's ancestors, and future generations will look to us for guidance' (2019, p. vii).

Notes

1 The Vakatabu Conference was held at Studio 6 in Suva, Fiji. It was hosted by the Pacific Theological College through its Institute for Mission and Research (31 July–2 August 2023).

2 DARE stands for Discernment and Radical Engagement. This forum was hosted by the CWM at the Novotel Bangkok Sukhumvit in Thailand (13–16 September 2023).

3 I have oversimplified Einstein's theory that one can only measure the distance between two points by 'idealizing or imagining the existence of simultaneity' which, to my non-scientific mind, means to assume that the two events actually happened at the same time. DiSalle posits this as the reason Einstein goes to great lengths to explain why 'reference frames' are arbitrary both in a conceptual and empirical way (2020).

4 There remains ongoing tension between the International Seabed Authority and local governments regarding how the EEZ (exclusive economic zones) laws will be policed in regard to seabed mining. After the ten-year venture between the Canadian-based Nautilus project and PNG's government ended in a high-profile collapse in 2019, the PNG government faced internal pressures on the transparency of its consultation processes. The reports of the failed venture revealed that the

country was now $375M Kina in debt (or $157M AUD). This was somewhat expected because the trade, which promised the country employment opportunities, was so specialized that the workforce was primarily outsourced. While it made other Pacific nations wary of the alleged benefits of seabed mining, island nations like the Cook Islands, Fiji, Tonga, the Solomon Islands and Vanuatu still entered exploration contracts to assess the mineral deposits in their territorial waters. In 2020, Nauru, Kiribati and Tonga also sealed a partnership with The Metals Company (formerly known as DeepGreen Metals), promising the said countries opportunities for employment, capacity building and royalties from future production. The company boasts that it is at the forefront of a more eco-friendly future that will be sustained with solar technology and, of course, more batteries. In 2014, Tuvalu entertained the possibility through its Seabed Minerals Act, mandating that a full consultation of coastal communities take place before any mining project is approved. This decision was reversed in 2022 after critical internal and regional discussions. It goes without saying that the mining of our ocean has been the topic of much debate in government forums and faith-based organizations throughout the Pacific. In a joint statement, the CWM endorsed not just a regional but a global ban on deep-sea mining together with the Pacific Blue Line comprising the Pacific Network on Globalisation (PANG), Pacific Conference of Churches (PCC), Pacific Islands Association of NGOS (PIANGO), World Wide Fund for Nature Pacific (WWF), and the Development Alternatives with Women for a New Era (DAWN).

5 For further reading, Penehuro Lefale (2010) provides a more detailed investigation of the traditional Samoan calendar drawing on the earlier works of Augustin Kraemer and George Pratt.

References

Barber, Keith, 2021, 'Science Versus Indigenous Knowledge? Toward a Dialogical Approach', *Sites: New Series* 18(1), pp. 1–24, doi: http://dx.doi.org/10.11157/sites-id470.

Bhagwan, James, 2020, 'Back to the Future: Reappropriating Island Time and a Return to Kairos', in D. Bhagwan, Elise Huffer, Frances Koya-Vakauta, Aisake Casimira (eds), *From the Deep: Pasifiki Voices for a New Story*, Suva, Fiji: PTC Press, pp. 37–48.

Brown, Marie A., 2019, 'Foreword', in N. Wilson-Hokowhitu (ed.), *The Past Before Us: Moʻokūʻauhau as Methodology*, Honolulu: University of Hawaii Press, pp. vii–ix.

Davis, Ellen F., 2009, 'Learning our Place: The Agrarian Perspective of the Bible', *Word and World Lecture* 21(2), pp. 109–20.

De La Torre, Miguel (ed.), 2022, *Shifting Climates, Shifting People*, Cleveland, OH: Pilgrim Press.

DiSalle, Robert, 2020, 'Space and Time: Inertial Frames', in Edward. N. Zalta (ed.), *The Stanford Encyclopedia of Philosophy*, https://plato.stanford.edu/archives/win2020/entries/spacetime-iframes/

Fakasiieiki, Ikani, 2022, '*Vahaʼa Ngatae*: A Pacific Island Response to the Global

Issue of Climate Change and Rising Sea Levels', in M. De La Torre (ed.), *Shifting Climates, Shifting People*, Cleveland, OH: Pilgrim Press, pp. 131–42.

Fraser, John, 1892, 'The Samoan Story of Creation: A "Tala"', *The Journal of the Polynesian Society* 1(3), pp. 164–89.

Harrison, K. David, 2007, *When Languages Die: The Extinction of the World's Languages and the Erosion of Human Knowledge*, New York: Oxford University Press.

Havea, Jione, 2013, 'From Reconciliation to Adoption: A *Talanoa* from Oceania', in R. Schreiter, Knud Jorgensen (eds), *Mission as Ministry of Reconciliation*, Oxford: Regnum Books International, pp. 294–300.

Latai, Latu, 2021, 'Failed Promise of Abundant Life: Revisiting 200 Years of Christianity in Oceania', in J. Havea (ed.), *Theologies from the Pacific*, New York: Palgrave Macmillan, pp. 153–67.

Lefale, Penehuro, 2010, '*Ua 'afa le Aso* Stormy Weather Today: Traditional Ecological Knowledge of Weather and Climate. The Samoa Experience', *Climatic Change* 100(2), pp. 317–35.

Mbembe, Achille, 2019, *Necropolitics*, Durham, NC: Duke University Press.

McLaren, Brian D., 2007, *Everything Must Change: Jesus, Global Crises, and a Revolution of Hope*, Nashville, TN: Thomas Nelson.

Pacific Conference of Churches (PCC), 2020, 'The Story of our Pacific Household in the New Normal: A Statement Issued by the Moderator, Rev. Dr. Tevita Havea', Suva, Fiji: Pacific Conference of Churches.

Rah, Soong-Chan, 2009, *The Next Evangelicalism: Freeing the Church from Western Cultural Captivity*, Downers Grove, IL: InterVarsity Press.

Rieger, Joerg, 2011, 'Alternative Images of God in the Global Economy', in J. Havea, Clive Pearson (eds), *Out of Place: Doing Theology on the Crosscultural Brink*, New York: Routledge, pp. 26–41

Roughan, John, 2021, 'The Economy Dictates the School Curriculum', in F. Pene, 'Ana Maui Taufe'ulungaki, Cliff Benson (eds), *Tree of Opportunity: Re-Thinking Pacific Education*, Nukualofa, Tonga: USP Institute of Education, pp. 66–70.

Smith, Adam, 1904 [1789], *An Inquiry into the Nature and Causes of the Wealth Nations*, 5th edn, London: Methuen.

Tanguay, Jamie, 2021, 'Vanuatu: The View from the Top of the Happy Planet Index', *Griffith Asia Institute*, https://blogs.griffith.edu.au/asiainsights/vanuatu-the-view-from-the-top-of-the-happy-planet-index/ (accessed 27.01.2025).

Uili, Afereti, 2023, 'Abraham and the "Curse" of James Cook', in Upolu L. Vaai, Aisake Casimira (eds), *ReSTORYing the Pasifika Household*, Suva, Fiji: PTC Press, pp. 29–50.

Vaai, Upolu L., 2023, 'We are Earth: reDIRTifying Creation Theology', in Upolu L. Vaai, Aisake Casimira (eds), *ReSTORYing the Pasifika Household*, Suva, Fiji: PTC Press, pp. 63–84.

Wesley, John, 'Sermon 116: Causes of the Inefficacy of Christianity', in Thomas Jackson (ed.), *The Works of John Wesley*, https://www.resourceumc.org/en/content/sermon-116-causes-of-the-inefficacy-of-christianity (accessed 13.04.2025).

5

De-imperializing 'Development as Happiness' by Re-appropriating *Atepzung*: A Southeast Asian Massif Experience

SHILUINLA JAMIR

These boys ... were taught to read and write ... Their slight *introduction into the world of knowledge* familiarized them more with the evil than with the *good of civilized life*. Many became mere hangers-on at the station, loafing about the local bazaar, drinking a deadlier liquor than their mountain *chu*, and acquiring other vices than those to *which they were born*. Their civilization was merely a veneer. The savage had been weaned from the jungle. He had learned to don a coat and to strut about the streets; but in *instinct, in passion, and in palate he was a savage still* (Carey, 1919, p. 52; my emphasis).

The transformation of the savage or the colonized other into the likeness of the masters, in thinking, in living and in making choices, has always been the assumed duty of the colonizers since colonialism. However, despite the introduction of the colonized people into the world of knowledge, as William Carey claims, of teaching the colonized the good of civilized life, the 'savage' continued to practise what according to the colonizers was reprehensible. After the decolonization process, the endeavour to transform the savage was reinvoked by the new empires in the name of development. These agendas were carried out through practices founded in the ideas of modernization, industrialization and development. But the stubborn 'savage' continues to resist the programmes of transformation that come in the name of change, strategically 'playing by the cracks in the system' to their advantage. This embodied staging is carried out despite their lives being rendered as non-lives.

This chapter is about how the Massif uplanders negotiate in the face of development-induced death. The discussion is limited to the north-east of India, considered as a part of the Southeast Asian Massif.

Methodological consideration

This chapter builds on the work of George Zachariah, who critiqued the discourse of development in his work *Alternatives Unincorporated*. His work was particularly critical of the way development was presented as redemptive and salvific, which he calls 'God-talk'. According to him, the result of development is not about bringing life to the subaltern communities but death. I build my critique on development on his work. I bring stories from the north-east Indian region that particularly focuses on the contradiction of the promise of development as happiness and its unhappy results (Zachariah, 2011). While Zachariah pays attention to the new social movements as theological text of resistance, I engage with women in the Massif who critically negotiate with the imperializing power of the neoliberal market economy in ways that help sustain their lives using their understanding of indigenous life worlds and knowledge. I study how these semi-literate women reconfigure the politics of death by using their home-grown skills and tools such as handlooms. My overarching question is: What are some of the practices among the grass-roots communities that can inform liberation theology to be life-giving and sustaining? The quest of the chapter is to engage with communities that are considered to be unhappy people by the dominant order and to bring out their ways of being theological. This approach also contributes to the ongoing study on the Massif societies, motivated by works done by scholars like Jean Michaud, Willem van Schendel and others. My approach is particularly motivated by the empirical work done by Sarah Turner and Michaud's work among the Hmongs in Northern Vietnam. While they analysed the practices of weaving looms and crafts from the livelihood perspective, this chapter looks at these practices as theological expressions of liberation.

The Southeast Asian Massif

The term 'Southeast Asian Massif' was proposed by the anthropologist Jean Michaud in 1997. It describes those places that occupy the Upland East of the Himalayan range stretching over ten countries including the north-east of India, south-west China and mainland south-east Asia. Both Willem van Schendel and Jean Michaud concluded that the upland Massif is made up of peoples practising a mosaic of cultures, social systems and linguistic traits. This place is also called the *Zomia*, a phrase coined by van Schendel and popularized by James C. Scott. According to the proponents of the idea of the Southeast Asian Massif, the peoples who make up this space are called uplanders, hillmen, hill tribes, Scheduled Tribes, stateless, nations, nationalities, minorities, national minorities and so on. Michaud, who has extensively studied this area, showed that these names given to the peoples in the Massif demonstrate the mindset that reflects geographical remoteness, the frontier spaces, and backwardness, including primitiveness with less political clout (Michaud, 2016).

People in the Northeast India Massif experience in their everyday lives the unfolding of this mindset over their bodies and spaces, more so if they are women. The Northeast India Massif societies also occupy the periphery of the nation states where the people are thought of as 'dangerous', 'unruly' and 'savage other', both by the state and the ruling elite at the centre of the state power. Thus, the governance of this region is shaped by a mindset of *difference.* Since the 1990s there has been an effort on the part of the state to erase the idea of difference through the introduction of various state-sponsored programmes like festivals, promotion of tourism and so on. Like most of the countries in the Massif, the north-east India uplands also have ministries aimed at 'developing' the people so that they can 'catch up' with the rest of the country and progress. The people here are subjected to programmes that are aggressively intrusive and aimed at changing their lifestyle, or forming their lives according to how the nation state and the empire see it. When people in the Massif resist the state-forming activities, their spaces are turned into a 'garrison state'. According to Franz Fanon, nation-building is inherently a capitalist project, so the Massif is like a female body that lies exposed to all forms of power and violence in the name of national development. Thus, in the case of the Massif, it is postcolonial India that also acts like an empire and as an agent of the neoliberal economy.

The idea of development is intimately linked to happiness. The idea is that if people are developed, they will automatically become happy. Studies done by scholars like Ruth Veenhoven further strengthen the discourse of development as happiness. In her work she analysed 245 studies in 32 countries and found that happy persons are more likely to be found in economically prosperous countries, countries that hold freedom and democracy. She further adds: 'The happy are more likely to be found in majority groups than minorities and more often at the top of the social ladder than at the bottom' (Veenhoven, 1991, p. 16). Which means bodies that live in the social, economic, political and geographical margins are unhappy people. So the Massif by default is an unhappy place, and its people unhappy people. The section that follows will briefly expose the banality of development and the conceited agendas that come clothed in the language of happiness.

Rituals of development as happiness

Colonialism was founded on the promise of happiness to brown men/women (Ahmed, 2010). In the neo-imperial age we see the same promise being packaged in the name of development. Prior to the introduction of the word 'development' as progress, the word in use was 'modernization'. The promise of modernization was based on the utilitarian injunction of happiness with the 'good' moral intention of helping those who lived in sheer darkness and backwardness. For instance, US President Truman's inaugural speech made on 20 January 1949, delivered at the Capitol, makes this connection clear:

> We must embark on a bold new program for making the benefits of our scientific advances and industrial progress available for the improvement and growth of underdeveloped areas. More than half the people of the world are living in conditions approaching misery. Their food is inadequate. They are victims of disease. Their economic life is primitive and stagnant. Their poverty is a handicap and a threat both to them and to more prosperous areas. (Truman, 1949)

Zachariah observed:

> Being a humanitarian project with a teleological vision of a better world, and a deontological commitment to bring in civilizational transformation at the peripheries, development has been considered as the panacea for the accumulated ills of societies and nations at the margins. (2011, p. 18)

As attested by Zachariah and other post-development theorists like Wolfgang Sachs, Arturo Escobar, Aram Ziai and others, the idea of modernization, change or development was always tied to the claim of improving the lot of the people, which we can today interpret as happiness, a happiness that means adapting to a capitalist way of looking at the world. This project is carried out systematically in cooperation with many other multinational corporations, such as the World Bank, the United Nations Development Programs and other regional and national organizations and mechanisms including state military. I call these 'rituals of development' because they are carried out in a systematic manner with a routinized set of practices, with clear boundary markers between happy and not so happy people. Development is offered to ward off human suffering with the supposed claim to ensure human well-being or happiness. Thus, two powerful ideas – development and happiness, both having universal appeal – are combined to remove the 'precarity of life' among the Massif highlanders. But the discussions that follow inform us that through these initiatives a situation is created in which the state, the ruling elites and the neo-empires instrumentalize the lives of the people and its spaces.

The section that follows will provide examples of how development is produced within the discourse of development and how that leads to the marginalization of the people. The first discussion revolves around the aggressive agenda of both colonialism and the postcolonial state to wean people away from *Jhum* (the traditional form of agriculture of the uplanders). The second example demonstrates how development agendas are pushed without the people, communities and stakeholders realizing it, via the ruling elites and the state, who acts as agents of neo-imperial powers. The third example highlights how the agenda of development as happiness actually brings death to the people.

The termination of *Jhum*

The *Jhum*, or swidden agricultural practice, is a way of life for the indigenous communities in the Northeast India Massif and other parts of the Massif highland. Even today there are discussions in the mainstream about the (un)feasibility of it in the context of the existing land pressure due to increase in population and the consequent impact on environment. Some are also concerned that *Jhum* is not economically viable. But a study of the context in which these discussions arose shows that the discussions were based on trying to make people change their lifestyles and adapt to a modernized way of life. Bela Malik, in her empirical study on *Jhum* in Garo Hills, concluded that the demonization of *Jhum* was more about conserving timber for commercial purposes than improving the lot of the people. Malik claims that *Jhum* has been a concern of various departments of the state, such as the Forest Department, the Tribal Areas Development Department, and since 1955 it became a concern of the Soil Department. Their primary focus was to limit and control the practice of *Jhum* to wean the indigenous societies away from it. Even in the 1990s, shifting cultivation or the *Jhum* continued to be seen as a problem that had to be done away with. Malik observed: 'The enduring image of the practice as inferior and wasteful, supporting an economy on the brink of impending collapse became the justification for interventionism, particularly in the post-Independence India' (Malik, 2003 pp. 287-315).

Debjyoti Das, who also did a critical study on the demonization of *Jhum*, observed that the studies that were done in order to provide an alternative to this primitive way of agriculture were premised on improvements of the quality life of those who practised *Jhum*, coupled with environmental concern for sustainable growth. The aim was to influence the state and different government agencies to act through a development model. The 'civilized' form of agriculture and leaving behind the practice of *Jhum* was considered as development, modernization and even civilization. For them, these changes were important for an improved quality of life and the world. However, Das notes that those who made the study on the unfeasibility of *Jhum* did not understand the complex system that supports the *Jhum* calendar, collective work (labour), ownership, mixed cropping patterns that diversified food grain choices and maintained self-sufficient livelihood options. He observed that the new dimension added to it the importance of market economy over community sharing and self-sufficiency. This also resulted in the creation of class division and social stratification (Das, 2006, pp. 4912-17).

The second example is the way illegal mining was sanctioned by the state and carried out by the ruling elites using local mafias to threaten the locals who objected to the illegal mining. This case shows how the ritual of development is carried out by the state, the ruling elites and capitalists.

The World Report 2007, titled 'India Development and Growth in Northeast India: The Natural Resources, Water, and Environment Nexus', stated that the objective of the report was to develop a broad vision for water and natural resource development and management leading to sustainable and equitable economic development and growth in the region. This report is said to have been made at the request of the Indian government for the World Bank to focus more of its attention on the Northeastern Region to support poverty reduction and development in the region. The Ministry of Development of Northeastern Region and the Bank accordingly devised a study that would focus on water and forest. The underlying logic is to extract as many available resources as possible so that the region can become rich. Now, contrast the World Bank's recommendation to extract resources with what is happening today. According to a newspaper report that appeared in 2020, the north-east continues to face a violent extractive regime by the Indian state (strongly armed with recommendations like that of the World Bank). It shows that Assam, Meghalaya and parts of other states have experienced extraction of coal, allied minerals and oil and gas since the occupation of the British. The current extraction by Coal India Ltd in Assam is at 465 million tons, out of the total coal prospect of 525 million tons. Compare this with another report that appeared in 2022, which claims that the government-owned North Eastern Coalfield (NEC), which was given a lease to extract coal in the region, was found to have been engaging in the activity illicitly for many years after its mining rights had expired. The Justice (Retd) B. P. Katakey Commission mentioned in its report that the NEC has illegally mined coal worth Rs. 48.72 billion. And there is a thriving illegal coal mining business that is going on rampantly in the region. The illegal mining of coal, which continued unabated for decades in Assam, is causing large-scale destruction to one of the country's finest rainforests (Bhattacharyya, 2022). There is a ban on rat-hole mining of coal in Meghalaya, one of the states in the Northeast Region, by the National Green Tribunal. But illegal coal mining continues, which has become a threat to the environment and to humans. According to Land Conflict Watch, nearly 60 people have either lost their lives or suffered injuries due to illegal mining since 2012. Several activists were attacked and threatened for looking into the illegal coal mining. These figures do not include the number of villagers affected due to environmental degradation such as polluted water bodies (East Street Journal Asia, 2024).

The question is: How are neo-imperial powers that promote the logic of development engaged in it? The development policies of the government entrenched in development road-map documents such as Vision 2020 and the World Bank's documents discussed earlier stressed the abundance of natural resources and the need to harness them for the benefit of the people and the region. These documents have sowed the seed of looking at natural resources as resources to be exploited. Simultaneously, bodies such as the Northeast Coalfield were created by the government so that through these institutions these resources could be extracted. Moreover, development of infrastructure under the Look East Policy, which later was changed to Act East Policy, provided the required infrastructure to transport both legally and illegally extracted resources. The logic is that the development model proposed by the government contained in it an inherent idea of extracting natural resources. The reports become a signal for capitalist agencies and the capitalists themselves, including the ruling elite from the region, to flock like vultures to the region to eat from the bodies of the people. During the colonial period, opium was used to 'domesticate' the native people in the region. Today drugs and alcohol are used in order to control and extract consent of the locals in the extractive business. According to Agnes Kharsing, a human rights activist in Meghalaya, the coal mafias would give alcohol and drugs to the local boys and train them to terrorize the locals who object to the aggressive coal mining work that is carried out in their surrounding villages. Similar cases were reported from Patkai Dehing in Assam, also known as the Amazon of the East and the seventh national park in Assam. According to a newspaper report, in the Patkai Dehing, in a place occupied by the indigenous community, a coal mining project was sanctioned by the Indian government during the pandemic in April 2020 (clearly indicating that the state itself is an empire today and the arms and legs of capitalistic forces). The report notes the ritualistic way the illegal coal mining was done. Initially, the mafia would encourage the people to clear the forest for *Jhum*; after that, they would encourage the people to lease out the land for tea plantation and, later, systematically the land would be handed over for open-cast coal mining. A local observed that the fact that it was previously a forest is pushed outside the public memory and people see it as if they were digging out a tea garden. The mafia also get people addicted to drugs to keep them from revolting against them. Potential troublemakers are identified and either killed or made addicted (A India Today NE, 2020). This is one way through which the spectre of development performs its ceremony of death.

The third example is that of the unseeming connection between militarization and development. The Dibang Multipurpose Project was designed as the world's tallest concrete gravity dam at 278 metres above sea level to generate 2,880 megawatts of power. By 2011 there were several protests against the project. The government, in response, deployed military to curb the protest. On 5 October 2011 the armed personnel entered a Durga Puja Pandal and opened fire at the gathering, during which at least nine people were killed. The government accused them of being anti-social elements, Maoist. One student leader remarked:

'Suddenly, we heard that Maoists were opposing the dams ... many feared that the government might use the Maoist excuse to apply the Armed Forces Special Powers Act. This broke the resistance' (Manju, 2019). Dibang became 'the threshold space where the rule of the law [is] effectively suspended' (Downey, 2009, pp. 109–25). The project was designed by AF Consult, now AF Poyry, a Finnish multinational company that was engaged to review the detailed project as well as the construction planning for the Dibang multipurpose project.

A comparison between how the process of development was carried out and what was promised in the development papers of the state shows divergences. Both the World Bank document and the Vision 2020 development road map stressed the importance of investment to exploit the available natural resources. Then projects were developed by multinational companies with the promise that this project will immensely enrich the region (happiness). But when locals resisted, they were silenced through the use of state machinery like the military, thereby showing a clear nexus between development and militarization. Looking at these three examples, one can conclude that what happens in the villages of the Massif uplands is different from what is promised in development. The next section discusses how women in the face of the empire of capitalism negotiate for life. This example is to elucidate that, despite the overarching power of capitalism, with the state acting as its agent and its infrastructures and institutions, including the military, as its legs and arms, people have found ways of negotiating with neo-imperialism, especially in the context of the inevitability of the empire. The cases discussed show that the empire of neo-capitalism cannot be evaded, but the question now is how we negotiate with it so that life becomes more liveable and less lamentable.

The practices and strategies of women weavers

This section, which is the constructive part, focuses on the way women, considered as 'unnormal bodies' in the Northeast Indian Massif societies, have interacted with the state's aggressive development process. I designate women of the Massif as 'unnormal bodies' because, due to their gender, they are seen as those who exist outside the 'normal' ordering of the world. In some parts of the Massif societies women are compared to crabs who can never learn to do anything right no matter how much they are taught, or seen as those whom even monkeys do not fear or whose knowledge amounts to that of a little girl. But these 'unnormal' bodies deploy their gendered roles and space strategically to de-imperialize the project of development as happiness. This work is informed by feminist theory of everyday resistance, in which coping mechanism, survival, accommodation and adaptability in the context of multiple power operatives are used with or without knowing whether their actions are political or not (Hollander and Einwoher, 2004, pp. 533-4). A study of their practices will inform this work, showing that the idea of happiness among women in the Massif is woven into the ways they perceive life and their cosmology. These women selectively make use of the opportunities that liberalization offers, maximize the 'local opportunities' available in their hands and exploit their gendered activities, something that they know and are familiar with, including gendered places, kinship and cultural mores. They make use of their 'homegrown tools to adapt ... while sustaining [their] identity and ensuring its social reproduction' (Turner and Michaud, 2008, pp. 158-90).

Traditionally, weaving is something that women in the Massif highlands learn at a young age. There was a time when, due to modernization, weaving activity had become marginal. However, with globalization, neoliberalization of the economy and the subsequent internal tourist flow to the Massif to see the 'barbarians within', there has been a resurgence of this activity. Today it is an important income-generating activity for women, especially in the rural areas.

For my research I had a conversation with four women from Unger village, Mokokchung district, Nagaland, about their livelihood means. This village also happens to be a village I originally come from, having spent a substantial amount of time there while growing up, and know all the research subjects individually. This village is important because the village and its people have been subjected to intense military torture, and the villagers were taken as part of the grouping – a form of securitization during which several of them died – whose names are engraved on a stone kept in the heart of the village. This stone acts as a reminder to its people of its resilience and its spirit to live and hope. According to the 2011 census, Unger village has a population of 1,394 people, out of which the male population is 724 and female population 670. While quite a few of the male members are employed in the government sector and a few are full-time businessmen, many are involved in the stone quarry as labourers earning around $10 a day. A few of them engage in *Jhum* cultivation. But all of them are in one way or another engaged in some form of diversified livelihood practices. It is the same with women when it comes to engaging in diversified livelihood practices. Many of the womenfolk are engaged in homestead farming, weaving, pickle-making, animal husbandry, and so on, indicating that in one way or another they are engaged in livelihood activities. Interestingly, almost all the women in the village are also active church members; some are choir members and are also involved in other community-building activities of the church and the village. This shows the intersecting roles that women and the people in the village play, integrating judiciously their community, religious and economic life into their very existence.

All four women I spoke to are weavers but none of them do that full time. One owns a shop attached to her house, the other weaver rears pigs, makes pickles and sells them, especially making use of the opportunity the growing number of adults who move outside the village for educational purposes provides; the third woman engages in *Jhum* but is also a homemaker, and the fourth one rarely weaves but actively engages in marketing the woven looms. She collects the finished looms not only from her village but also from women living in the surrounding villages and takes them to urban areas to sell. Two are married and the other two are widows. Two are in their sixties, one in her fifties and the other in her forties. One of them is a deaconess in the church, two are members of the church choir and the other one is an active church member, while her husband is a deacon. When asked how they market their products, they said that they do it as and when they get orders from friends and shopkeepers who run handloom and handicraft shops in the nearby towns and sometimes from faraway places like Dimapur. They said that, through word of mouth, customers get to hear from them and accordingly place orders. After they make the shawls/looms (they said it takes three days to make one shawl/*mekhala*), they send the finished product through someone from their village travelling to that particular place (use of kinship). Sometimes they would travel especially when they needed to buy thread for their next batch of weaving. During those visits they also buy household items, including pig feeds, milk, sugar, dry fish and other household needs. They would go early in the morning from their village in a minibus and return the same day. If it was to nearby towns and villages, they would wait on the highway for the buses that ply through the village and hitch a ride. One of the weavers who runs the shop (attached to her house) often needs to go to the nearby towns to restock her shop. So among the four of them, she is the one who travels outside the village more often than the other three. When she gets more orders, she would let other weavers, including the other three women mentioned here, weave and she would buy from them and sell. Or sometimes, when she travels, she would carry the looms of two of them and deliver them. When I asked whether there is a sense of competition among them, they answered that they don't see competition but a sense of considerate living and transaction in their everyday lives, at least when it came to weaving and marketing their products. The woman who does *Jhum* said that when it is sowing, weeding or harvesting season, she would put away her weaving activity and concentrate on *Jhum*. In between the weeding and harvesting or sowing, she weaves.

All four of them said that they do travel to Dimapur with their looms at least once in a while, or to Mokokchung. It is not just to sell but to meet families who are there, or to buy items like fridges, pressure cookers, electric cookers or other fineries. They also take this time to visit friends and families, especially those families who have experienced death or sickness. When they go to the urban areas they also carry with them locally grown vegetables from the village as gifts to their friends and families. We see here a network of activities being regenerated and rekindled. While adapting to the market strategically, they also keep intact the ways in which their social and cultural life is built. One might see this as a mundane activity but in the midst of an imperializing market economy and an aggressive developmental model that does not pay attention to the happiness of the people, for these women to rely on their home-grown skills, their gendered skills and place itself, is resistance. As Michaud and Turner found in their work among the Hmongs in Vietnam, the women in the Northeast Massif also 'have developed a creative spirit of tenacious resistance to assimilation and subordination' (2008, pp. 158–90).

We can learn from the Northeast Indian Massif women that happiness is what everyone desires. Yet to pursue one's happiness without regard for the happiness of others is morally wrong. Therefore, unlike the imperial project of happiness that thrives on the death of others and renders lives as malleable lives, women in the Massif display a form of life that lives in intentional awareness of one's being and its landscape, flourishing together.

When I asked them from where they draw their sense of living considerate lives and thriving, they said that since their childhood they have been taught in their *atepzung* how to live life as members of a community. They said that things that they have learned in their *atepzung*, including weaving and the formation of an ethical, moral world, inform their ways of living and their conduct. This response pushed me to enquire about the importance of *atepzung* in liberative theologies, which I discuss in the next section.

Atepzung as a liberative political place and process

This chapter looks at liberative theologies through a sense of place. A sense of place resuscitated through the re-appropriation of *atepzung* reminds us of our connectedness to each other and the larger creation, more especially to a place called home, the *Oikos*. It reminds us of our belongingness and therefore the obligation to preserve life and adopt solidarity practices in our everyday life so that human existence becomes meaningful, and life is acknowledged as a gift from God.

The proposal of *atepzung* as a liberative political process is driven by the need to rethink contemporary ways of doing liberation theology. Despite liberation theology being around for more than four decades, as acknowledged in the concept note of DARE 2023, one has not been able to see the fruit of liberation theology. Liberation theology unfortunately has become an exercise largely confined to academia, especially in the South of the globe and particularly in India. There also seems to be a hypocrisy in the way one engages with liberative theologies. The fact that the empire continues to grow unabated both in the South and the North, and the fact that the resources of the South through exploitation of bodies including geo bodies are plundered, demonstrates that our engagement with liberative theologies both in the North and South needs renewal. For this reason, this chapter tries to look at *atepzung* and bring out some practices that might help enrich our liberative thinking and practices. The foundation of *atepzung* is based on its everydayness. Therefore, this chapter calls for liberative practices in our everyday life.

Among the indigenous Ao communities, *atepzung* literally means the hearth in the kitchen place. Families sit around this place every morning and evening. This is the place where food is cooked, shared and served. The hearth as a place has its importance in relation to the fire that is within it and the people who come around it in need of warmth, food, friendship and conversation. This is also a place where families and friends come together for prayer and other aspects of social and political life. This place is also important because it is where children are taught to be good citizens of the community. In this chapter, I use *atepzung* in a specific sense – as a place within the house that is the nerve centre of a family, which extends to community as well. However, while engaging with it theologically, I use it in a metamorphic sense so that a relevance of *atepzung* is built for contemporary theological articulation.

Atepzung is a political place because in this place teaching on how to be a good citizen is done and shaped; families strategize sitting here about how best to engage in the world and make meaning. Liberation, when understood through *atepzung*, helps us understand solidarity as an everyday practice. This is especially true when people or communities or movements say that their goal is to come together when there is a need. This might look as if one waits for violence to occur and, when it happens, the group comes together to protest. But solidarity practices must move beyond needs-based practices and incorporate them into our everyday lives.

Liberative theologies should be like the *atepzung*, nurturing the marginalized victims and the poor. bell hooks writes in her memory of homeplace that 'houses belonged to women, were their special domain, not as property, but as place where all that truly mattered in life took place – the warmth and comfort of shelter, the feeding of our bodies, the nurturing of our souls' (2014). Likewise, liberative theologies should be the soul from which the victims can draw their energy to resist and the perpetrators can learn the right ways of living as human beings and not as agents of capitalism, as those who understand life as a gift, therefore to be respected.

A liberative theology informed by *atepzung* can become a source of hope for those who are engaged in resisting the empires. Tired people should find in liberative theologies and practices sources of hope. They should be places that have in them the fire from which resisting people and communities draw energy to continue to struggle against the regime of death. In today's context, movements like the World Social Forums can be considered as *atepzung* in which people from across the globe fighting against globalization, imperialism and neoliberalism come together to learn, reflect, speak and create solidarity across the globe – necessary tools needed to continue to struggle for life. Places like the Plaza de Mayo, around which Argentinian mothers marched in silence claiming the ones who became victims of enforced disappearance, can be considered as *atepzung* in which life is pursued, justice is taught and learned. *Atepzung* is therefore not just a place but a political place of liberation and solidarity that can be transnationally linked to people's movements.

Liberative theologies and practices should be life-giving and life-generating. This has become more important because the language of the empire also comes in the language of liberation, or the way the discourse of development is packaged as happiness.

References

A India Today NE, 2020, 'The Tai Phake: Dehing Patkai and Roots of Ingenuity', 16 July, https://www.indiatodayne.in/perspective/story/tai-phake-dehing-patkai-and-roots-indigeneity-404586-2020-07-16 (accessed 27.01.2025).

Ahmed, Sarah, 2010, *The Promise of Happiness*, Durham, NC: Duke University Press.

Bhattacharyya, Rajeev, 2022, 'Why is India Unable to Check Illegal Coal Mining in Assam's Rainforest?', *The Diplomat*, 24 January, https://thediplomat.com/2022/01/why-is-india-unable-to-check-illegal-coal-mining-in-assams-rainforests/ (accessed 27.01.2025).

Carey, William, 1919, *A Garo Jungle Book or The Mission to the Garos of Assam*, Philadelphia, PA: The Judson Press, p. 52.

Das, Debojyoti, 2006, 'Demystifying the Myth of Shifting Cultivation: Agronomy in the North-East', *Economic and Political Weekly* 41(47), 25 December, pp. 4912–17.

Downey Anthony, 2009, 'Zones of Indistinction: Giorgio Agamben's "Bare Life" and the Politics of Aesthetics', *Third Text* 23(2), March, pp. 109–25.

East Street Journal Asia, 2024, 'Unbridled Illegal Coal Mining in Meghalaya Despite Court Ban', Anupa Sagar Kujur, 3 January, https://www.landconflictwatch.org/conflicts/unbridled-illegal-coal-mining-in-meghalaya-despite-court-ban (accessed 27.01.2025).

Hollander, Jocelyn A., and Einwoher, Rachel L., 2004, 'Conceptualizing Resistance', *Sociological Forum* 19(4), December, pp. 533–54.

hooks, bell, 2014, *Yearning: Race, Gender, and Cultural Politics*, 2nd edn, London: Routledge, https://doi.org/10.4324/9781315743110.

Malik, Bela, 2003, 'The "Problem" of Shifting Cultivation in the Garo Hills of North-East India, 1860–1970', *Conservation Society* 1(2), July–December, pp. 287–315.

Manju Menon Manju, 2019, 'How Consent for Dibang was Manufactured by Terrorizing the People of Arunachal Pradesh', *Scroll.in*, 25 July, https://scroll.in/article/931504/how-consent-for-dibang-dam-was-manufactured-by-terrorising-the-people-of-arunachal-pradesh (accessed 27.01.2025).

Michaud, Jean, 2016, 'Introduction: Seeing the Forest for the Tree: Scale, Magnitude, and Range in the Southeast Massif', in Jean Michaud, Meenaxi Barkataki-Ruscheweyh and Margaret Byrne Swain (eds), *Historical Dictionary of the Peoples of the Southeast Asian Massif*, 2nd edn, Lanham, MD: Rowman & Littlefield, pp. 1–40.

Scott, James C., 2009, *The Art of Not Being Governed: An Anarchist History of Upland Southeast Asia*, New Haven, CT: Yale University Press.

Truman, Harry S., 1949, 'Inaugural Address', https://www.trumanlibrary.gov/library/public-papers/19/inaugural-address (accessed 27.01.2025).

Turner, Sarah and Michaud, Jean, 2008, 'Imaginative and Adaptive Economic Strategies of Hmong Livelihoods in Lao Cai Province, Northern Vietnam', *Journal of Vietnamese Studies* 3(3), pp. 158–90.

Van Schendel, Willem, 2002, 'Geographies of Knowing, Geographies of Ignorance: Jumping Scale in Southeast Asia', *Environment and Planning D: Society and Space* 20(60), pp. pp. 648–68.

Veenhoven, Ruth, 1991, 'Questions on Happiness: Classical Topics, Modern Answers, Blind Spots', in Fritz Strack, Michael Argyle and Norbert Schwarz (eds), *Objective Well-Being: An Interdisciplinary Perspective*, Oxford: Pergamon.

Zachariah, George, 2011, *Alternatives Unincorporated: Earth Ethics from the Grassroots*, London: Equinox.

6

The Resilience of Indigenous Women in the Midst of Development

MOAKUMLA LONGKUMER

The indigenous Ao-Naga women[1] exhibit remarkable resilience as their communities undergo various developmental changes and modernization. This chapter explores their challenges and their exceptional ability to assert their rights, preserve their cultural heritage and participate in decision-making processes. The resilience of these women serves as a testament to their strength, perseverance and adaptability despite being in a male-dominated set-up.[2] By actively engaging in cultural preservation, pursuing economic empowerment, advocating for education and awareness, participating in social and political spheres, building networks and demonstrating environmental stewardship, Ao-Naga women navigate the complexities of development while upholding their identity and contributing to the well-being of their communities.

The present generation of Nagas have ventured into different aspects of life, reproducing fabrics that represent the ancestral motifs blended with modern advancement and development. In reality, the Ao-Nagas still live in independent villages, having their independent village council of elders in all the decision-making,[3] where their decisions are considered final and binding in all matters of policy, defence, administration, settlement, marriage, warfare and so on. Matters like marriage, divorce and adoption, inheritance and property disputes are settled by the clan elders,[4] who are comprised of only male members. Thus, the rights of women are ignored and neglected because someone decides on their behalf, which amounts to the denial of basic human rights. In other words, indigenous women have no financial or property decision-making rights. Ironically, over seven decades of post-independence, development and complete dominance of Christianity in the life and affairs of the Nagas have not changed the status of women. Women, even though mostly educated, continue to live under the clutches of patriarchy, yet surprisingly have developed a resilient attitude towards this dehumanizing attitude of Naga society.

No doubt the state has developed in different aspects since attaining statehood.[5] However, this chapter will focus only on educational development and the contributions of the womenfolk in promoting the importance of education by actively involving themselves in different capacities. Many Ao-Naga women have risen to leadership positions in educational institutions, including schools and colleges. They have contributed to the development of education policies and the improvement of educational facilities in their state. The Ao-Naga women have actively promoted literacy in their communities by encouraging children, especially girls, by advocating the right to girls' education and have been at the forefront of efforts to break down gender-based barriers to education. They have worked to eliminate stereotypes and traditional norms that may have hindered girls' access to education. Many Ao-Naga women have actively participated in community-based educational initiatives, contributing to the development of educational infrastructure and resources within their villages and towns. They have been instrumental in bridging the gap in literacy rates and making education more accessible to the younger generation, even though they continue to live under the dominant patriarchal structure.

Arju[6] and Tsuki[7] or the traditional education

The Arju, also known as the boys' dormitory in the Ao-Naga community, was a traditional learning and social centre that played an important part in the community's cultural and educational life. It was a crucial institution as well as the social hub for all unmarried male members of society, where they learned about social behaviours and ideas from their elders. The Arju was a vital institution where young boys could be educated, learn traditional values and get practical skills. It was a communal residence that was usually positioned in the centre of the village and acted as a central hub for many activities. It was often a massive structure over 50 feet long, 30 feet high, and lavishly ornamented.[8] Married men and minor children did not become members of Arju, and women and strangers were not allowed to come near Arju to maintain its sanctity (Jamir, 2022, pp. 101–3).

One of the key functions of the Arju was to keep an eye out for attackers. It also met societal demands such as social security, cultural advancement and master workmanship. It was, in fact, a true training institute that fostered the socialization process of people in general and men in particular. A male who had not lived through Arju life was not chosen for village council leadership. As a result, an Ao-Naga male had to go through such rigorous training in order to pass the fundamental exams required to be acknowledged as a responsible and respectable member of the community. Arju was one of the best instances of rural social institutions where a man's socialization occurs. It had separate sections for different purposes, such as sleeping quarters, storage areas and central gathering spaces. Each Arju was overseen by experienced elders, who served as mentors and educators for the young boys. The other function of the Arju was to educate young boys about the history, traditions, war tactics, agriculture, folk songs, customary laws and cultural practices of the Ao-Naga community. Elders would impart knowledge through storytelling, discussions and hands-on experiences. The curriculum at the Arju included teachings on moral values, social responsibilities, survival skills, traditional craftsmanship and the importance of community cohesion (Jamir, 1993, p. 82). Apart from education, the Arju also served as a space for communal activities and celebrations. It was a place where important decisions were made, conflicts were resolved and ceremonies and rituals were conducted. The Arju fostered a sense of belonging, unity and cultural pride among the Ao-Naga community. Therefore, Arju was the anvil of the Ao-cultural heritage. According to Mills, the Arju was a 'Public School' (Mills, 1926, p. 10).

As the Arju serves to train unmarried bachelors, the Tsuki serves the needs of unmarried girls. Thus, Arju is a male institution whereas Tsuki is a female institution. It is as old as the Arju and is an absolute feminist social-cultural institution. In modern terms, it is nothing more than a 'girls' hostel'. Therefore, the term 'Tsuki' can be translated as a girls' dormitory where the unmarried girls used to sleep under the guardianship of an experienced widow, or normally an unmarried woman of the same clan known as Tsukibutsula.[9] As a customary practice, only girls belonging to the same clan were allowed to sleep in a particular Tsuki (dormitory), reflecting the way of clan exogamy, where marriage within the same clan was strictly prohibited. The members of these institutions were called Tsukir, which can also be translated as the members of a small garden of beautiful flowers. In Ao dialect, Tsuki or Atsuki means 'garden'. Therefore, when one speaks about Tsuki, it refers to the garden of young girls where their socialization takes place under a qualified matron. In the Ao-Naga tradition, flowers, *naro*, denote the young girls. Therefore, Tsuki refers to 'encircling or protecting young girls' in the form of a well-fenced garden or Tsuki/Atsuki. It was, in fact, a learning institution for the girls (Jamir and Lanunungsang, 2005, p. 102).

Only the bona fide girls were entitled to become members of this institution; that is, in terms of age and clan affiliation and so on. It is up to Tsukibutsula or the matron as to who should be bona fide members of the Tsuki under her direct control. She was not only in charge but also the owner of the house where a group of beautiful and unmarried girls assemble and sleep. Normally it was established in the house of a widow who served as matron. She was known as the real owner of the key under whose responsibility a group of unmarried girls sleep in her house. It was a small institution where five to seven, or barely a dozen, girls could be accommodated. Therefore, in the past, there existed several institutions in every locality in a given Ao village (Jamir and Lanunungsang, 2005, pp. 103–5).

The function of Tsuki

The main functions of the Tsuki were as follows:

1 To train Tsukir (members) into womanhood.
2 To strictly discipline them to maintain the dignity of a woman regarding family norms, social-cultural activities and proper placement in society.
3 To educate the members on the dignity of labour, such as weaving and the method of cultivation.
4 To initiate the process of courtship between partners, bridging the gap between parents.
5 Often to act as the meeting place for unmarried boys and girls, particularly in the evening hours. This is the joyous moment for Tsukir and Arju members, where they exchange their views normally through songs after the day-long tiresome work in the field. Thus, the functions of a Tsuki were manifold towards shaping the adulthood of a woman.

In this way, this institution played the most significant role in shaping young girls into real womanhood. For this, the Tsukibutsula became an important figure in the village. She was indeed respected by Tsukir and also by the young boys, especially those who were in search of a life partner. Normally the boys select their partners from these institutions where Tsukibutsula act as the consultant or advisor. The members willingly run all the errands for her, like fetching water and collecting firewood, including hard work that women could not do. The members of Tsukir used to do many of her menial works, where even the boyfriends of the young girls lend a hand ecstatically. She commanded respect especially among the youngsters as she acted as instructress. She was the most respected woman by common people and was regarded as the lady of the village (Jamir and Lanunungsang, 2005, p. 106–8).

Relationship between Tsuki and Arju

As mentioned above, Tsuki was purely a female institution. However, there was an indirect relationship between Tsuki and Arju. The Arju members used to visit the Tsuki very frequently but no Tsuki members were allowed to visit the Arju. In other words, Tsuki and Arju were the two institutional lovers. In this way, Arju and Tsuki were considered two distinct social institutions. Tsukir were honoured by regular visits of the Arju men. This was in fact a meeting place for young men and women in the evening hours after they returned from the fields. Some girls and boys hastily leave their houses and proceed to the Tsuki to meet their friends there. However, their visit was not meant for sexual relations but for social interaction. Normally no man was allowed to visit Tsuki in the absence of Tsukibutsula (Jamir and Lanunungsang, 2005, pp. 109–11).

The sanctity of the Arju was so highly kept that even the members of the Tsuki were not allowed to enter the bachelors' dormitory, though the Arju members could enter the Tsuki. The Tsuki, though it was a women's dormitory, had an indirect impact on Arju's life as both the institutions were the centre of learning and disciplining. Moreover, since the members of Arju have direct interaction with the members of the Tsuki, its effect on the life of Arju was tremendous, especially on psychological fronts. The men have to select the best members from Tsuki to be their life partners. At the same time, the Tsukir would prefer the most handsome, rich and talented bachelor from the Arju. In this way, the moral discipline in both institutions was helped to improve with efficiency of the Arju system. The members of Arju became more active and smarter, and this attracted the members of the Tsuki. In the olden days, the warriors were preferred more by the women, who considered that they would protect them safely in times of war. The cowards were not liked, because even the women looked down on them. There was heavy competition among the Arju of different colonies, or *mepus* or *khels*, and so it was also in the case of Tsuki. Whatever experience the boys got in Tsuki was shared in Arju among their co-friends with much hilarity.

The songs sung by the girls in Tsuki were rehearsed and the elderly members of the Arju corrected those songs (Jamir and Lanunungsang, 2005, pp. 110–11).

The members of Arju were compelled to be very competitive in terms of physical achievements and the development of inner qualities as those were the qualities that attracted the members of the Tsuki. The activities of Tsuki and its function became a source of energy and good strength to the members of the Arju in every village. In this way, there was a tremendous effect of Tsuki on the life of Arju in Ao society in the past. Arju and Tsuki have served as the best instructional institutions in Ao society since time immemorial. Unfortunately, in the present, the working systems of Arju and Tsuki do not exist. One of the main reasons for the disappearance of such traditional institutions is the impact of Christianity and formal education. In other words, the Ao-Naga indigenous traditional educational system was significantly impacted by colonialism. Western-style education was brought in by colonial rule, mostly through Christian missionary schools that prioritized English and western ideals. Indigenous knowledge and cultural practices were not being transmitted as intended, and because of this, society gradually moved away from traditional educational systems like Arju and Tsuki, which were considered a 'Public School' (Mills, 1926, p. 10). The indigenous cultural and spiritual features were further impacted by the conversion to Christianity and the marginalization of indigenous languages and rituals. Christian religion brought by the colonial powers could not accept many of the traditional practices of the Naga, like the working system of Arju and Tsuki in Naga society. Gradually after the inception of Christianity, such traditional institutions disappeared during 1950s and 1960s. Unfortunately, the features and value systems of Arju and Tsuki, especially the teaching, learning and disciplining system, could not be adopted well when the formal or modern educational system was introduced (Jamir and Lanunungsang, 2005, p. 112). Thus, the Arju and the Tsuki learning, or the traditional learning of the Ao-Nagas, experienced a drastic change with the first coming of the British in 1832, followed by the American Baptist Missionaries in 1872. With the introduction of formal education and the influence of Christian missionaries, the significance of the Arju system gradually declined (Imtimangyang, 2017, p. 78). However, its legacy and influence on the Ao-Naga community's cultural identity and educational values remain. Efforts have been made to revive and preserve the Arju system, with some communities establishing replicas of traditional Arjus as cultural and educational centres.

Formal education

The introduction of formal education in Nagaland is credited to the American Baptist Missionaries who came into the Hills nearly half a century after the British. Formal education in Nagaland was first introduced in the Mokokchung district[10] with Dr Clark's arrival, an American Baptist Missionary, in 1872. However, their main objective was evangelism. The missionaries considered the initiation of education to be their main priority since this would facilitate evangelization (Imtimangyang, 2017, p. 78).

In 1878 the first formal school was established at Molungyimsen village[11] by Mrs Mary Mead Clark. It was a Sunday school and initially for girls.[12] The instructional materials were portions of the Bible and hymns; students were taught using English, Assamese and the Ao-Naga language initially, and gradually English became the medium of instruction. In subsequent years, boys were also enrolled and gradually the road map to formal education in Nagaland was created. The Revd L. Kijung Ao records that by the year 1886 there were eight mission schools in eight villages with 56 pupils (*A Priceless Legacy*, 2020, pp. 16–24).

In 1895 the Impur[13] Mission Training School was established by the Revd S. A. Perrine at Impur with nine people. By 1899 there were 40 students in the Impur Mission Training School and within a short time the enrolment rose to 60 (Longkumer, 2022, pp. 671–2). In 1901 the charge of Headmaster of Impur Mission School was shouldered by the Revd W. F. Down, an educationist missionary who was considered one of the best educationists of the time. It was under his guidance and direction that some Naga boys on completion of the course of study at Impur attended the Mission School at Jorhat (Clark, 1907, p. 109; Sharma and Ao, 2000).

Gradually, Nagas were appointed as teachers and headmasters who worked alongside the American missionaries in the development of education in Naga Hills.[14] With the passage of time, Impur Mission Training School was upgraded to Middle English (M.E.) School and was renamed Impur Mission Training and Middle School, and the government allotted a grant-in-aid of 50 rupees (Jamir, 1993, pp. 164–7). By 1938, Impur Mission Training and Middle School grew to be the biggest M.E. school. The school started offering subjects like geography, geometry, English and grammar. In the year 1950 the school was named Christian High School, with the inclusion of classes till seven, and in 1954 the school was renamed Clark Memorial High School. In the same year the school became a fully fledged High School and was recognized by the Assam Education Board (Kiremwati, 2020, pp. 64–6). The school was upgraded to Higher Secondary in 1999. In 2020 Clark Memorial Higher Secondary School attained 125 years of its existence, the oldest surviving American missionary school in Nagaland.

Education, which was imparted by the American missionaries, is still considered a fundamental aspect of development, empowering individuals and communities. The Ao-Naga have taken initiatives to improve access to quality education. Hence, though a small district with a population of 101,092, today educational institutions have increased reasonably over the years. Presently there are 14 pre-primary schools, 286 schools (primary, upper primary, secondary and higher secondary schools), six colleges (four general colleges, a teacher education college and a law college), two theological colleges, a Bible school, a DIET centre, an Institute of Communication in Information Technology (ICIT), a National Institute of Electronics and Information Technology (NIELIT) extension, an Industrial Training Institute (ITI), and an Institute of Higher Studies has been established by Tata Institute of Social Science (TISS) in collaboration with Nagaland Gandhi Ashram (NGA). However, Mokokchung district is yet to have a university, engineering college, medical college, agricultural college or other professional institutions (Longkumer, 2022, p. 673). Mokokchung district has a literacy rate of 91.62%, the highest in the state with 92.18% among males and 91.01% among females (Govt of Nagaland, 2023; Census, 2023). Thus, despite being a male-dominated community, the influence of education on Ao-Naga women has been transformative, empowering them to challenge traditional gender roles, pursue their aspirations and contribute to their community's socio-economic development. Education has played a crucial role in breaking down the barriers that have historically limited the opportunities available to women in Ao-Naga society (Das, 2019).

Theological education

Theological education among the Ao-Nagas has a rich and fascinating history that spans over a century. Along with formal education, people also accepted the new religion brought by the American missionaries. As a result, the new believers formed Christian communities and churches, leading to a growing need for trained pastors, teachers and evangelists. Dr Edwin Winter Clark recognized the importance of theological education to nurture the Christian faith and equip local believers for ministry (Clark, 1891, p. 275). In 1938 he laid the foundation for the theological institution by starting the Mokokchung Bible School. The primary purpose of this school was to provide basic biblical and theological training to local believers and potential church leaders. The Bible school aimed to deepen their understanding of the Scriptures and prepare them for effective ministry. As the Bible school grew and its impact increased, Dr Clark's vision for a more comprehensive theological institution became a reality. On 19 March 1948 the Mokokchung Bible School was officially transformed into Clark Theological College. The college was named after Dr Clark in recognition of his dedicated service to the Ao-Naga community and his passion for theological education. Clark Theological College was inaugurated with the aim of offering a more comprehensive and formal theological education programme (Ao, 1972, p. 22).

Over the years, Clark Theological College continued to grow and evolve. It expanded its curriculum, introduced postgraduate courses and enhanced its facilities. The college's impact extended beyond the borders of Nagaland, attracting students from various Naga tribes and other states of north-east India. Clark Theological College has played a vital role in equipping generations of pastors, evangelists and Christian leaders, not only among the Ao-Nagas but also among other Naga tribes and ethnic communities in the region. Its commitment to theological education has contributed significantly to the growth and spread of Christianity in Nagaland and neighbouring states. Today, Clark Theological College remains an essential institution in the field of theological education in north-east India. It continues to uphold its mission of training and preparing men and women for Christian ministry, nurturing a deeper understanding of the Christian faith and fostering its students' spiritual and intellectual development.

The resilience of Ao-Naga indigenous women despite being in a patriarchal society

Being born as a male child is an honour in a patriarchal society, but being born as a female is just celebrated and welcomed. In the Ao-Naga society, women are still grouped in the category of *Tetsur Tanur* (women and minor children), which indicates the general position of women in the society. A common statement *Tetsur Tanur-alidak* (in the presence of women and children) is popularly used even today, differentiating the status of women from that of the menfolk, sometimes rating them as minor citizens irrespective of their status, age and qualifications. In order to defame or defend women, the very common words used are *Parnok-tetsur-tanur-i-kechimetet?* ('What do these women and children know about?'). Such usage refers to the dominating attitude and nature of the male folks and is also an insult to the gender. In fact, women are regarded as inferior to men in society and in family circles because the Ao-Naga live under a patriarchal structure.

However, the resilience of the indigenous Ao-Naga women serves as a testament to their strength, perseverance and adaptability despite being in a male-dominated set-up. Here it is important for us to understand the three following concepts that act as a witness to the resilience of the indigenous Ao-Naga women.

Strength

The concept of strength is multifaceted and can be understood in various ways, depending on the context in which it is applied. In the context of the resilience of the indigenous Ao-Naga women, strength is understood to be a particular aspect of strength related to endurance, mental fortitude and the ability to overcome adversity. The Ao-Naga women have displayed this strength in different capacities at different points of time, enduring hardship, overcoming obstacles and maintaining their composure in challenging situations. To claim one's own right and make a place in a male-dominated society, women need qualities like resilience, determination and a positive mindset. Strength, in the context of Ao-Naga women, refers to their inner fortitude and resilience in the face of adversity. It encompasses various forms of strength like emotional strength, which the Ao-Naga women have exhibited by remaining composed and resilient in challenging situations. They have faced hardships and their voices and rights have been suppressed and denied; they have experienced the impacts of conflicts but their ability to manage their emotions and stay focused on positive outcomes is a testament to their emotional resilience. Ao-Naga women have been at the forefront of advocating for gender equality. They challenge traditional gender norms and stereotypes that may limit women's roles within the community. Through awareness campaigns and community discussions, they work to change attitudes and perceptions regarding the capabilities and rights of women (Longkumer, 2019, pp. 7–9). They have also initiated and participated in empowerment programmes aimed at enhancing the status of women in their society (Kumar and Shobana, 2021, p. 218).

These programmes may include skill development, leadership training and educational initiatives designed to empower women to take on more prominent roles in decision-making and community development. Ao-Naga women have been actively involved in conflict resolution and peace-building efforts within their communities. Their social strength is evident in their ability to mediate disputes and promote reconciliation. They work to maintain social harmony and prevent conflicts from escalating.

Ao-Naga indigenous women have exhibited their strength through their cultural identity by preserving and promoting their indigenous culture. It is a well-known fact that Ao-Naga women have historically played significant roles in cultural preservation. They have served as the primary bearers of cultural knowledge and traditions within families. Like many other societies, Ao-Naga women are also responsible for teaching children about their cultural practices, passing down oral histories and maintaining traditional arts and crafts, which they have been faithfully doing. They also actively participate in all cultural celebrations, rituals and ceremonies. They contribute to the preparation and execution of these events, ensuring that cultural traditions are carried out with authenticity and reverence. They also keep the artistic and craftsmanship traditions alive despite being in a developed and advancing society. The artistic and craftsmanship traditions such as weaving, pottery and textile work such as silk worming are still practised today. These skills are integral to many cultural practices and are passed down through generations of women. Thus, their cultural strength is evident in their commitment to preserving and promoting their indigenous culture (Aier, 2018, p. 4901).

Ao-Naga indigenous women have also exhibited their strength through social network support within their communities. These networks provide a platform for women to share experiences, seek advice and offer emotional support to one another. Such networks are essential for fostering solidarity and resilience. They also help in the advocacy against discrimination in various aspects. In this way, they work to create a more inclusive and equitable society where all community members have equal opportunities and rights, especially in the field of education. This is one of the reasons why many Ao-Naga women are at the forefront when it comes to education. They are also involved in awareness campaigns on various social issues, including health, sanitation and environmental conservation. Their social strength is evident in their efforts to improve the overall well-being and quality of life in their communities. Thus, through their participation they get access to community development projects, addressing issues such as infrastructure development, healthcare access and poverty alleviation. Their social strength is reflected in their dedication to improving living conditions for all community members. This, social strength demonstrated by Ao-Naga women highlights their resilience, determination and commitment to creating positive social change within their communities (Nukshirenla and Dhanaraju, 2021, p. 2). Their efforts contribute not only to gender equality but also to the overall development and well-being of Ao-Naga society. Their advocacy and leadership serve as an inspiration to future generations, emphasizing the importance of active participation and social strength in shaping a better future.

Perseverance

Perseverance is the determination to persistently pursue goals, even in the face of obstacles or setbacks. For Ao-Naga women, perseverance is evident in several aspects of their lives, such as in leadership, because Ao-Naga women have broken through gender barriers to assume leadership positions within their communities and organizations. Despite facing resistance and scepticism in traditionally male-dominated roles, their perseverance in their leadership roles, especially in different educational institutions, has been remarkable. Their determination to lead and advocate for positive change serves as an inspiration to others. Many Ao-Naga women have shown remarkable perseverance in pursuing education. Despite limited access to quality educational resources and traditional gender roles that may discourage education for girls, they continue to strive for knowledge (Longkumer, 2019, pp. 5–6). Their determination to overcome these barriers underscores their commitment to personal growth and empowerment. Though a man is considered to be head of the family, women equally take responsibility when it comes to the economic stability of the family (Tianenla, 2020, p. 2400). Thus, the Ao-Naga women are often actively involved in economic activities, such as agriculture and handloom weaving. They work diligently to contribute to their family's income and economic stability. Their economic perseverance reflects their dedication to improving their living conditions and ensuring the well-being of their families. The economic perseverance of Ao-Naga women is a testament to their determination and resilience in contributing to their family's income and economic stability. They engage in various economic activities and play a crucial role in the economic well-being of their communities.

Many Ao-Naga women actively participate in agriculture, which is a significant source of livelihood in their communities. They engage in tasks such as farming, planting, harvesting and tending to livestock. Despite the challenges of agricultural work, including labour-intensive tasks and weather-related uncertainties, they persevere in ensuring food security for their families. Handloom weaving is another essential economic activity among Ao-Naga women. They create intricate and beautiful traditional textiles and garments. Weaving is a skill that is passed down through generations, and women persevere in honing their craft and producing marketable products. Some Ao-Naga women are involved in pottery and craftsmanship. They create pottery items, baskets and other handicrafts that are not only functional but also hold cultural and economic value. These women demonstrate perseverance in preserving and adapting these traditional arts to contemporary markets. The Ao-Naga women also exhibit entrepreneurship (Ozukum, 2019) by establishing small businesses, such as food stalls, local shops and trading activities. They take on the responsibility of managing these enterprises and contribute to the local economy by providing goods and services to their communities (Longkumer, 2019, pp. 10–13). Thus, through all such economic activities, the Ao-Naga women contribute significantly to their family's income and economic self-reliance. They understand the importance of economic stability and work diligently to ensure that their households have the resources they need to thrive.

It is interesting to know that despite challenges related to market access and transportation in remote regions, the Ao-Naga women persist in finding ways to connect with markets for their local products. They strive to collaborate with local cooperatives or organizations to improve market linkages, which is how the local products are made available in different marketplaces. All these contribute to the economic and financial uplifting of the family in particular and society in general by demonstrating perseverance in small-scale business, budgeting, saving and making financial decisions that benefit their families and future generations. In this way, Ao-Naga women are empowered through economic activities that are closely linked to empowerment. By contributing to their family's income, Ao-Naga women gain a sense of economic independence and decision-making power within their households. Economic perseverance also involves adaptation to changing economic conditions, where the Ao-Naga women recognize the importance of adapting their economic activities to contemporary demands while preserving their traditional values and practices (Ezung, 2021, p. 2). Thus, many of the Ao-Naga women engage in multiple income-generating activities simultaneously, diversifying their sources of income. This resilience strategy helps them cope with economic uncertainties and fluctuations. The economic perseverance of Ao-Naga women reflects their dedication to improving the economic well-being of their families and communities. They overcome various challenges, including limited resources, geographical isolation and market constraints, to ensure a stable and sustainable livelihood. Their economic contributions play a pivotal role in poverty alleviation, food security and the overall development of their communities.

Adaptability

Adaptability is the ability to adjust to new or changing circumstances effectively. The Ao-Naga women demonstrate adaptability in various areas in the midst of development, modernization and globalization. They embrace new technologies and communication tools to bridge the gap between tradition and modernity, ensuring that their cultural practices remain relevant and accessible to younger generations. Adaptability is a crucial quality that plays a significant role in enhancing the resilience of Ao-Naga women, as it does for individuals and communities facing various challenges and changes. The adaptability of Ao-Naga women in a male-dominated setting amid development is crucial for their empowerment and progress. Here are four key aspects that highlight the significance of adaptability in this context.

Development often brings about changes in cultural norms and practices, which can be both positive and negative, and they are a natural part of the process of social and economic development. This typically involves the adoption of modern technologies, infrastructure and economic systems. This can lead to changes in traditional ways of life. However, the Ao-Naga women have played a crucial role in preserving their cultural heritage while embracing aspects of modernization. Today there are many Ao-Naga women engaged in traditional art forms and cultural expressions (Temsukala, 2023). They adapt these traditions to contemporary contexts, incorporating new designs and styles while preserving the essence of their cultural heritage. This adaptability ensures that their artistic expressions remain vibrant and appealing to a broader audience. This also shows that they can find a balance between tradition and progress, ensuring that cultural values are respected and passed down to younger generations, even in the face of changing dynamics, by adapting to cultural preservation and modernization.

The Ao-Naga women have adapted to the challenges of living in a male-dominated society through various means, demonstrating their resilience and resourcefulness as many Ao-Naga women have recognized the importance of education in gaining knowledge and skills that can empower them in male-dominated settings. They have adapted by pursuing higher education and vocational training, equipping themselves for various roles in society beyond traditional gender roles (Temsukala, 2023). They have given importance to economic empowerment in order to exhibit their resilience because many Ao-Naga women have ventured into entrepreneurship, agriculture or other income-generating activities as a means of economic empowerment. They have adapted by diversifying their sources of income and gaining financial independence, thereby making their way more secure and conventional despite the patriarchal clutches. This has paved the way and uplifted their status to leadership. Hence, today we can see several Ao-Naga women who have taken up, or who are in, leadership roles in community development initiatives and advocacy efforts. They have adapted by using their voices and influence to challenge discriminatory practices, promote gender equality and advocate for women's rights.

Since the Ao-Naga women belong to a communitarian set-up, they still believe in the significance of networking and support systems. Thus, building strong networks and support systems has been a key strategy for Ao-Naga women. They adapt by connecting with like-minded individuals, support groups and organizations that provide mentorship and resources to navigate male-dominated environments. It is true that, with the changing context, Ao-Naga women have engaged in negotiations within their households and communities to challenge and renegotiate traditional gender roles (Chowdhury, 2019, p. 288). This involves discussing and distributing responsibilities and decision-making more equitably, giving them the opportunity to be involved in conflicts and disputes. Conflict resolution is an essential skill adapted and practised by Ao-Naga women within their communities. The Ao-Naga society has a rich tradition of conflict resolution methods that have evolved over generations. Thus, the Ao-Naga women often serve as mediators in various types of conflicts, both within families and at the community level. They use their interpersonal skills and cultural understanding to facilitate dialogue and negotiations between conflicting parties. They also play a significant role in resolving family disputes, such as conflicts between spouses, siblings or extended family members. They offer advice, counsel and emotional support to those involved and work towards finding amicable solutions. They also emphasize restorative justice approaches, where women contribute by helping to restore relationships and harmony within the community after conflicts are resolved. In situations of larger-scale conflicts or inter-community disputes, Ao-Naga women participate in peacebuilding efforts. They may engage in dialogue with other communities, advocate for peaceful solutions, and promote reconciliation by being proactive in preventing conflicts by fostering understanding and tolerance within their communities. They may organize community gatherings, workshops or awareness campaigns to address potential sources of tension (Majumder, 2023).

However, despite the endless efforts and tremendous contributions, when it comes to decision-making, the voices and opinions, thoughts and ideas of women always feel deaf in the ears of the Ao-Naga indigenous society. But although men are the decision-makers for all important matters both in public and private life, and although women's roles are strictly confined and defined by tradition, Ao-Naga indigenous women's contribution cannot be denied, especially in the field of education. Here is some present leadership and some contributions of the indigenous Ao-Naga women in the district of Mokokchung in some of the notable institutions:

1 The oldest school (1895), Clark Memorial Higher Secondary School, is headed by an Ao-Naga indigenous woman, Mrs Chubaienla, as the Principal, with 13 out of 20 Ao-Naga indigenous women teaching staff.[15]
2 The second-oldest school (1941), Mayangnokcha Higher Secondary School, is also headed by an Ao-Naga indigenous woman, Mrs Lipokienla, as the Principal, with 40 Ao-Naga indigenous women teaching staff out of 75 teaching faculty members.[16]
3 The oldest college (1959), Fazl Ali College, has 35 Ao-Naga indigenous women teaching staff out of 74 teaching faculty members.[17]
4 Jubilee Memorial College (2015)[18] has 13 Ao-Naga indigenous women teaching staff and five male teaching faculty members.[19]
5 Clark Theological College (1948) has 20 faculty members, out of which seven are Ao-Naga indigenous women.[20]
6 The oldest hospital (1904), Imkongliba Memorial Civil Hospital, is headed by an Ao-Naga indigenous woman, Dr S. Marina Yaden, as the Medical Superintendent, where six Ao-Naga indigenous woman serve as full-time medical doctors out of 18 doctors.[21]
7 The first publishing house (2008), Heritage Publishing House (HPH), was founded by an Ao-Naga indigenous woman, Lanusangla Tsudir.

Apart from this, Ao-Naga indigenous women continue to strive and claim their place, even in the religious sphere, despite opportunities seeming seldom. Under Ao Baptist Arogo Mungdang (ABAM), the Ao-Naga have 285 ordained pastors, of whom 20 are women and 167 are associate women pastors. Unfortunately, there are no women pastors, only associate women pastors. However, when it comes to theological education, the Ao-Naga indigenous women have immensely and equally contributed as the men, or probably even more. As per the ABAM record, altogether there are 125 theological educators in different theological institutions, out of which 57 are women.[22] Thus, 'Not only publishing but the entire intellectual spectrum is dominated by women' (Das, 2019).

Conclusion

This is a society where women have been denied political space for centuries. It is only this year for the first time that two women candidates have been elected as members of the Nagaland Legislative Assembly (Shekhar, 2023). It is a society where it is difficult for women to even speak out about their basic rights. Yet the Ao-Naga indigenous women continue to occupy a unique status, as there is no other state in the country where women dominate the intellectual landscape in this way. In addition to formal education, Ao-Naga women have been instrumental in preserving and passing down traditional cultural knowledge. This knowledge is often transmitted through storytelling, songs and other cultural practices, which play a role in education. They have passed on their knowledge and culture to younger generations, ensuring the preservation of traditional wisdom. Ao-Naga women have been role models and mentors for young girls in their communities, inspiring them to pursue education and personal growth. They encourage girls to aspire to greater achievements and to be self-reliant. It is important to recognize that while some of these contributions have taken place within the formal education system, many have occurred informally within the community. The Ao-Naga women's contributions to education are part of a broader effort to strengthen their community, preserve their culture and ensure a brighter future for the next generations. In the midst of development, Ao-Naga women have demonstrated remarkable resilience and adaptability, making significant contributions to their communities and society at large. Their roles encompass a wide range of domains, including education, economic empowerment, leadership, cultural preservation and conflict resolution. These women have not only adapted to the changing landscape of development but have also actively shaped the trajectory of their communities. The contributions of Ao-Naga women highlight the importance of gender equality and the recognition of the valuable roles they play in the holistic development of their society. Their adaptability is a testament to their strength, determination and capacity to overcome challenges, break down gender barriers and foster positive change. As Ao-Naga women continue to adapt, innovate and thrive, they serve as inspiring examples of how individuals can be agents of progress within their communities, even in the face of complex social, economic and cultural dynamics. Their resilience and contributions are essential for achieving inclusive and sustainable development in the region and stand as a testament to the power of adaptability and determination in the pursuit of progress.

Notes

1 This chapter will give special reference only to the Ao-Naga indigenous women. The Ao-Naga is a dominant indigenous tribal community in Nagaland that lives in the north-eastern part of India – the sixteenth state of the Union of India. Nagaland is one of the seven states in north-east India where the majority of those who reside are from an indigenous background. It is one of the most Christian states in India where almost all the Nagas are Christians. There are 14 major Naga tribes in Nagaland. They are: Ao, Angami, Chakhesang, Chang, Khemungan, Konyak, Lotha, Phom, Pochury, Rengma, Sangtam, Sema, Yimchunger and Zeliang (see https://www.capertravelindia.com/nagaland/nagaland-tribes.html, accessed 27.01.2025).

2 The Ao-Nagas practise a rudimentary system of delivering justice and decision-making based on the 'Customary Law'. It states that the Parliament cannot legislate in matters of Naga religion or social practices, Naga Customary Law and procedure, administration of civil and criminal justice involving decisions according to Naga Customary Law and ownership and transfer of land without the concurrence of the State Assembly.

3 The village council, which consists of the elders, is the supreme decision-making body with representations from every clan but only men.

4 Clan elders do not include the female/women. It is to be noted that in all such proceedings, it is solely the male who decides for themselves and even for the women.

5 Nagaland got its statehood on 1 December 1963. Some of the developments are as follows: *Infrastructure Development*: post-statehood, there have been efforts to improve infrastructure in Nagaland. Roads, bridges, and other transportation networks have been constructed or upgraded to improve connectivity within the state and with neighbouring regions. *Economic Development*: the state has witnessed some economic growth, but there are ongoing efforts to diversify the

economy and attract investments in sectors such as tourism, handloom, handicrafts and horticulture. *Culture and heritage*: Nagaland takes pride in its diverse and rich cultural heritage. The state government, along with various organizations, promotes cultural events, festivals and activities to preserve and showcase the unique traditions of different tribes in the state. It is also known as the 'Land of the Festivals'.

6 Arju, or the boys' dormitory, was a traditional learning academy where boys who had reached adolescence were required to join the Arju or dormitories and sleep there (Jamir and Lanunungsang, 2005, p. 26).

7 Tsuki, or the girl's dormitory. Just like the Arju, which was for the boys, the village also maintained a dormitory for the girls of the village called Tsuki (Jamir and Lanunungsang, 2005, p. 28).

8 The Arju was lavishly ornamented and richly decorated with carvings representing hornbills, tigers, mithun and human heads and sometimes with projecting barge boards representing wings or horns that physically dominate an Ao-Naga village. (The mithun is a semi-domesticated bovine animal. It is a symbol of social status used in rituals and cultural ceremonies by the rich.)

9 Tsukibutsula is an Ao dialect, which means the owner of the house whose function is similar to that of the matron.

10 Mokokchung district is mainly inhabited by the Ao-Nagas. The Ao-Nagas represent one of the major Naga tribes with a population of 101,092 (2011 census). The formal system of education had its foundation laid in the Mokokchung district in the late nineteenth century by American missionaries and gradually spread to other parts of Nagaland.

11 Molungyimsen is the first Ao-Naga Christian village in Nagaland. It was in Molungyimsen that the first Naga Christian Association was held. Molungyimsen is also known as the 'Cradle of Education' because the first school in Nagaland was established in this village in 1878. The first book in Nagaland was written and printed in Molungyimsen. In 1894, Clark moved the Naga Mission Center to Impur, which is now known as the Ao Baptist Arogo Mungdang (Ao Baptist Church Association).

12 The names of the first batch of girls who were enrolled were Tongpangkokla, Noksangla, Jongmayangla, Purla, Punayula and Taripisü. L. Temjen (*College Souvenir*, 2009, pp. 162–4).

13 Impur is a town and an assembly constituency in Nagaland, India. It was established as a mission centre in 1894 by American missionaries. In 1897, when the Ao Baptist Arogo Mungdang (Ao Baptist Church Association) was formed, it became its headquarters and continues to be so. It is 15 kilometres away from the heart of Mokokchung town. It is also the headquarters of Ao churches (ABAM) in Nagaland, which has about 159 churches under its fold.

14 Kiremwati (1995), pp. 63–4. In this book he pays tribute to the first four Naga headmasters for their invaluable contribution towards the growth and continuity of Impur Mission Training School. They were Gwizao Meru Zeliang (1915–17), the Revd Pehlielie Angami (1918–19), Kumbho Angami (1919–27) and Mayangnokcha Ao (1927–40).

15 In a telephone conversation with the writer on 22 July 2023. Tekatemjen Imchen, Youth Co-Ordinator, ABAM, Impur.

16 In a telephone conversation with the writer on 22 July 2023. Lipokienla, Principal, Mayangnokcha Higher Secondary School, Mokokchung.

17 In a telephone conversation with the writer on 22 July 2023. Dr Limasenla Jamir, Assistant Professor, Department of Sociology, Fazl Ali College, Mokokchung.

18 Jubilee Memorial College is a college established in 2015 by the Mokokchung Town Baptist Church (MTBA) to commemorate its Platinum Jubilee in 2012. The college is an integral part of the church's mission to provide holistic, quality education to students at college as well as at the school level.

19 In a telephone conversation with the writer on 23 July 2023. Dr Merensangla Jamir, Assistant Professor, Department of Sociology, Jubilee Memorial College, Mokokchung.

20 In a telephone conversation with the writer on 23 July 2023. Dr Toshitemjem Aier, Associate Professor, Department of History of Christianity, Clark Theological College, Aolijen.

21 In a telephone conversation with the writer on 23 July 2023. Dr S. Marina Yaden, Medical Superintendent, Imkongliba Memorial Hospital, Mokokchung.

22 In a telephone conversation with the writer on 22 July 2023. Dr Moanungsang Tzudir, Literaure Secretary, ABAM, Impur.

References

2020, 'The Creation of the Greater Story: A Priceless Legacy', in *A Priceless Legacy – Quasqui Centennial Souvenir, Clark Memorial Higher Secondary School, Impur (1895–2020)*, Impur, Mokokchung.

Aier, A., 2018, 'Cultural Continuity and Change Among the Ao Nagas', *International Journal of Social Science and Economic Research* 3(9), pp. 4897–902.

Ao, L. K., 1972, *Nokinketer Mongchen*, Impur: Ao Baptist Arogo Mungdang (ABAM).

Census, 2023, 'Literacy in India', https://www.census2011.co.in/literacy.php (accessed 9.07.2023).

Chowdhury, P. D., 2019, 'Women in the Ao-Naga Family and Community: A Study of Temsula Ao's *Aosenla's Story*', *An International Journal of English Language, Literature and Literary Theory* 8(1), pp. 279–89.

Clark, E. W., 1891, 'The Naga mission Molung', *The Baptist Missionary Magazine* 71(7), p. 275.

Clark, E. W., 1907, *A Corner in India*, Philadelphia, PA: American Baptist Publication Society.

Clark, M. M., 2000, *A Corner in India*, Philadelphia, PA: American Baptist Mission Publication Society.

College Souvenir: Celebrating Fifty Glorious Years 1959–2009, 2009, Fazal Ali College, Mokokchung.

Das, Y. S., 2019, 'Why Women Dominate the Entire Intellectual Spectrum in Nagaland', *The Times of India*, 18 September.

Ezung, J., 2021, 'Role of Women in Economic Contributions with Reference to Lotha Nagas', *Journal of Humanities and Social Science* 26(8), pp. 1–3.

Govt of Nagaland, 2023, 'Department of Higher Education', https://education.nagaland.gov.in/contact-us/ (accessed 9.07.2023).

Imtimangyang, 2017, 'A Brief Historical Account: Christianity Among the Ao Nagas of North-East India', *National Journal of Multidisciplinary Research and Development* 2(3), pp. 77–82.

Jamir, A., 2022, 'Ethnography of the Nagas in General and Aos in Particular: Limapur/Animist and Modern-Christian Context', *Journal of Emerging Technologies and Innovative Research* 9(5), pp. 94–119.

Jamir, N. T., 1993, *Asen Sobalibaren*, 2nd edn, New Delhi: Neeta Prakashan.

Jamir, N. T. and Lanunungsang, A., 2005, *Naga Society and Culture*, Nagaland: Nagaland University Tribal Research Centre.

Kiremwati, 2020, 'Education and the Nagas – with Special Reference to the Ao Nagas', *Commemorating the Centennial of the Clark Memorial High School, Impur (1895–1995)*, Impur, Mokokchung.

Kumar, J. S. and Shobana, D., 2021, 'Status of Women Empowerment in Nagaland', *International Journal of Advance and Innovative Research* 8(4)(VII), pp. 217–22.

Longkumer, I. W., 2019, *Naga Women's Perspective on Gender Roles: An Analysis of Literary Narratives*, New Delhi: Zubaan Publishers Pvt. Ltd.

Longkumer, M., 2022, 'Development of Formal Education in Nagaland with Special Reference to Mokokchung District', *International Journal of Creative Research Thoughts (IJCRT)* 10(8), pp. 669–70.

Majumder, S. S., 2023, 'Warriors of Peace: Naga Women in/and a Conflict Zone', https://www.academia.edu/52589127/Warriors_of_Peace_Naga_Women_in_and_a_Conflict_Zone (accessed 14.10.2023).

Mills, J. P., 1926, *The Ao Nagas*, Bombay: Oxford University Press.

Nukshirenla, N. and Dhanaraju, V., 2021, 'The Status of Ao Naga Women: Reflections on the Recent Debates in Nagaland', *Shodh Sanchar Bulletin* 11(41), pp. 1–5.

Ozukum, R., 2019, 'Women Entrepreneurship in Nagaland', *Eastern Mirror*, 22 June.

Sharma, R. P. and Ao, N., 2000, *The Ao-Naga Tribe of Northeast India: A Study in Anthropology and History*, New Delhi: Mittal Publications.

Shekhar, K. S., 2023, 'Meet First 2 Women MLAs of Nagaland: Hekani Jakhalu and Salhoutuonuo Kruse', *The Times of India*, 3 March.

Temsukala, 2023, 'Influence of Education on Naga Identity: From Women Perspective', *Asian Journal of Multidisciplinary Research & Review* 2(2), pp. 467–79, https://thelawbrigade.com/wp-content/uploads/2021/06/AJMRR_Dr.-Temsukala.pdf (accessed 14.10.2023).

Tianenla, 2020, 'The Role and Position of Women in Traditional Ao Society', *International Journal of Creative Research Thoughts (IJCRT)* 8(10), pp. 2396–402.

PART 3

Theological Models

7

'Sola' Mining, 'Sola' Profit, 'Sola' Development Gloria: Extractivist Theology and Heretical Spiritualities

NANCY CARDOSO
(translated by Francis McDonagh)

Introduction: theologies of rivers and mudflows

> We've been fighting against mining for 200 years. Our land is on the bank of the river. I have many emotional memories associated with the river, We call it 'Watu', 'the river that flows', 'the river that speaks'. For many people it's just flowing water. For us it's as though it was a living being that used to talk to us every day. We don't call what has happened to Watu a disaster, we call it a crime. On 5 November 2015, when the Mariana dam burst ... And a few days later, when the mud reached my community's territory ... It was very fast, it went around smashing everything. (Shirley Djukurnã, from the Krenak people)[1]

The theology of the 'river that speaks' and the 'mud that comes up' – these two narratives constructed out of territory and power are in confrontation in normal life in Latin America and other regions of the Global South as a political and liturgical struggle. The 'mud that comes up' is part of extractivism's creed, *All Glory to Mining, All Glory to Profit, All Glory to Technology, All Glory to Progress*, and disasters – capitalism as religion in theological mode. The 'river that speaks' is an expression of historical acts of resistance, familiar knowledge and sacred rituals going by many names in many cultures with many languages of what we call in Latin America *R-existence* (Porto-Gonçalves, 2002) – 'For us, land is something more than a resource: it is an origin' (a Mixe indigenous, Oaxaca, Mexico) (Toledo, 2008).

In this chapter I want to share Latin American reflections, authors and activists on extractive projects following the path of the debates about capitalism as a religion (Coelho, 2022; Sung and Coelho, 2019, p. 651), and those of Latin American feminism about body and territory (Cardoso, 2023), widening the challenge to the theologies of liberation in their opposition to the gods of patriarchal and racist capitalism, especially the theology of extractivist activities and their liturgies of power.

Extractivism: ecology, world and power

Intensive mining has been the main motor of colonial business activity since the sixteenth century and has produced radical geological, social and metabolic changes, which, associated with the intensive exploitation of plant and water resources, has impacted life on the planet by altering the conditions of life rapidly and fundamentally (Porto-Gonçalves, 2012). Colonialism produced and was produced by an ecology or world of power, capital and nature: 'Capitalism is an ecology or world that combines with the accumulation of capital, the quest for power and the co-production of nature in successive historical configurations' (Moore, 2023).

Colonialism is an extensive and intensive system for extracting life in all its forms:

- extracting territories, their materials, compromising life-forms and biodiversity (Brandão, 2023);
- extracting people – men and women – and their labour force, their creativity and existence (Quijano, 2000);
- epistemicide and extracting communities' ways of relating to their environment, through culture and ways of learning and forms of wisdom that follow the movements of the land (Pessanha, 2019).

Latin America was inserted into the international colonial economy through mechanisms of extraction and usurpation of the land, which became a 'trade' in raw materials; this system has come to characterize even today our model of peripheral capitalist development – a product of colonial exploitation updated by neocolonialism (Cavalcante, 2021).

> Resources were extracted from Latin America that fuelled the capitalist interests of European countries such as Spain, Portugal and England, placing the territories 'discovered' in a subordinate position in the international division of labour as exporters of raw materials. Accordingly, even after more than five centuries, this region of the American

continent continues to serve the hegemonic interests of the rich industrialised countries as a supplier of raw materials. (Gonçalves, 2016)

In recent years Brazil has suffered the impact of at least two great disasters involving the mining company Vale do Rio Doce, with large numbers of deaths among the populations of the territories affected and dramatic damage to the environment that still continues.

On the afternoon of 5 November 2015 the tailings (or residue) dam at Fundâo, in Mariana, Minas Gerais, burst. A wave of mud and stone the height of an eight-storey building wiped out whole neighbourhoods, killed 19 people and polluted two thirds of the estuary of the Rio Doce, the largest estuary in the south-east of Brazil.

Four years later, in January 2019, Vale's dam at Brumadinho, 120 kilometres from Mariana, burst. This destroyed everything around it, killed 262 people – eight of them have still not been found – and invaded the estuary of the River Paraopeba, the source of the water supply for Belo Horizonte and fifty-odd neighbouring towns … Fish disappeared six years ago, and life changed completely for more than a million people on the banks of the 675 kilometres of rivers in the southeast of Minas Gerais as far as the coast of Espírito Santo. (Casado, 2021)

Reparation for and the recovery of the communities and the territories is still pending and dragging through the courts (Dotta, 2021). Even so, Vale reported a net profit of US$3,886 billion in the third quarter of 2021, an increase of 34% over the same period of 2020.[2] The contradiction between the environmental and social crimes and the preservation of mining activity shows that mining companies are above society, that there are no adequate and efficient control mechanisms, and that the tragedies do not affect the profitability of the companies. This situation is repeated not only in Brazil but throughout Latin America with different companies, national, regional and international.

Berta Cáceres was a leader of the Lenca communities in Honduras in the fight against businesses and the government, which wanted to install huge hydro-electric projects on the River Gualcarque; she was murdered in March 2016. Her daughter, Berta Zúñiga, says:

We have pointed out that there is something very important to show, namely that not only are they projects that violate the rights of the indigenous peoples, they are violent, they take over territories, but also that they are corrupt projects, approved through corruption, the manipulation of the state. One of the documents the company had said that the project wasn't viable because of its impact on the environment, and still they gave them the concession. (Gómez, 2020)

Development and extractivism: eliminating ways of life and ancestral knowledge

In a history marked by conquest by Portugal and Spain with an economic model that extracted value from nature and labour, pre-existing social relationships were disrupted and a territorial and social control imposed that was expressed by the supremacy of the white European male and his structures. In this way, through the imposed model of development, two violent processes were also imposed:

- the breakdown and disruption of the ways of life of the native peoples (with all their contradictions);
- the imposition of a different model of social organization based on social inequality, racism, sexism and the exploitation of other life forms.

There is no need to idealize life in the precolonial cultures and imagine a world of equality and functioning tribal structures. The important thing is to understand the impact of a systematic process of social disruption and the crushing of hierarchies, and the structural cost of this for the social body throughout history. In many ways in Latin America we are still living with this choking effect of social relationships based on patriarchal, racist and sexist power that persists in social and cultural structures.

We have learned from Alberto Acosta that:

> The predominant school of thought leads us to believe that an economy without growth is an impossibility and that the only means of achieving development is through economic growth. In turn, this growth requires ever-larger amounts of natural resources to sustain increasing global demand, while generating revenue for the global South to overcome its 'underdevelopment'. Reality nevertheless tells us that moving beyond this vision is the most pressing challenge of our time: to overcome 'the religion of economic growth' and make room for new approaches that will enable us to escape the extractivism 'trap'. (Acosta, 2017, p. 100)

'SOLA' MINING, 'SOLA' PROFIT, 'SOLA' DEVELOPMENT GLORIA

To understand 'the religion of economic growth' and move on from the inevitability of capitalism as the only recognized model in extractivist practices, it is necessary to recover the visions, the values, the experiences and the ecologies of knowledge in the varied forms of R-existence of peoples and territories. These ecologies and forms of knowledge were, and continue to be, denied legitimacy and authority. The word 'development' is old, worn out and ill-intentioned. It always was! I am going to take the word to pieces to bite into its meanings and trace a genealogy of its interests.

The first recorded use of the term is from 1756, as *develop + ment*, from the French *développement*, which in turn comes from the old French *desvelopemens*, 'unrolling', connected with the French *enveloppe*, and so, in the strict sense, the action of freeing a thing from what surrounds it, a wrapper, a boundary. In the eighteenth century the word acquired a figurative sense, and referred to the act of evolving, which required first freeing oneself from some protective wrapping (Delaisse, 2020). The underlying idea is of something kept, retained, wrapped up; the dominant idea of development depends on natural and social phenomena – with their expansion contained by the awareness of the limit – that need to be opened, broken open, brought out. This understanding was consolidated in the modern period as 'infinite progress', as the continuing linearity of evolution, which required to be stimulated, with the 'wrapper' of containment rejected.

Another development paradigm, however, had already reached its peak in the nineteenth century, under the form of social evolutionism. The term 'development', in this new paradigm, was dominant in concepts such as modernization or liberation. An apparent alignment of theories of modernity can now be distinguished by its perception of social groups as a single species and therefore presenting similar developmental paths (Soares and Quintella, 2008).

The narrative is now complete. Development marked by the project of colonial and neocolonial expansion is understood as offering opportunities for societies regarded as slower to advance on the path to civilization. For this to happen their territories would need to be taken out of the envelope, de-enveloped, the wrapping, the barrier, taken away, that is, developed – that was development.

The 'envelopes', the 'shells', the 'wrappings' are a population's own mechanisms for finding solutions, for defence, for intervention in an environment or territory with a solution that is based on the labour, techniques and culture proper to each territory. These co-cultural mechanisms have an awareness of limits and prohibitions, which are dealt with in cultural and ritual ways. When they have been forced to respond to the 'generous' imposed development arrangements they have lost their own mechanisms for finding solutions, for defence, for intervention in an environment or territory. It is precisely these 'wrappings' that explained the ways of life, the material and immaterial modes of production and reproduction that were sacrificed in the name of development.

Unprotected by their 'envelopes', the peoples and their territories could be plundered and made subject to the interests of an economy that had become a story of unquestionable totality, and radically directed to the interests and 'envelopes' of North Atlantic brands of capitalism.

> 'Developed' is not being involved, not being connected, with anything. So when we buy a product, we are not involved in the history of that product, of the raw material used, the work undertaken and all the plagues that product brings with it for society. As a result we confuse ourselves with the things we buy. Our planet is limited and unlimited growth doesn't work. It is the suicide of human society itself. Development, as well as being ecocidal, is suicidal. The societies that are most resistant to capitalism are those that existed before capitalism. We have to learn from them. (Miranda, 2017)

This violence against ways of life and eco-cultural practices also damaged the rituals for relating with the territory; it also plundered the forms of belief and the feelings for limits. The River Watu full of mud, the end of the forests, the extermination of species, the rejection of native forms of agriculture – all these are forms of un-development, of removing involvement, of breaking down a community's mechanisms for protecting itself and its territory. Religion is an important battleground on which deities fight for control of life and death.

In the intensive extraction of ways of life and their rituals, the development model also imposed its religion and its rituals. When we talk about capitalism as a religion, that is not a metaphor or an allegory. It is what it is.

A theology of extractive projects – rock taken hostage by capitalism

> Capitalist entrepreneurs are devotees of this metaphysics, treating it as the framework of their religious faith. And those among them who claim to have no religion subscribe to this same metaphysics.

Entrepreneurial metaphysics is a metaphysics of commodities, money, marketing, and capital. (Hinkelammert, 1983, p. 165)

Despite being engaged in an invasive activity that has a serious social and environmental impact, mining companies float over society as untouchable bodies, impossible to control or to subject to social interests. Extractivism is a model of development based on the massive exploitation of natural resources such as minerals, oil, crops, farm animals and forests. All these economic activities – especially when carried out intensively and extensively in terms both of territory and finance – enjoy special protection as performing the role allotted to Latin America in peripheral capitalism, to be a supplier of raw materials.

This protective and almost religious cloak that covers mining in particular and extractive projects in general is what we must now discuss – theologically!

The Uruguayan author and activist Eduardo Gudynas (2016) has been one of the main voices to criticize and denounce the religious character of extractive projects. Number 24 of the review *Tabula Rasa* takes its title from the introduction by Gudynas entitled 'Teología de los Extractivismos' ('The Theology of Extractive Projects'), which asserts that it is impossible to maintain that mining activities generate economic well-being because they are always in the poorest areas of the region; nor can it be maintained that they are a safe activity for communities because the ecological disasters and land exhaustion they cause in areas affected by extractive projects are obvious.

Gudynas says:

> But, despite all this evidence and the civic resistance campaigns, extractive projects nonetheless keep advancing. They are defended by the companies, as we all know, but the same argument is made, and very fiercely, by almost all politicians, most universities and much of public opinion.
>
> This forces us to recognize that extractive projects rely on deeply rooted beliefs, shared by political and party positions ranging from conservatives to progressives, from right to left. These are acts of faith that make them immune to all evidence of impacts or accidents. (2016, p. 13)

The religious character of 'faith' in extractive projects as an indispensable activity is based on the developmentalist culture that sees and promotes the productive capacity of industry on the monopolist model

– controlling not only the raw materials but also the technology and the applications directed at consumption. But if we considered extractivist activities closely and with strict criteria, we would be forced to recognize that this is not a 'productive' sector but an activity directed at exports. According to Gudynas: 'To consider the extraction and exportation of iron, for example, as "production" is a gross distortion, since nothing is being "produced": it is being extracted (and so amounts to a net loss of natural heritage)' (Gudynas, 2016, p. 391).

Asserting the sector's productivity, which is reflected in the various applications of the resources extracted, confuses the whole with the part and does not disclose the reality of who it is that benefits from the extractivist economy, who receives the resources extracted, what the activity adds to the local economy allowing for the loss to the environment or the natural heritage. What is being envisaged are the results of the activity, with no consideration of the impacts of the activity. Everything is based on the ends justifying the means: the ends are the maintenance of the reproduction of the consumption base shaped by the market, and the means are the impacts on the immediate area of extraction (and its various systems, land, vegetation, animal, water and others), which are not part of the assessment of loss and damage.

> The labels 'production' and 'industry' are, no doubt, an attempt to justify these activities socially and politically in the eyes of the public and place extractivists in the same category as industrialists in people's minds. The repetition of these terms by academics reveals, apart from the intentions, a rather simplistic treatment of extractive projects and particularly of their ecological and political connotations. (Gudynas, 2019a, p. 389)

The economic reality of extractive projects needs ideological alchemy to support it and to have objective and subjective conditions for the reproduction of what it does. In his *1844 Manuscripts*, Marx relates nature, mining and the capitalist mode of production to the five senses, the spiritual and practical senses (desire, love):

> Only through the objectively unfolded richness of man's essential being is the richness of subjective human sensibility (a musical ear, an eye for beauty of form – in short, senses capable of human gratification, senses affirming themselves as essential powers of man) either cultivated or brought into being. For not only the five senses but also the so-called mental senses, the practical senses (will, love, etc.), in a

word, human sense, the human nature of the senses, comes to be by virtue of its object, by virtue of humanised nature. (Marx, 2009)

Marx's text offers two examples, food and minerals:

The dealer in minerals sees only the commercial value but not the beauty and the specific character of the mineral: he has no mineralogical sense. Thus, the objectification of the human essence, both in its theoretical and practical aspects, is required to make man's sense human, as well as to create the human sense corresponding to the entire wealth of human and natural substance. (Marx, 2009)

A mineral subjected merely to market values has no beauty or particular sense of rock with a meaning in the natural world that creates human meaning when the whole wealth of the *human and natural* being is maintained. Rock intercepted by capital and turned into a commodity loses the correspondence and organic quality of the wealth of the relationship between human being and nature. Capitalism makes human forms of meaning inviable, and rock turned into a commodity no longer belongs to the natural world because it is restricted to the 'immense accumulation of commodities' (Marx, 2018, p. 3). The extractivist mode of production, which is an economic mechanism of a specific historical process, passes for a productive subject, a producer of value in itself, by making the forms and mediations with the natural world disappear. Marx says:

In the extractive industries, such as fishery, mining, labour merely consists in overpowering the obstacles in the way of the seizure and appropriation of the raw products or primary products. There is no raw material to be worked up for production; rather, the existing raw product is appropriated. (Marx, 1973, p. 634).

It is precisely this appropriation that has to be veiled, disguised: appropriation of significant portions of the natural world that have no designated owner and, strictly speaking, belong to the place. Extractivist capitalism needs to hide this improper appropriation: the raw material is taken over in a private manner, removing its attachment to the place. As Vitor Bartoletti Sartori argues: 'We have the raw material as a free present' (Sartori, 2019).

This *metaphysics* of extractive practices is supported by various sectors that maintain the supremacy of the extractivist narratives over and above reality and outside any social mechanism of control. In a relationship of complicity and corruption between companies, the state, political groups and – in some cases – also militias outside the law, mining controls not only the territory but also the social mechanisms, making any attempt at resistance difficult and unfeasible.

The super-protective mechanisms used by extractive activities include:

1 laws and policies favourable to the entry of investments and firms into countries;
2 violation of the right to free, prior and informed consultation and, in general, civil participation, which allows projects to be established despite opposition;
3 the protection of company installations through the militarization of territories and action planned with armed groups and organized crime;
4 the action of judges and prosecutors, who deny any responsibility on the part of companies, so allowing a situation of impunity to prevail. (based on Gudynas, 2019b)

The capitalist economic model and its perspective of modernity destroy any organic relationship or delight in the relationship with nature on the part of the cultures in the territories. This technological and developmentalist 'secularization' has the following results:

- economic growth becomes something sacred to underpin development;
- a state of imperative necessity is created requiring the exploitation of nature to avoid an economic apocalypse;
- we are surrounded by extractivist liturgies, that is, media strategies;
- 'it creates community', that is, large mining, oil and agribusiness associations;
- opposition is impossible, but moreover it is almost unthinkable. (Gudynas, 2019b, p. 16)

Extractivist theology operates with its myths of development and modernity, polluting territories and democracy, making participatory processes impossible and sacrificing lives, species, forms of knowledge. The altar of sacrifice required by the maintenance of the extractivist model is in the global South, in areas extensively and intensively excavated, buried and destroyed by extractivist economic projects in mining, agribusiness and water business.

For [Walter] Benjamin, however, 'The modernity that occurred historically represents the reign of myth and not of development,' according to Rouanet: 'Instead of awakening human beings from their mythical sleep, capitalist modernity plunged them into a new mythology.' (Bellesa, 2016)

Anti-extractivist prophecies and heresies

The Brazilian sociologist and activist Moema Miranda has stressed the need for prophecy in facing down the 'religion' of the extractivist firms when she argued during the 'Meeting with Communities Affected by Mining in Latin America' that was held in Brasília in 2018:

> What the affected communities expect is a firm and prophetic position from the churches. As Pope Francis has said, this economy kills, and we see this every day in the communities. It is a moment when a Prophetic Church, in favour of the poor and of the land, is becoming urgent and necessary. (Miranda, 2018)

Eduardo Gudynas too, in a meeting with the Churches and Mining movement, set out his theses about the theological character of extractivist projects in his talk 'Extractivist Theologies and Heretical Spiritualities':

> I am referring to a political theology, by which I mean the production of policies that, contrary to what they proclaim, are neither neutral nor rational, but immersed in beliefs and spiritualities. In them a sort of sacredness is created that is used to legitimate and underpin systems and political practices between human beings and in our relationship with nature. (Gudynas, 2019b)

Together with religious, theologians and activists from different pastoral ministries organized in the movement Churches and Mining, Gudynas points to the need to expose the 'religious' character of extractivist movements by revealing the *deep core of concepts, sensibilities and spiritualities* that form part of the phenomenon. He argues that this theological critique is fundamental for creating and promoting a 'heretical' activism and spirituality whose aim and motivation would be:

- to break down the place of extractivist theologies in the common sense of societies;

- to recover the ability to imagine alternatives and to decide other paths;
- to experiment with or even want another form of relationship with nature and people;
- conviviality and depatriarchalization;
- ecumenical and intercultural spiritualities;
- listening to the rocks, the soil, the trees ... and not to the 'market';
- the greatest heresy – affirming the rights of nature. (Gudynas, 2019b)

Against extractivist movements and the repatriarchalization of territories: feminist heresies

In Latin America we territorial and community eco-feminists say that the defence of the territory is the defence of the body lived in community. It is the 'body-land territory' in three dimensions of life: the personal body, the social body and the body of the world (the planet).

> To experience in my life and in the community's territorial space the historical and structural forms of oppression created by the patriarchates to dominate my life, as they dominate the lives of the world's women, has led me to write and rethink ... some of the elements of community feminism that, as the process of epistemic construction goes on, are taking shape out of this historical territory, my body and its relation with the land. (Cabnal, 2010)

Territorial and community feminisms identify extractivist projects and policies as part of a system that produces inequality and spatial injustice that violently targets women's bodies and their territories. Even while we recognize that the impacts of extractivist activities are experienced by whole communities, feminists stress that on women these impacts have the effect of repatriarchalizing the territory in the following ways:

> The interconnection between patriarchal and colonial violence associated with the current cycle of capital's expansion in the continent, which of course includes the response women are making in a combined struggle against:
> 1 the territorialization of megaprojects;
> 2 the neocolonial methods of expelling people from life spaces;
> 3 the reconfiguration of the colonial patriarchy required by the extractivist model. (Colectivo Miradas, 2019)

Apart from all the destructive effects of extractivist activities, feminists denounce an intervention in the methods of dialogue and decision-making used by companies and governments in implementing extractive activities that attack community structures and compromise participative forms of discussion in which women – albeit with contradictions – can exercise power and leadership.

> Extractivism therefore favours the reconfiguration of spaces of discussion and decision-making as male-dominated, which are superimposed on previous patriarchal political structures. As a result, one of the factors that led to the processes by which women mobilized and organized politically against extractivist projects was precisely their historical exclusion from decision-making spaces and the cooptation of male leaders, who were more favourable to extractivist logic. (Colectivo Miradas, 2018)

This gives us five dimensions of the repatriarchalization of territories:

1. the political dimension: male-dominated decision-making;
2. the ecological dimension: the breakdown of the cycles by which life is reproduced;
3. the economic dimension: the formation of patriarchal labour structures;
4. the cultural dimension: the intensification of sexist images and stereotypes;
5. the bodily dimension: male social control and violence. (Colectivo Miradas, 2018)

Feminists' political and organizational responses to these enormous challenges occur both in study, protest, the formation of alliances to oppose extractivist activities and also, and simultaneously, in the development of respect, recovery and renewal of women's ancestral and communitarian forms of knowledge. These forms of knowledge are expressed in the 'incarnational' expression of spiritualities and in the methods of popular education. The feminists introduce themselves in this way:

> We think of our bodies as our primary territory, and we recognize the territory in our bodies: when the places we live in are violated our bodies are affected, and when our bodies are affected violence is done to the places in which we live. We insist on the importance of sensory experience; it is our bodies that embody our lives and our memories,

and they are the senses that connect us with the territories. Our bodies retain the mark of what happens with the territories: sadness at the exploitation, anguish at the pollution, and joy because we are creating 'other worlds' despite so much violence. (Goméz, 2020)

It is important to stress that the forms of resistance and 'embodied' living in a territory demands a different understanding of the process of politicization and organization, one that is able to bring together dimensions such as the spirituality of 'women guardians of the territories', 'women guardians of ancestral knowledge', 'women who pass on the languages and cultures of their peoples' (Goméz, 2020). These self-understandings imply a different configuration of the space of political representation that is not as present as it should be in the state and legal system, and neither properly understood yet in the sphere of feminism nor that of the social and popular movements.

Notes

1 https://oglobo.globo.com/epoca/sociedade/lutamos-contra-mineracao-ha-200-anos-diz-indigena-que-vive-as-margens-do-rio-doce-23878269 (accessed 28.01.2025).

2 *Istoé Dinheiro*, 'Vale registra lucro líquido de US$ 3,886 bi no 3° trimestre', 28.10.2021, https://www.istoedinheiro.com.br/vale-registra-lucro-liquido-de-us-3886-bi-no-30-trimestre/ (accessed 4.11.23).

References

Acosta, A., 2017, 'Post-extractivism: From Discourse to Practice – Reflections for Action', in G. Carbonnier, H. Campodónico and S. Tezanos Vázquez (eds), *Alternative Pathways to Sustainable Development: Lessons from Latin America*, Leiden/Boston: Brill/Nijhoff, https://library.oapen.org/bitstream/handle/20.500.12657/37966/9789004351677_webready_content_text.pdf?sequence =1&isAllowed=y (accessed 4.11.2023).

Bellesa, Mauro, 2016, 'Rouanet analisa a concepção de modernidade de Walter Benjamin', Instituto de Estudos Avançados, Universidade de São Paulo, https://www.iea.usp.br/noticias/walter-benjamin-versus-max-weber.

Instituto de Estudos Avançados da Universidade de São Paulo, http://www.iea.usp.br/noticias/walter-benjamin-versus-max-weber (accessed 27.11.2023).

Brandão, P., 2023, *Colonialidade do Poder, Biodiversidade e Direito: raça, classe e capitalismo na construção da legalidade*, São Paulo: Lumen Juris, https://outraspalavras.net/descolonizacoes/colonialidade-do-poder-biodiversidade-e-direito/ (accessed 2.11.2023).

Cabnal, L., 2010, 'Acercamiento a la construcción del pensamiento epistémico de las mujeres indígenas feministas comunitárias de Abya Yala', in *Feminismos diversos: el feminismo comunitário*, ACSUR-Las Segovias, https://porunavida vivible.files.wordpress.com/2012/09/feminismos-comunitario-lorena-cabnal.pdf (accessed 18.11.2023).

Cardoso, N., 2023, 'Corpo, território e religião: leituras e tramas', *Revista Coisas do Gênero*, Programa de Gênero e Religião, EST, São Leopoldo, https://revistas.est.edu.br/periodicos_novo/index.php/genero/article/view/2277/2117 (accessed 1.11.2023).

Casado, J., 2021, 'Para se livrar do ônus do desastre, Vale e BHP renegam até Aristóteles', *Veja Abril*, 8 November, https://veja.abril.com.br/blog/jose-casado/para-se-livrar-do-onus-da-samarco-vale-e-bhp-renegaram-aristoteles/ (accessed 4.11.2023).

Cavalcante, G., 2021, 'Extrativismo mineral e os sentidos da colonização', *Outras Palavras*, 11 November, https://outraspalavras.net/crise-brasileira/extrativismo-mineral-e-os-sentidos-da-colonizacao/ (accessed 2.11.2023).

Coelho, A., 2022, *Capitalismo como religião*, São Paulo: Editora Recriar.

Colectivo Miradas Críticas del Territorio desde el Feminismo, 2018, '(Re)patriarcalización de los territorios. La lucha de las mujeres y los megaproyectos extractivos', *Ecología Política, Cuardenos CLACSO*, 10 January, https://www.ecologiapolitica.info/?p=10169 (accessed 19.11.2023).

Colectivo Miradas Críticas del Territorio, 2019, 'Repatriarcalización de los territorios. La lucha de las mujeres y los megaproyectos extractivos', https://dialnet.unirioja.es/servlet/articulo?codigo=6292625 (accessed 18.11.2023).

Delaisse, Julie, 2020, 'Comment se développer?' *alternego*, May, https://alternego.com/comment-se-developper/ (accessed 4.11.23).

Dotta, Rafaela, 2021, 'Após STJ anular ação da barragem de Brumadinho, vítimas da Vale protestam na Justiça Federal', *Brasil de Fato*, 21 October, https://www.brasildefato.com.br/2021/10/21/apos-stj-anular-processo-da-barragem-de-brumadinho-vitimas-da-vale-vao-ao-df-lutar-por-justica (accessed 4.11.23).

Durán, T. G., 2021, 'Interview with Berta Zuñiga', *Mongobay*, 15 November, https://es.mongabay.com/2021/11/entrevista-berta-zuniga-caceres/ (accessed 4.11.2023).

Gómez, M., 2020, 'Nosotras sin intermediarios: Acciones colectivas de mujeres indígenas contra los extractivismos y en defensa de sus territorios', *Revista Etnografías Contemporáneas* 6(11), pp. 318–418, https://revistasacademicas.unsam.edu.ar/index.php/etnocontemp/article/view/541 (accessed 19.11.2023).

Gonçalves, C. W., 2002, 'O Latifúndio Genético e a R-existência Indígeno-Camponesa', *GEOgraphia* 4(8), pp. 30–44, https://periodicos.uff.br/geographia/article/view/13431 (accessed 1.11.2023).

Gonçalves, R., 2016, 'Capitalismo extrativista na América Latina e as contradições da mineração em grande escala no Brasil', *Cadernos Prolam/USP* 15(29), pp. 38–55, https://core.ac.uk/download/pdf/268360329.pdf (accessed 20.11.2023).

Gudynas, E., 2016, 'Teología de los Extractivismos: Introducción', *Revista Tábula Rasa* 24 (January–June), pp. 11–23, http://www.revistatabularasa.org/numero24/teologia-de-los-extractivismos-introduccion-a-tabula-rasa-no-24/ (accessed 8.11.2023).

Gudynas, E., 2019a, 'Development and Nature: Modes of Appropriation and Latin American Extractivisms', *The Routledge Handbook of Latin American*

Development, ed. Julie Cupples, Marcela Palomino-Schalscha and Manuel Prieto, London: Routledge, pp. 389-99.

Gudynas, E., 2019b, 'Teologías extractivistas y espiritualidades herejes, Iglesia y Mineria', https://iglesiasymineria.org/2019/03/01/eduardo-gudynas-teologias-extractivistas-y-espiritualidades-herejes/ (accessed 23.2.2023).

Hinkelammert, F., 1983, 'The Economic Roots of Idolatry: Entrepreneurial Metaphysics', in P. Richard (ed.), *The Idols of Death and the God of Life: A Theology*, Maryknoll, NY: Orbis Books.

Igreja y Mineria, 2019, *Teologías Extractivistas y Espiritualidades Herejes*, 1 March, https://iglesiasymineria.org/2019/03/01/eduardo-gudynas-teologias-extractivistas-y-espiritualidades-herejes/ (accessed 17.11.2023).

Marx, K., 1973, *Grundrisse: Foundations of the Critique of Political Economy (Rough Draft)*, London: Penguin.

Marx, K., 2009, *Economic and Political Manuscripts of 1844*, 3rd Manuscript, Moscow: Progress Publishers, https://www.marxists.org/archive/marx/works/1844/manuscripts/comm.htm (accessed 20.11.2023).

Marx, K., 2018, *Capital, Vol. 1 – Part I, Commodities*, London: Penguin.

Miranda, M., 2017, 'Mesa sobre Conflitos pela Água encerra programação da Tenda Multiétnica, II Tenda Multiétnica – Povos do Cerrado', https://www.cptnacional.org.br/index.php/publicacoes-2/destaque/3849-mesa-sobre-conflitos-pela-agua-encerra-programacao-da-tenda-multietnica (accessed 12.12.2023).

Miranda, M., 2018, 'Igrejas e Comunidades Afetadas pela Mineração devem Construir Alternativas para Defender a Vida e a Terra', *CIDSE*, 7 August, https://www.cidse.org/pt/2018/08/07/churches-and-communities-affected-by-mining-must-build-alternatives-to-defend-life-and-the-earth/ (accessed 2.12.2021).

Moore, J. W., 2023, 'Introdução', in J. W. Moore (ed.), *Antropoceno ou Capitaloceno? Natureza, história e a crise do capitalismo*, https://outraspalavras.net/crise-civilizatoria/o-antropoceno-ou-capitaloceno (accessed 2.11.2023).

Porto-Gonçalves, C. W., 2002, 'O Latifúndio Genético e a R-existência Indígeno-Camponesa', *GEOgraphia* 4(8), pp. 30-44, https://periodicos.uff.br/geographia/article/view/13431 (accessed 1/11/2023).

Porto-Gonçalves, C. W., 2012, 'Colonialidade do poder e os desafios da integração regional na América Latina', *POLIS Revista Latinomericana* 11(31), pp. 295-332.

Porto-Gonçalves, C. W., 2023, 'Lutamos contra mineração há 200 anos, diz indígena que vive às margens do rio Doce', *O Globo*, https://oglobo.globo.com/epoca/sociedade/lutamos-contra-mineracao-ha-200-anos-diz-indigena-que-vive-as-margens-do-rio-doce-23878269 (accessed 1.11.2023).

Pessanha, E., 2019, 'Do epistemicídio: as estratégias de matar o conhecimento negro africano e afrodiaspórico', *Problemata: International Journal of Philosophy* 10(2), pp. 167-94, https://dialnet.unirioja.es/descarga/articulo/7856557.pdf (accessed 2.11.2023).

Quijano, A., 2000, 'Colonialidad del poder, eurocentrismo y América Latina', in E. Lander (ed.), *La colonialidad del saber: eurocentrismo y ciencias sociales. Perspectivas latinoamericanas*, Buenos Aires: CLACSO, pp. 201-46.

Sartori, Vitor Bartoletti, 2019, 'Marx, natureza e mineração: da indústria extrativa pura às sociedades por ações', *Revista Culturas Jurídicas* 6(14), pp. 79-117,

May–August. English version, https://periodicos.uff.br/culturasjuridicas/article/view/45224 (accessed 16.11.2023).

Soares, J. and Quintella, R. H., 2008, 'Development: An Analysis of Concepts, Measurement and Indicators', *BAR*, Curitiba 5(2), art. 2, pp. 104–24, Apr./June, https://www.scielo.br/j/bar/a/5SHFxh5cBhrQtBM6GXWy3tp/?format=pdf&lang=en (accessed 12.9.2023)

Sung, J. M. and Coelho, A. da S., 2019, 'Capitalismo como religião: uma revisão teórica da relação entre religião e economia na modernidade', *Horizonte – Revista de Estudos de Teologia e Ciências da Religião* 17(53), pp. 651–75.

Toledo, Alejandro, 2008, *Geopolítica y desarrollo en el istmo de Tehuantepec*, Mexico, Centro de Ecología y Desarrollo, p. 149, https://books.google.com.cu/books?hl=ptBR&id=oVGOAAAAIAAJ&focus=searchwithinvolume&q=origen (accessed 1.11.2023).

8

The Brazilian Favelas: Territories that Challenge Us to Think About the Meaning of Liberation in Contemporary Latin American Neoliberal Society

PRISCILA SILVA

Introduction

Development and coloniality are two very painful concepts to the ears of any Latin American scholar who is critical of the precepts of the free market or capitalism. This is because at various times in Latin American history the notion of development has concealed, justified and validated the worst pains inflicted on our people. From indigenous genocide to the enslavement of African peoples, from various military dictatorships to the exploitation of the human body and nature, we live under the statute of a development that never arrives. What comes to our bodies and minds is only pain, police control, exploitation, in exchange for survival, food insecurity and so many other violations of our human power. In the specific case of Brazil, especially the territories of poverty and extreme poverty called favelas, this scenario of exploitation and domination is enhanced by precarious infrastructure.

The favela in Brazil, especially in Rio de Janeiro, is a product of colonialism and now a product of coloniality that insists on imprisoning us in the dictates of consumer culture, in mentalities that perpetuate our existence in the poorest layers. In this way, we live doubly captive: tied to an economy that shapes society through the constant and irrepressible massive exploitation of bodies for the production of accumulation by the few; in addition to mental captivity, which acts through ideologies of consumption, meritocracy and even theologies co-opted by capitalism, through which people not only accept the idea that life is constant suffering, but that they find meaning in being instruments of their own martyrdom.

Thinking from the realities of territories of poverty in Rio de Janeiro, its subjects and contents of faith, this chapter discusses how liberation is a challenge that is posed not only by political issues but also finds barriers in the very current religious-theological configuration in the country. In three topics we will present what the favela is, its history, how the issue of racism is involved in the formation of these territories that operate marginalization and vulnerability; and we will see how theological-political liberation initiatives, initially linked to the Roman Catholic Church, today are forced to deal with a setting much more motivated by evangelical morality than by the development of a religious ethic concerned with the dignity and quality of life of the populations most vulnerable. Finally, we will see how some new voices can already be heard, how some cries are formed amid the chaos of the favela, so that another theology more committed to human life, more embodied, is placed as a seed of liberation, promoting what we can celebrate as resurrection from social death.

What is a favela?

For a person like me, born and raised in a favela, talking about this subject is like talking about something that everyone knows. It's like talking about breathing, water and fear. But some time ago, I asked a man in the United States if he knew what a favela was, using the term slums. And he replied, 'I've never heard of it.' I promptly took out my phone, googled images and showed him some pictures of Brazilian favelas. After looking closely at the photo, he asked me, 'Does anyone live there?' I smiled, and replied, 'Yes, thousands of people.'

Taking this experience as a standard, I will not behave as if my readers know what a favela is. The favela is a territory historically formed by the agglomeration of poor people who do not have sufficient financial conditions to occupy spaces in the formal, legalized city, and survive in precarious housing in spaces not used by either the government or private initiatives. The first territorial occupations that gave rise to the favela as we know it today occurred at the end of the nineteenth century in the city of Rio de Janeiro, caused by two converging factors dependent on capitalism at the time: the industrialization of the Brazilian productive sector (which emptied the fields and crowded the cities, leading to a rural exodus) and the lack of broad social policies aimed at the poorest (who in this period were the former slaves and their descendants).

It is important to emphasize that it was Christian imperialist colonialism that inaugurated the idea of America, and consequently of the Brazil that we have today (Dussel, 1994). It was liberal capitalism that indirectly invented the favela. And it was Christian sacrificial theology that justified and validated these two processes. In the first case, Christian imperialist colonialism, through racism, sexual abuse and the extraction of wealth, made Brazil a land of enriching the wealthy through the exploitation and death of the poorest. In the history of Brazil, according to Aimé Césaire, 'Europe is indefensible' (1978, p. 17). In the second case, liberalism indirectly invented the favela simply because the dignified maintenance of human life was not in the interests of relations of production. It was more feasible and economical to allow the poor to live in the newly created favelas than to create housing programmes, for example. The idea of accumulation, associated with a growing loss of the notion of human dignity, of basic needs, consolidated a poor country, with relative indifference to social, economic and territorial misery.

It is important to highlight that the name 'favela' is directly connected to the history of Brazil and, initially, did not designate a geographic space marked by precariousness and socio-political margins of society, as is the case today. Favela is a plant from the Brazilian flora, very common in the north-east region, the location of many formerly enslaved, poor and black men during a war between rural workers and the Brazilian Army over agrarian issues (known as the War of Canudos). With the end of the war, the men returned to Rio de Janeiro and settled on a hill that also had many favela trees. Hence the historical name, *morro da favela* ('hill of favelas'). It is in this place that many poor, unemployed and war-scarred families gathered and began trying to seek better living conditions in the centre of Rio de Janeiro in the initial phase of Brazil's industrialization.

In English, the closest correspondence to the noun 'favela' is 'slum', which refers to the industrial clusters that emerged on the outskirts of London. However, the word 'favela' is not well known and the association between the term and the territory is not immediate. Therefore, it is important to emphasize that 'favela' and 'slum' are not synonymous. These are terms that emerge at different historical moments, and that is why I prefer to use throughout this chapter the word that is directly connected to the Brazilian reality, which is 'favela'.

In 2003, in an effort to think of viable solutions to the social inequality that was growing alarmingly in the world, the UN produced a document entitled 'The Challenge of Slums – Global Report of Human Settlements', which included Rio de Janeiro as a field of study. The document already noted that it was necessary not only to think of the favela as an infrastructure problem but as a territory that lacked public policies that encourage a more dignified life based on better working conditions, quality of mobility and, mainly, co-opting the life technologies of poor populations, their survival strategies, so that they could escape a life of informality. According to this document:

> In general, slum policies should be integrated with, or should be seen as part of, broader, people-focused urban poverty reduction policies that address the various dimensions of poverty, including employment and incomes, food, health and education, shelter and access to basic urban infrastructure and services. It should be recognized, however, that improving incomes and jobs for slum dwellers requires robust growth of the national economy, which is itself dependent upon effective and equitable national and international economic policies, including trade. (UN, 2003, p. xxvii)

The problem with this document is that it does not indicate the roots of each urban poor agglomeration, and neither does it design practical solutions to reduce social gaps such as salary differences, illiteracy and fairer work policies. That is, the homogenization proposed in the document ends up promoting a utopia in which social problems are the same in all favelas around the world and the free market is the saviour of all of them.

In the specific case of Brazil, the term 'favela' returned in 2024 as official terminology used in the development of studies that can provide support for the design of effective public policies for the population of Brazilian favelas. Since 1991, official documents have registered and enumerated favelas using the term 'subnormal agglomerations'. This term is extremely technical; it is related just to infrastructure issues and does not take into account human conditions, such as housing, for example. It means that favelas, historically, are perceived as an infrastructure problem that must be solved and not as the result of centuries of exploitation and neglect of the poor, the working class.

The concepts adopted were aimed at identifying deficiencies and/or precariousness in urban infrastructure, in the provision of essential public services and in the land and urban planning adequacy of the mapped areas, and terms such as 'irregular', 'illegal', among others, were sometimes used, which highlighted the positioning of these populations within the scope of an impractical and unattainable normative apparatus for vulnerable social groups. (IBGE, 2024b, p. 5; author's translation)

This current change, returning to the use of the term 'favela', is precisely an attempt to refer to this territory in a more assertive way, but also to consider the people who live there. In other words, what their profiles are, where they work, whether they have access to basic health, sanitation and transport services, what faith they profess. In short, what is sought in this new stage in the use of the term is to advance not only in the recognition of the favela as an urban, socio-political issue but in the development and acceptance of its specificities as a place that is formed by human groups that develop technologies of survival in the market society, which is ours, including adopting the Christian religion as a way of life. In numbers, we are talking of around 16 million people in Brazil, and 1 billion people around the world, living in favelas, slums, informal settlements and their synonyms (IBGE, 2024b, p. 5).

In short, when I say 'favela', socially speaking I am referring to a territory that arose from the abandonment of the enslaved black masses to death on the margins, from the abandonment of the populations of the countryside, and foreigners who migrated to urban centres. Economically speaking, I am referring to a territory that emerged indirectly because of ideas that valued accumulation and exploitation more than the notion of human dignity (we will see more about it in the next part). In my book *Religion and Violence in the Favela* (Gonçalves, 2020), I produced a genealogy of the favela, trying not to point out the most evident milestones in the formation of this territory, as in the case of the war mentioned above, but seeking to outline distinct parameters that would point out how the economy directly involved the construction of a society where living humanity was not the foundation of economic practices and so-called development. Taking this parameter as a research guide, I pointed out that three distinct moments were crucial in the formation of Brazilian favelas, revealing a causal relationship between economy and *favelização* (the process to form the favelas): in 1770, the agglomeration of slaves in the port region already made the city centre an unhealthy space, where only the poorest travelled and set up commercial establishments. Brazil's proto-favela was born there. Second, in 1893, there was a political milestone and the beginning of a long battle against favelas, when the mayor of the city ordered the demolition of houses considered an aesthetic and social disease. Those houses can be compared to the slums in London, as only those workers in extremely precarious situations lived in them, crowded together without minimum hygiene conditions. They lived in these spaces to be close to their places of work but they did not receive enough to maintain their lives. Finally, the aforementioned War of Canudos, which was also a war of a religious nature (Facó, 2009), resulted in an irreversible occupation of the hills and peripheral regions of the city, which was tolerated because the proximity of workers to their jobs decreased costs and avoided the establishment of social rights and better working conditions.

This genealogy is fundamental because it highlights that the favela did not emerge organically in Brazil's urban scenario; it demonstrates that the factors that converged towards its emergence are directly linked to a notion of an economy focused on accumulation, the extraction of wealth, and that it demanded the enslavement of the body (Africans and indigenous people) and cheap labour (natives, ex-slaves, foreigners). Faced with an economy that only produces inequalities, the result could not be very different. That is, the favela is the result of a disregard for human life and dignity.

Ideologically speaking, the favela is primarily the result of racism, because from it the greatest social differentiations were established in Brazil, not to mention the issue of fetishization, which transforms life into a thing, even though the thing has the status of a living being. Just to illustrate, Figure 1 below shows the map of Brazil and the population density of each region. The dark grey parts represent the states with the most crowded population, and it is not surprising that they are the states with the most black residents: Rio de Janeiro and Bahia, states that were capitals of Brazil in the colonial period. Without racism we would not have Brazil and its favelas. Enslavement was the base of the economy of Brazil for 388 years, and it produced waves of inequality until today. The favelas are formed basically of black people. For this reason, racism results in favelas, and favelas are targets of violence that rise from racism. It's almost a circle.

Religiously speaking, a certain image of God, always sovereign, powerful, indifferent to suffering, inflexible, rich and dominating, contributed to the powerful of all periods feeling represented and validated both in heaven and on earth. Thus, humiliating the poor, the slum dwellers (*favelizados* in Portuguese), or even having an indifferent stance was

Figure 1: Demographic density of Brazil, considering race, 2024.
Source: IBGE (Instituto Brasileiro de Geografia e Estatística), 2024a.

nothing less than exercising the dominance that God himself bestowed. Even today this theological construct is used, preached, and the liberation we seek in text and practice is above all a response to it. In this sense the convergence of religion and capitalism produces a mentality that can bring liberation or captivity.

Catholic liberation theology in action in the favelas and the challenge today

Is Brazil a Christian country? Yes, for sure. The latest development in light of the data we have since 2010 is that Brazil is in a process of changing its religious matrix. We are turning into a country of Evangelicals. The expectation is that in 2030 the number of Evangelicals will be greater than the number of Catholics. Recent research has shown that there are more churches than schools and hospitals together. It may sound strange, but Pentecostalism and neo-Pentecostalism constitute massive channels of communication with poor people. More than that, the main narrative of pursuing material things, the roots of the Gospel of Prosperity, entails more than accumulation or consumerism. To evangelicals in poor communities, it can represent the opportunity of these people to have access to basic things, such as food. And theologically speaking, the belief is that God is responsible for that. Second, social problems are avoided inside the churches because these themes are related to political ideas, so they are considered not to be 'spiritual things'. On the other hand, the precariousness that people in favelas face every day becomes the perfect scenario for them to create new ways to survive, the attitude we described above in terms of strategies for survival. Figure 2 below presents the most recent data about religion in Brazil. It does not specify how many churches are Evangelical, Catholic or even of other religions, but it demonstrates how religion is a pillar of relationships and of daily life. The dark grey parts represent the regions with greater density of religions. The megachurches, Pentecostal churches and others like Baptists closely related to politics are inside these regions. In other words, all those denominations cited above are in the centre of power – religious and political – and, despite all the historical impoverishment of the population, stand as servers of the market. It is important to mention that these churches are also inside favelas, but the theological discourse reinforces their service to capitalism.

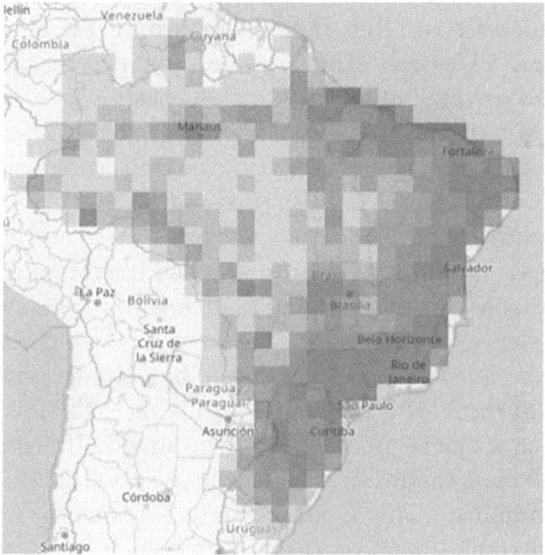

Figure 2: Religious establishments in Brazil, 2024.
Source: IBGE, 2024a.

The problem is the correlation of an economy that exploits the poor but is interpreted as the will of God, like a new spirit of capitalism. How can we build liberation facing this kind of theology that spreads individualism rather than collectivity? Why are there so many churches while there is a deep concentration of wealth and profound social differences?

Considering this panorama, in the 1960s, in the midst of a difficult period at the beginning of the Brazilian military dictatorship, the favelas were consolidated as part of the urban scenario, and the situation, which had previously been precarious, was getting worse and worse because of the agglomeration of people that kept happening. Politically speaking, the state had already tried to solve the 'favela problem' in three ways: sanitation, removal and urbanism. In the first solution, this space and its people were seen as a place where diseases could arise; they were unhealthy. In the second solution, the attempt was made to remove, to place people in other spaces to 'clean' urban centres from the sight and presence of poverty. In the third solution, the attempt was to alleviate the precariousness with the construction of squares and living spaces. None of the three political moments flourished, and the favela remained stigmatized and a target of racism and violence.

It is known from documents that the first movements aimed at giving dignity to favela residents were made by the Catholic Church, under the leadership of Dom Helder Câmara, in the action known as the São Sebastião Crusade. This crusade sought to sensitize the public authorities and private initiatives to make investments in the precarious infrastructure of the favelas – issues such as the creation and implementation of sanitary sewage services, drinking water, health services, access to education, garbage collection and so on. Dom Helder, who went down in history for being persecuted as a heretical communist only because he served among the poorest and had liberation theology as his foundation, was a pioneer in trying to change the lives of hundreds of people in the slums, and also to change the way in which God, Jesus and the church were lived in a society marked by extreme poverty. If today it is possible to think of a theology that liberates the favelas and their residents, much is due to Dom Helder, who stated: 'If I give bread to the poor, they call me a saint. But if I ask why the poor have no bread, they call me a communist.' This famous phrase is for us the motivation for thinking contextual, liberationist theology, which is not complicit with the powers of this world but which is food for people with potential dignity.

One of the challenges I need to mention here, however, has to do with two historical issues: the first is the low acceptance and spread of liberation theology and similar theologies, like integral mission theology, among the impoverished masses. Due to the controlling efforts of the churches, both Catholic and Protestant, both Latin American theologies were stifled and accused of dialoguing with communism. Because at this historical moment there was a very strong political force promoting dictatorships in Latin America, even liberation theology's religious representatives were silenced and forced to leave the country. In other words, the development of liberation theology took place under suspicion, although it flourished. The second challenge is related to the changing of the religious matrix that we have mentioned before. Associated with this, unfortunately, what we notice is a growing phenomenon of theological inversions in favour of the market and fundamentalist religious policies. People in favelas are also part of this movement. Evangelical fundamentalism in Brazil is perceived mainly in the construction of narratives where gender issues, climate issues, racism, patriarchy, increasing poverty, increasing food insecurity have, respectively, been accused of being communist themes and secular (earthly) themes, and so they should not be discussed. A theological fatalism becomes legitimate.

In a very paradoxical way, what we point out here is that the greatest obstacle to liberation in Brazil, to the weakening of the imperialist mentality, is the church itself, mostly the Evangelical one. Historically co-opted by the powerful, there is currently a repetition of narratives that prevents deep discussions about, as Dom Helder pointed out, the reasons for poverty. That is, the religious situation in which we find ourselves can be summarized in these ways: religious fundamentalism, co-option of religious discourse for economic and political purposes, focus on metaphysical issues, and avoidance of contemporary themes. In more objective terms, to talk about issues of liberation we have to recognize that there are places, like Brazil, where the church is also a power to be overcome and not a space where liberation is nurtured.

Dignity as social resurrection: it is time to hear the liberation outcries

Despite this, unlike a theology co-opted by empires and the powers of this world (Míguez, 2012), there are people in the favelas who understand God and that God reveals the structures of domination that plague their lives. In a recent survey of Christian people from the favelas in my doctoral work, I observed that even with the panorama exposed above, there are people trying to develop other ways to believe in God

(Gonçalves, 2023), to build communities that think about social issues and produce solutions to them. Although they still move through sacrificial elements (cross, blood, sins, payment of spiritual debts), there is also an idea that Jesus was killed because of his positions, and represented the Father in trying to promote justice in the world. Jesus made himself weak (cf. the notion contained in Philippians 2.7) to build another way of life in society. According to the interviews conducted, people assume the life and work of Jesus to be the guide of faith, the foundation and the paradigm under which they base their theological reworkings. Thus, everything they profess has a tone more connected with ordinary life, not least because Jesus took upon himself the judgements of his time (of the Romans and the high priests), and not just metaphysical sins (Boff, 1972; Alves, 1987; Gebara and Sung, 2020).

The people interviewed, a total of six from different favelas, have a deep discomfort with their immediate realities, not only because they are poor but because they are sometimes not recognized as persons or are going through various internal conflicts and conflicts with the world. For example, a mother interviewed is concerned about her son because she does not want to see him working in drug trafficking, even though the profits are good and it is very attractive for the youth in these places (it does not mean that poverty is a consequence of criminality). What can she do about that? Her answer is that she is praying and trying to give him another option in life. In the cases I identify, the discomfort is not about poverty itself but in the lack of prospects for overcoming it. And overcoming poverty here does not mean getting rich but living with dignity and recognition of humanity. We are talking about the possibility of eating salad; to live in a house that is really a shelter and will be strong enough to keep out the rain; we are talking about having the opportunity to learn to read, to write properly and get a good job; to have access to culture; to not suffer for matters of gender or race.

To exemplify a little bit more in material terms how poor people want to overcome poverty, let's see an example. Professor Jung Mo Sung, in a recent paper, says that Jesus spoke about the bread but highlighted that people could not live just by eating bread alone. Why is bread not enough? For Sung,

> The hunger of the poor has two aspects, or in other words, the poor, like all human beings, have two types of hunger. First is the immediate and obvious: killing hunger to avoid dying little by little. But, as Jesus said, human beings do not live on bread alone. 'Bread' is the condition of material possibility for the poor, without food no one lives,

but human beings have another basic need: recognition as 'people'. People who don't feel recognized by anyone end up going down the path of suicide. ... Oppressive societies establish a boundary between who humans are and groups that are not recognized by society as such. In current neoliberal capitalism, non-humans or sub-humans are the poor, those who are excluded from the market. The truth that God reveals to humanity is that all human beings, regardless of their social condition, are worthy of being recognized as such. (Sung, 2023; author's translation)

Feelings of not belonging, inadequacy, frustration, fear of rejection and even mental fatigue were revealed during the interviews. Everyone pointed out situations and feelings that indicate a certain level of not belonging to a world where dignity can be experienced. In other words, poverty is not just a present situation, it affects generations, the future, the possibility of living another reality with health, education and security.

In this direction, Professor Jung Mo Sung again, when considering the nefarious advances of neoliberalism and the place of the poor in today's society (2023), discusses the idea of social death, which can be understood as an existence lacking recognition, legitimacy. The favela dwellers, by exposing their feelings, express a pain related to social death. In a certain way they are only seen when they are killed in shootings, in massacres, when they are arrested for some petty crime. They are people who exist as avatars because they do not feel they belong to any world. They are not recognized in their potentialities and needs.

In this same discussion, Sung deals with the idea of social resurrection, following the line that overcoming death, for liberation theology, is a more relevant fact than death itself. In other words, Christianity is a religion that was built on the idea that death is somehow surmountable. And not the biological death but the unjust one, the one that occurs before the time to experience abundant life; a death that happens to people still alive. By expressing their pain, the interviewed slum dwellers reveal that they are under the yoke of this social death, of non-recognition and legitimacy. By expressing their pain, they cry out for dignity.

Somehow, either by the power of the Spirit or by discernment, the people interviewed managed to realize that they are worthy of experiencing the best of this life, and not just being treated on the margins as cogs in systems where liberation is a distant dream. Thirsty and hungry for meaning, the social death that afflicts them is gradually overcome when they are recognized and acknowledged as people loved by God and within the koinonia, who are capable and who do not deserve to chronically face the hardship of life in poverty and slums. They are innocent of their own harsh reality. They are victims. The interviews reveal that God is more Emmanuel (With Us) than YHWH (The Absolute), and it is from this theological shift that the liberation of these people begins.

The final topic of my research is 'God is with us' and it is a phrase used by a young theologian from a favela. In practical terms, believing in another image of God may seem like an isolated, small element, but this possibility carries a very large potential for change. Thinking about ethics, a Christian faith that cares about social issues, that thinks from contexts of poverty how religion and capitalism connect and promote ties to the lives of the poor, that criticizes theologies that are clearly allies of contemporary empires, is a very significant advance. We saw above that Brazil is becoming a country of Evangelicals and, for the most part, the theology that is spreading has an elitist character, a language of prosperity that serves the market more than human life. In spiritual terms it can be said that this type of theological possibility increases the critical stance and encourages the creation of small communities of faith that are not willing to validate the status quo. Here we mention the *Igreja do Caminho* (Church of the Caminho), which is a dissident group but which has a community practice based not only on social actions but on thinking and suggesting social policies that increase the quality of life of vulnerable people. To create and be part of a faith community in this format, it is necessary that another image of God, another type of theology, be established and cultivated, and that is what my research captured. For those people from favelas, liberation is not a better place to live but a process that begins at the very moment that they understand that they can believe in a God who is not interested in their sacrifices (symbolically or real) but in a better life for them, their sons and daughters. They are up against a process that might never end, just be softer, because the empire is always seeking to conquer.

In sum, resurrection from social death, life in liberation is an ever-unfinished reality. Within their stories, even at this time, they are in the process of discerning, maturing and sharing a faith that is not only useful for the post-mortem but is useful for the present: in the loving treatment given to others, in the hope for better days, in the transformative contact with people who encourage and contribute to the improvement of structural conditions, in the perception and intentional change of oppressive structures. Even if they are victims of convergent sacrifices – in economics and theology – they are freed day by day when they can perceive themselves as being worthy and being endowed with dignity. Those who have ears to hear, listen, because the cries are going out.

References

Alves, Rubem, 1987, *Da Esperança*, Campinas: Papirus.
Boff, Leonardo, 1972, *Jesus Cristo libertador: Ensaio de cristologia crítica para o nosso tempo*, Petrópolis: Vozes.
Césaire, Aimé, 1978, *Discurso sobre o colonialism*, Lisboa: Sá da Costa.
Dussel, Enrique, 1994, *Historia de la filosofía y filosofía de la liberación*, Bogotá: Editorial Nueva América.
Facó, Rui, 2009, *Cangaceiros e Fanáticos: Gênese e Lutas*, Rio de Janeiro: Editora UFRJ.
Gebara, Ivone and Sung, Jung Mo, 2020, *Direitos humanos e amor ao próximo: Textos teológicos em diálogo com a vida real*, São Paulo: Recriar.
Gonçalves, Priscila, 2020, *Religião e violência na favela: A fé e o cotidiano lavados pelo sangue de Jesus*, São Paulo: Editora Recriar.
Gonçalves, Priscila, 2023, *Deus tá com a gente: Reelaborações teologais favelizadas não sacrificiais*, São Bernardo do Campo.
IBGE, 2024a, 'Censo população', https://censo2022.ibge.gov.br/panorama/mapas.html?tema=especies_cnefe&localidade=&recorte=N3 (accessed 27.01.2025).
IBGE, 2024b, 'Favelas e Comunidades Urbanas: Notas metodológicas n. 01. Sobre a mudança de Aglomerados Subnormais para Favelas e Comunidades Urbanas', https://biblioteca.ibge.gov.br/visualizacao/livros/liv102062.pdf (accessed 27.01.2025).
Míguez, Néstor, 2012, in N. Míguez, J. Rieger and Jung Mo Sung, *Para além do espírito do Império: novas perspectivas em políticas e religião*, trans. Gilmar Saint Clair Ribeiro and Bárbara T. Lambert, São Paulo: Paulinas.
Sung, Jung Mo, 2023, 'A fome, o mercado e a palavra', https://www.ihu.unisinos.br/categorias/626663-a-fome-o-mercado-e-a-palavra-artigo-de-jung-mo-sung (accessed 27.01.2025).
UN, 2003, 'The Challenge of Slums: Global Report on Human Settlements, 2003, United Nations Human Settlements Programme' https://unhabitat.org/sites/default/files/download-manager-files/The%20Challenge%20of%20Slums%20-%20Global%20Report%20on%20Human%20Settlements%202003.pdf (accessed 27.01.2025).

9

Land, Labour and Liberation: Conversion, *Theosis* and Material Pneumatology in the Capitalocene

LUKE LARNER

'Woe unto them that join house to house, that lay field to field, till there be no place, that they may be placed alone in the midst of the earth!' Isaiah 5.8, KJV

Introduction

My reflections in this chapter begin with my 'job' as a Church of England parish priest in the heart of Luton, a town about 30 miles north of London. I have had a *strange* love affair with this town, because despite its marvellous richness (including our underdog football team's promotion to the Premier League!) it has been voted the worst place to live in the UK many times, has the worst air pollution in the UK, the highest rate of child poverty outside London, and is the only non-city among the top ten most deprived places in the UK. Some of Luton's bad press is undoubtedly shaped by thinly veiled racism and Islamophobia: in the parish I serve, 70% are Muslim by faith, 70% are of Asian heritage, 17% are of white British/European heritage, and 5.1% are of Black African and/or Caribbean heritage, and 56% of the population were born in the United Kingdom. Luton is also the birthplace of controversial media figures Andrew Tate and Tommy Robinson.

Proximity to London and excellent transport links make Luton ripe for development into lucrative real estate, with various plans and schemes often funded by our airport. All this adds up to a context where ministerial and theological considerations posed by challenges of class struggle in a cost-of-living crisis, decolonial and anti-racist struggles in the wake of Brexit, and environmental struggles in a climate catastrophe, are lived and *breathed* on a daily basis. As a white, male priest in the established church from a working-class construction-trade background, my place in all this is rather complex.

The morning I started this chapter, I was digging test holes to investigate the soil quality for planting of a small fruit orchard in our church garden, part of a wider project to help our parish church to re-engage with the local community and join with others who are promoting peace, well-being and social justice. One of our project partners, the doctors' surgery next door (developed on land formerly owned by the church), shared a paper with me highlighting the need for a joined-up approach in tackling some of the material woes of our town: healthcare inequality, high rates of violence, pollution and urban decay, and the lack of access to safe green spaces, all of which affect people's well-being (Marmot et al., 2022). Planting a few apple and pear trees might seem a trite act in the face of these and broader international struggles, but for me and our congregation and allies it is an act of faith and commitment that a better future is possible that does not rely on the development of our town in line with neocolonial capitalist interests. My hope is that through cultivating beauty in this way we will start to fall in love with each other and our local area again, while building the community power to resist its colonization and development. That morning, I was preparing orders of service for the feast of the Epiphany and our first-ever blessing of the local river to celebrate the baptism of Christ. These two festivals capture this chapter's theological reflection: the Holy Spirit's transformation of relationships, between people and their created siblings (in this case the polluted River Lea half-buried in culverts under the local shopping mall), and between different groups of people (in this case through celebrating the visitation of Christ by Gentile 'wise men from the East').

In the next section of this chapter, I will argue why land and labour are the fulcrum of twenty-first-century liberation struggles, where theological reflection on decolonial liberation struggles, class liberation and eco-struggles for the liberation of our Mother Earth meet. I will do this through arguing for an emphasis on material analysis in liberation theologies, exploring how this highlights both *land* and *labour* as important foci for liberation praxis and theological reflection on decolonizing and development. I will do this in a contextual manner, addressing the 'wound' in my own Church of England tradition and its failure to prioritize these struggles. Following on from this will be a section looking at how the Holy Spirit's work of conversion, in conversation with the Orthodox theology of *theosis*, might help theological reflection on what Joerg Rieger describes as a 'deep solidarity' (Rieger, 2022, p. 175). I will conclude by pointing to praxis, considering what these theological reflections might bring.

Why land and labour?

I locate my work in the broad field of liberation theology. A critique might rightly suggest that as a white, male, Church of England priest, I've got some nerve identifying myself or my work in this way. My introduction to this field came ten years ago when I started a theology diploma while still working as a precariat bricklayer. I have elsewhere, including in a chapter in my edited volume *Confounding the Mighty* (2023, pp. 3–22), explored in more depth the relationship between power, privilege and my working-class roots; however there is no room to repeat all that here. I would define social class as *a set of unequal labour relationships and the socio-cultural frameworks and institutions that reproduce them.* For me, social class is primarily *material* – it is rooted in the way the labouring (including reproductive labour and non-human labour) masses of the world are exploited by those of the middle and upper classes. To address these unequal relationships of labour means more than analysis of identity, rather engagement with critical material *analysis* of the material *conditions* of those labouring masses of the world, and the factors and webs of relationship that cause and replicate their unfair, unjust and intolerable material conditions. This, of course, is a vast oversimplification but will have to do for now.

Liberation theology and material analysis

With this material emphasis in mind, the kind of liberation theology I am interested in addresses these material conditions, responding with both liberatory praxis and liberatory theological reflection. Sadly, this emphasis on material analysis and indeed material praxis often seems underemphasized in contemporary scholarship. In 2008 the Argentinian liberation theologian Ivan Petrella decried a major failure in liberation theologies in both Latin America and the United States, in that they shared a 'common inability to deal successfully with the material context' (Petrella, 2008, p. 82). So if not dealing with material context, what are these liberation theologies doing? He suggests that the widening variety of axes for liberation struggle (for example, race, gender, sexuality) blurs the 'fact that material deprivation, that is, the deprivation that comes from one's class standing in society, remains the most important form of oppression' and that while the 'economic poor bear the brunt of oppression' they 'fall by the wayside of liberation theologies in the Americas' (2008, p. 82).

Reading these words in the present, particularly with my own intersections of identity, feels a little uncomfortable. I hear the critic say: 'Of course you think class is the most important thing!' I fear the problem here is that the very concept of class has become synonymous with whiteness in contemporary identity politics and is often a dog whistle for white supremacist populist politics (Reddie, 2019, p. 171, and 2021; Larner, 2023, pp. 9, 15–16). Petrella, however, suggests that 'Class is involved in all social arrangements of oppression.' He cites works of medical anthropology which, like the research paper on healthcare inequality in Luton I mentioned above, recognize that 'nothing occurs without implicating the material conditions that shape the way individuals and groups locate themselves, and are located, within their societies' (Petrella, 2008, p. 81). This is a recognition that living in circumstances of material deprivation of the person and community (that is, class deprivation) results in poorer health outcomes. If, as I have described above, class is a set of unequal labour relationships and the socio-cultural frameworks and institutions that reproduce these relationships, class is not just an abstract identity, it is the materially unequal, insufferable and unjust conditions in which the labouring and poor majority of the world live, both in the Global South and, as Petrella recognizes, the deprived communities of the Global North. Class analysis in my own context in Luton, therefore, means taking into account the material conditions in which 45% of children here live in poverty, the majority of whom are from global-majority heritages, and the way that our society causes their ethnicity, gender, social class and other factors to compound these material conditions and result in unequal education and healthcare outcomes.

Material class analysis, then, cannot be either dismissed as (or abandoned to) white populist identity politics. Rather, liberation theologies of all stripes must include a deep analysis of the relationship between class, the unjust material conditions in which many people live, and the structures that create those conditions: structures shaped by the interests of neocolonial globalist capitalism. This is not to ignore or even minimize other intersections of oppression; rather, it is to see that we must look to the material, and therefore to class, if we are to speak of real liberation.

Here, of course, I mean material in a broad sense: material analysis of labour includes reproductive labour; material analysis of oppression includes the impact of oppression on the bodies of the oppressed, including their brain chemistry. Material in this wholistic sense means to consider the whole of the person and the multiple impacts of oppression.

At a recent conference on 'Inclusivity in the Church of England', I spoke about how I don't want the church to be inclusive towards working-class people, I want the unjust structures that allow there to be class differentiation and exploitation to be dismantled. As both Petrella (2008, p. 81) and Rieger (2013, p. 11) recognize, while it makes sense to celebrate a diversity of genders, sexualities, ethnicities and other intersections of *identity* in the church and society, it makes absolutely no sense to celebrate a diversity of *class* relationships that depend on one class being exploited by other classes. It is a sinful diversity built upon injustice and exploitation, not the beautiful diversity of God's creation – sinful because this injustice and exploitation, finding its ultimate contemporary manifestation in neocolonial global capitalism, has a demonstrably negative impact on the well-being and dignity of not only the labouring classes of the human family but also our created siblings and our Mother Earth.

Liberation in the Capitalocene – land, labour and climate

Joerg Rieger refers to our present climate epoch not as the Anthropocene but the 'Capitalocene' – an age and epoch where 'the economic interests of a small and privileged group of humans rule both people and the planet', whereby the 'ecological devastations of our age' are 'shaped by the dynamics of capitalism' (Rieger, 2022, p. 175). The need for constant growth, development and production through neocolonial capitalist exploitation of land and labour is literally killing our lands and the lives they sustain. Here then we can conclude that the labouring human and non-human masses of the world, alongside the suffering lands of our Mother Earth, share the struggle against further capitalist development and colonization. Recognizing this relationship between neocolonial capitalist development and the climate crisis, Rieger shows that something more than 'reduce, reuse, recycle' is needed in terms of praxis (Rieger, 2022, p. 207). Indeed, to address development and decoloniality in this volume, a material analysis of liberation must include the colonizing and capitalist 'development' not only of labour but of the lands where we live and the lives and materials those lands produce.

Pope Francis (2015, §49) reflects on the relationship between labour and land in his 2015 encyclical *Laudato Si'*. He argues the stewardship of the world granted to humankind in the first chapter of Genesis implies not so much a 'dominion' but rather a responsibility to 'till and keep' – tilling meaning 'cultivating, ploughing or working', and keeping meaning 'caring, protecting overseeing and preserving'. This relationship between land and labour is not one of domination, greed, exploitation and perpetual growth, as found in capitalism and colonialism, but rather is a relationship characterized by a 'mutual responsibility between human beings and nature'. In accordance with Catholic social teaching, this is all undergirded by a challenging of greed, as 'God rejects every claim to absolute ownership' – for to God belongs 'the earth with all that is in it' (Deut. 10.14, ESV). Pope Francis (2015, §49) demonstrates the very practical nature of this aspect of Old Testament law, that 'The land shall not be sold in perpetuity, for the land is mine. For you are strangers and sojourners with me' (Lev. 25.23, ESV). Land and labour are intimately connected, so 'a true ecological approach always becomes a social approach', integrating questions of justice, hearing 'the cry of the earth and the cry of the poor' (Pope Francis, 2015, §49). Drawing from *Laudato Si'*, I would suggest that given the kind of material analysis I am arguing for in this chapter, to address the struggles of the poor and of the climate we must begin to address not only the exploitative *development* of land but also its *ownership*, particularly where this ownership is obtained by unjust means.

Decolonizing land and labour

This is a book about decolonizing and development, so an obvious place to start thinking about greed and land ownership is in the decolonial struggles of the colonized peoples of the world. My friend and comrade the Sri Lankan-born theologian Anupama Ranawana argues for a strong correlation between the ecological struggle of *Laudato Si'* and decolonial liberation struggles in her excellent book *A Liberation for the Earth*. Part of the inspiration for this chapter comes from our work and conversations, alongside Professor Rieger and others, at the 2023 European Academy of Religion conference. Here I began to develop, in no small part thanks to Anupama and other colleagues, a deep shared frustration that in the 'different discussions surrounding climate activism, there [is] limited conversation around colonialisms, both historical and present', and that the 'idea of some humans being seen as lesser [is] fundamental to how the land was expropriated and extracted' (Ranawana, 2022, p. 3). In these conversations, and those that took place at DARE 2023 in Bangkok, Thailand, with my friends and contributors to this book, I also began to see with some clarity that the intersection between class, colonialism and climate would be a powerful place to do some theological reflection. Ranawana states her case with great clarity:

> The struggle for ecological justice cannot be separated from the struggle to overturn systems of enslavement, expropriation, colonization and Indigenous genocide. Imperial projects that were centred on the expansion of empire also focused attention on the dominion over land such that entire landscapes were subjected to control and exploitation, and colonies were created in order to maximize extraction of natural resources. (2022, p. 3)

Here 'colonization' refers to both the historic and ongoing imperial projects of western nation states *and* the contemporary forces of neocolonial capitalism. In both cases, the desire for growth and development that feeds the insatiable greed of the colonizer is the basis for the exploitation and expropriation of both lands and people. This is a relationship based on the desire to dominate and extract, one that does not recognize the dignity and liberty of peoples and lands but only the opportunity to feed the greed of the colonizer. This simultaneous exploitation of people and land often occurs through forced labour and/or enslavement in order to extract the natural resources from the land, or indeed the removal of existing people whose labour is exploited either in other colonized lands or the homeland of the colonizer.

One example would be the colonization of much of Africa and the Americas, and the evil injustice of the transatlantic slave trade that trafficked colonized labour to extract resources from colonized land. As Ranawana observes, underlying this process is a theology that dehumanizes the colonized to such an extent that both their individual rights and their rights to their land are rejected due to their perceived status as less-than-human, or at least less than the supremacist colonial *ideal* of humanity (2022, p. 3). I could go on citing numerous other excellent works on decolonial theology, alongside the other chapters of this present volume, but what I want to emphasize here is that the enactment of unjust land and labour relations based on this logic is not limited to the class and decolonial struggles of the peoples of the majority world, or indeed those of majority-world heritages living in the colonial heartlands of the Global North. A very similar logic has been applied to the exploitation of land and labour within these colonial heartlands themselves and against their own peoples, as I will now argue by giving two examples from the history of the Church of England.

Land enclosure, class struggle and colonization – a Church of England case study

Let me start by stating clearly, I am by no means wishing to suggest that in the exploitation of the working classes in the 'Global North', their suffering and struggle has been the same or even equal to those who suffered the horrors of the transatlantic slave trade and the ongoing impact of the wider colonial project on the indigenous peoples of the majority world or 'Global South'. Neither am I in any way trying to absolve myself from complicity in the ongoing legacy of white supremacist racism. I recognize that as a white person and a clergyman in the Church of England (whose financial resources are deeply implicated), I too am deeply implicated and shaped by this ongoing history and have gained from my own white privilege. But as Rieger (2022, pp. 162–78) describes, privilege and *power* are not the same thing. England's involvement in the exploitation of land and labour did not begin when English ships transported African slaves in the seventeenth century. For a thousand years (if not longer) England's own common lands were stolen by the *power*-full from 'common' people through a process called 'land enclosure'.

Land enclosure and class struggle

Between 1604 and 1914 alone, 5,200 parliamentary enclosure bills enabled the seizing of over a fifth of England's lands, which, combined with previous informal enclosures, resulted in over half of all the land in England being taken into private ownership for landowners to 'consolidate, dictate and *develop*' (Oxford Centre for Global History, 2022, p. 1; emphasis mine). These were common lands on which the common people had exercised their common land rights, to graze their livestock, draw water and chop wood (UK Parliament, 2025), drawing the three essentials for human life from Mother Earth's bounty: food, water and warmth. According to Oxford University's 'Global History of Capitalism' project (Oxford Centre For Global History, 2022, p. 1), land enclosure 'revolutionised private property as a concept, largely introduced the concept of land as a commodity, and came to define the economic priorities of the last five hundred years'. It was also the beginning of a greater move towards *wage-labour*. The very history of capitalism, the Industrial Revolution and the removal of the means of production from the labourer, all sits upon the theft and exploitation of common lands. This history of land theft leads directly into the history of colonialism, for:

> The effects of enclosure were immensely far-reaching. It underpinned modernity, catalysing urbanisation, the Agricultural and Industrial Revolutions, and the modern understanding of property. It also rippled outwards across the world: Britain was the earliest industrialising nation and the first great colonial power. The British Empire replicated its rural land-use policies across Asia, Africa, and the Americas, codifying new property rights worldwide. Some historians laud it as one of history's greatest steps towards economic efficiency and liberal freedom; others lament it as one of history's most egregious and destructive instances of *class-based injustice*. (Oxford Centre for Global History, 2022, p. 1; emphasis mine)

In his bestselling publication *The Book of Trespass*, Nick Hayes (2020, p. 35) describes this further. The 'goldrush' of private property wrought by enclosure was rooted in the desire for '"improvement", a euphemism for privatisation', which saw supposedly unowned and un*developed* land as 'a waste of potential profit' and that 'society at large could be bettered by the private regulation of land'. Here we see once again the very same type of relationship to land (and, as I will go on to explain, labour) as we saw critiqued by Pope Francis in *Laudato Si'* – one based not on respect, solidarity or even stewardship but rather on domination, greed and exploitation – a relationship that sees only resources to be extracted and profit and power to be gained. Hayes recognizes that this new relationship to land was undergirded 'by a moral prohibition that stemmed from the other great shepherds of England, the Church' (2020, p. 65). Indeed, the church's involvement was not restricted to mere moral prohibition of trespass. In most cases the enclosure acts required specific endorsement by the clergy, who were often rewarded handsomely for their efforts, often with a parcel of the enclosed land. The British historian Matthew Cragoe describes this involvement in his case study centred on Northamptonshire, the northern-neighbouring county to my own context. While not wishing to take an ethical stance on the enclosure, he notes that the 'prime motivation' for enclosure was 'the desire for profit' based on the belief that 'a more scientific, productive, and ultimately profitable form of husbandry' was possible where enclosed fields came under the ownership of an individual, in contrast to the 'more communal modes of organisation, as in the open fields' (2016, p. 2). Whether these methods did indeed increase productivity is a matter of some debate, but what is clear is that enclosure was ultimately about resource extraction through development. He also notes that despite much debate on the topic, its relationship to the Church of England has had 'remarkably little scrutiny', despite the church's material/economic interest in the process.

Historically, Church of England clergy such as myself depended in part on the income from glebe land, property that was farmed to support the living of the parish priest (a hugely unequal system where some clergy became rich and those in parishes with little or no glebe land lived on a pittance). The other income clergy received was largely from the tithe – at the time a mandatory payment of one-tenth of the harvest from the lands of the parish. This method of extracting income from local lands was, according to Cragoe (2016, p. 11), a source of much tension and often lengthy legal battles between clergy and local people. Land enclosure and subsequent changes to farming practice were expected to bring a huge increase in profit, and therefore in the value of the tithe, so some landowners would 'exonerate' or exempt themselves from the tithe by paying a fee to the parish. In order for enclosure to be passed, the support of the tithe 'owner', often the rector of the local parish, was needed.

Given the anticipated profits, as Cragoe puts it, 'the promoters of an enclosure were willing to offer extremely generous terms to bring the tithe owners on side' (2016, p. 14), usually in the form of a parcel of the enclosed land, free of the significant costs of the enclosure itself. The result of this, combined with the huge increase (often double) in land rent charged to tenant farmers associated with enclosure, meant that clerical incomes rose significantly. Put plainly, clergy became wealthy through the exploited labour of tenant farmers labouring on expropriated common lands. There was, of course, some resistance to all this, including from other Christians, most notably the proto-communist group the Diggers, who occupied and farmed former common lands. The well-known Digger Gerard Winstanley sang of the clergy who 'say it is a sin that wee should now begin, o[u]r freedom for to win', greedy as they were for tithes, and acting in cahoots with lawyers:

for Tyrants they are both,
even flatt against their oath
to grant us they are loth,
free meat & drinke & cloth
Stand uppe now diggers all. (Winstanley, 1650)

Not all clergy in the Church of England were lucky enough to have ownership of significant glebe lands or tithe claims. In recognition of this, a fund was set up known as the 'Queen Anne's Bounty', which was initially used to purchase 'bounty lands' to subsidize the income of poor clergy, and there were 'large additions' to these bounty lands 'by allotments under the Inclosure Acts'. The bounty later became more like an investment fund, producing interest (Le Fanu, 1921, pp. 21–2). The Church Commissioners – the modern body that inherited management of the Queen Anne's Bounty and other church endowment funds – has recently published research into the history of these funds (Church Commissioners, 2023). Links were found between the Queen Anne's Bounty and transatlantic chattel slavery: between 1723 and 1777 'it invested almost exclusively in South Sea Company', which traded in enslaved people (2023, p. 39). In the 111 years that the church held these annuities, they generated £783,846 in income through interest and dividends, approximately £1.3 billion pounds in today's money.

Colonial exploitation of land and labour

As I have briefly surveyed here in my discussion, the wealth of the Church of England is, in part at least, bound up in the illicit enclosure of common lands and exploited labour in England, and in the colonized and exploited lands and labour of the majority world. As noted above, there is a direct relationship between the enclosure and development of common lands as an act of class injustice, the colonization and development of lands in the majority world through the exploitation and enslavement of indigenous people, and the rise of neocolonial capitalism. Both rely on the denial of basic rights and exploitation of people through their dehumanization, in the case of enclosure through their social class, and in the case of colonialism due to white supremacism. This relationship runs even further – as Hayes demonstrates (2020, p. 67). Those 'robbed of their homes and natural resources that now lay within the fences of the new lords of the manor' had to go *somewhere*. They often took to the roads looking for gainful labour, leading to the passing of 'vagrancy acts', whereby those found out of their hometowns 'whether unemployed, begging or just simply walking' could suffer vicious punishment including branding, whipping, having 'a hole of an inch diameter bored into the cartilage of your ear' and, if caught twice, execution. Vagrants were something lesser, 'children of Belial, without God, without magistrate, without minister'. As the colonialization of the so-called new world began, to improve their diminished humanity through work, some were 'shipped abroad, transported to the colonies of Virginia and the Caribbean to work as feudal serfs'. This continued until the colonial farmsteads dropped any 'pretence of moral improvement for the cheaper alternative: African slaves' (Hayes, 2020, p. 106). It is here, then, I wish to argue that the dehumanization and exploitation of land and labour that Ranawana and many other decolonial theologians describe did not, of course, arrive in a vacuum, but was, in part at least, a natural development from the dehumanization and exploitation of the land and labour of poor and working-class people in the colonial heartlands themselves.

Kenan Malik explores this further in his book *Not So Black and White*. Taking the example of American plantations, he recognizes that during the initial decades of the seventeenth century they were mostly worked by indentured white European servants (2023, p. 67). The status of these bonded labourers was 'as close to slavery as it was possible to get'; they could be 'bought and sold like livestock'. It is important to recognize here, as does Rieger (2022, p. 204), that slavery is an extreme form of *labour* exploitation, generally rooted in the dehumanization of the slave and the removal of their rights in order to extract profit. While it would, of course, be ludicrous to claim that the plight of these indentured servants was the *same* as that of the victims of chattel slavery, Malik argues that there were striking similarities, not least that 'it was common to be beaten, maimed, even killed with impunity'. When it came to the exploitation of their labour to work the land, the skin tone of these servants mattered little: 'what mattered was that they were poor and exploitable' in a system that treated human beings as *things* (Malik, 2023, p. 68). As times changed and fewer Europeans were sent off to the colonies as indentured servants, 'more slaves were being imported, and at a cheaper price, from Africa', which wrought a substantial change to the 'brutal economics of plantation labour' (Malik, 2023, p. 69). While the plantation labour economy began based on 'class distinctions, not racial divisions', over time it became more racialized in tandem with both the ideological and pragmatic development of anti-black, white supremacist racism. In my 2023 edited volume *Confounding the Mighty*,

I trace further the use of racism by wealthy elites to divide working-class people racialized as white and working-class people racialized as black in order to exploit both (albeit in differing ways). There is not space to rehash that here, although it is worth repeating that this does not excuse the racism present among poor and working-class white people, it merely explains one of the reasons for the development of the ideology of anti-black racialization – the exploitation of labour and the development of power.

Behind the Church of England's profiting from the enclosure and colonization of lands and the exploitation of labour is a theological rationale that places the white dominant class of Britain (from whom the clergy have typically been drawn) as superior to those whom they exploit and rob, both at home and overseas. This theological notion of exceptionalism and superiority lies behind the complicity of the Church of England's mission in the colonization of the majority world in what is known as the 'white man's burden': the three 'Cs' that the supposed superior colonial Anglo-Saxon must bring – 'Christianity, commerce and culture' – to the 'undeveloped' majority world. The godfather of British black liberation theology Professor Anthony Reddie recognizes this notion of superiority and exceptionalism and its ongoing legacy in post-Brexit Britain in his book *Theologising Brexit*. For Reddie, the 'relationship between mission Christianity and Black people' has been rooted in the 'relationship between empire and colonialism' – indeed the failure of British Christianity to 'take a preferential option for the marginalised' is almost certainly rooted in 'the collusive relationship that the historic churches, especially the Church of England, have with the operational activity of imperialism and colonialism' (Reddie, 2019, pp. 15, 27). The sense of supremacy and exceptionalism inherent in the elites of the British Empire was combined with the missiological drive of Matthew's Gospel's 'Great Commission', reflected in a 'mercantilist expansion', and 'resulted in the exploitation of non-white bodies' and a missiological justification of 'imposing Eurocentric values on the cultures of non-European peoples across the world' (Reddie, 2019, p. 67). It is, here, important to trace the specific role of the Church of England as the established church. Reddie underlines the way 'White English Anglicanism becomes the archetypal, embodied ideal that defines authentic notions of being in the body politic of the nation' (2019, p. 92). Based on what I have argued above, we can trace this beyond the role of the Church of England in imperial mission back to the role of parishes and rectors in land enclosures, and the complicity of the Queen Anne's Bounty in the same, in addition to investment and profiteering from the transatlantic slave trade. All of this is only possible through a theological rationale of the superiority and exceptionalism of the church as part of the body politic and national establishment, which views the land and labour of its lesser 'others' as ripe for 'improvement' or 'development' through exploitation.

Land ownership and climate – the impact of ill-gotten gains today

I have, here, traced the complicity of the Church of England in class and decolonial struggles, but what of climate change (which disproportionally affects the poor and colonized)? According to research published on the land reform blog *Who Owns England?* by the environmental campaigner and author Guy Shrubsole (2019), the £10 billion fund managed by the Church Commissioners owns a rather secretive portfolio of approximately 105,000 acres of land and property (in addition to the significant land and property owned by individual dioceses, parishes and other bodies). A 2022 report by the Christian climate charity Operation Noah, drawing from Shrubsole's research, suggests that churches own approximately 500,000 acres in the UK, around half of which belongs to the Church of England more widely (Hall, 2022, p. 6). The report notes that in the Church of England's net-zero 'route map', the carbon footprint of this land is mentioned only in passing, the focus being mainly on changes to church energy use, which considering that the 'agricultural lands owned by the Church of England is likely to create more greenhouse gas emissions than all Church of England church buildings combined' seems a major oversite (Hall, 2022, p. 3).

I'm indebted here to conversations during the 2023 Society for the Study of Theology conference with fellow Church of England priest and theologian Alison Walker. Walker reflects on this in her 2023 paper 'Resisting the Building Project of Whiteness: A Theological Reflection on Land Ownership in the Church of England'. Walker's paper offers a strong argument for the white supremacist and colonial nature of the church's land use and theology, drawing from James Cone and Willie James Jennings. Walker also recognizes the history of the Queen Anne's Bounty and its use to purchase church lands (2023, pp. 3, 7–10, 13–14). Missing, however, from Walker's reference to the process of land enclosure is any reference to the Church of England's complicity and benefit from it or its role in *class*-based injustice and the ongoing history of capitalism. While Walker's deconstruction of a white and Anglican theology of place is commendable in considering a decolonial climate theology, there is a need, as I have argued above, to bring in the material *class*-based analysis of liberation theology here. This becomes especially clear when we recognize that it is not only white supremacy but *class* supremacy that led to the Church of England illegitimately obtaining land and profit from the exploitation of the labouring classes.

Section conclusion – towards conversion

In this section I hope I have exposed the theological *wound* I am attempting to address – the sinful exploitation of land and labour aided by theologies that dehumanize and belittle those 'other' to the white-establishment-class ideal of personhood. Is there, therefore, any hope of proposing a theology of liberation that, through reclaiming a material analysis, can address this wrong relationality and transform it? In the next section, I will explore the notion of conversion in *Laudato Si'* and, prompted by Pope Francis, I will explore in greater detail what an Orthodox theology of *theosis* might offer, suggesting that *theosis* might lead us to the notion of *deep solidarity* as a goal of conversion and expression of its ultimate *telos* in *theosis*. I will then, drawing from its own eucharistic liturgy, offer a challenge to the Church of England to address its historic and ongoing failure in this area.

Conversion, *theosis* and deep solidarity

As I have outlined above, drawing from one context and one church tradition as a case study, the situation is somewhat dire. While some might talk of western church involvement in the colonization and oppression of land and labour as a thing of the past, this is clearly not the case. How, then, might we reflect theologically on this great sin, perpetrated by those whose interests align with neocolonial global capitalism, including many western churches who continue to profit from it? Is all hope lost – has the right hand of the Most High lost its strength (see Ps. 77.10)?

Conversion

In *Laudato Si'*, conversion is seen as the way to a new kind of relationship with land and labour, and as Pope Francis (2015, §5, §9) recognizes, it is the turn taken by both Pope John Paul II and Patriarch Bartholomew in their own writings. Reflecting on conversion (a 'Converting Ordinance' according to Methodist tradition) through the lens a eucharistic theology of 'becoming what we receive', Ranawana suggests it 'entails working for justice' (2022, p. 23). The 'encounter anoints us' and 'sends us out into the world with a gaze that is renewed', the gaze of awe and wonder associated with Francis of Assisi. This new way of seeing leads us to seek 'to be in right relationship with God, neighbour and Creation', our eyes opened to 'the mystery of being and the Divine'. I have argued that behind the exploitation of land and labour, and the class, colonial and climate struggles of our time, is a wrong relationality, shaped by exploitation and extraction. As Ranawana powerfully argues, to have an encounter with the divine (in this case in the Eucharist) is to be converted, to work for justice, to seek right relationship with God, neighbour and creation. Concerned as I am in this chapter with material analysis and material solutions, how might we paint a clearer picture of the outcome of this sense of conversion? What are we being converted to?

A conversion into deep solidarity

The outcome I envisage here is characterized by Joerg Rieger's conception of *deep solidarity*. As Rieger suggests:

> Things do not need to be this way, and alternatives already exist: instead of promoting disembodied ideas (that have too often not materialized for very long, and sometimes never), economics can be reconstructed from the ground up, in touch with the ecological, sociological, and political dynamics described ... The same is true for religion and theology. (2022, p. 56)

Deep solidarity, for Rieger, takes us beyond abstract notions of one-ness into a very practical response – it makes Jesus' teaching to love one's neighbour something very practical, managing to 'employ differences for the common good and the power of resistance' (2022, p. 175) across the various struggles I highlight in this chapter. In the earlier volume,

Occupy Religion, Joerg Rieger and Kwok Pui Lan describe deep solidarity very much in terms of the Occupy movement of the time; it 'begins with an understanding that we are all in the same boat: we are the 99 percent, and we challenge the 1 percent to stop building their power and wealth at our expense and invite them to join us' (2011, p. 79). In this sense, deep solidarity is not so much the creation of something *new* but rather the revelation-to and living-out-of something that already exists – a commonality that the greed, exploitation and extraction of capitalism seeks to hide (Rieger, 2022, p. 170). Indeed, as I have traced above, this recognition of commonality is noted by Pope Francis in *Laudato Si'*, and is what both he and Ranawana are pointing to by using St Francis of Assisi as a model of one who has been made alive through a 'conversion' experience leading to a deeper sense of communion with all creation and a recognition of the 'inseparable bond' between 'concern for nature' and 'justice for the poor' (Pope Francis, 2015, §10–11). But this does pose a question for further theological reflection: How does this conversion take place? It is not enough to point to the Eucharist as a 'converting ordinance' in this sense; after all, there were Eucharists going on in the churches complicit in the atrocities I have mentioned above. This, as I will now go on to argue, requires some reflection on the work of the Holy Spirit as the agent of conversion.

Conversion and *theosis* – an Orthodox perspective

In his 2008 book *Beloved Dust*, the American Episcopalian theologian Robert Davis Hughes argues that conversion is rightly reflected upon as within the category of pneumatology, the work of the Holy Spirit (2008, p. 6). He points to three 'tides' of the Spirit in the Christian life: conversion, transfiguration and glory. Drawing from this analysis, in this section I will argue for a movement from conversion to transfiguration (or *theosis*) in reflecting on the work of the Holy Spirit as a means of the formation of deep solidarity, and, therefore, claiming a liberation impetus rooted in the *mission* of the Spirit.

Pope Francis (2015, §9) references Orthodox Patriarch Bartholomew in *Laudato Si'*, not least his notion that Christians are called 'to accept the world as a sacrament of communion, as a way of sharing with God and our neighbours on a global scale' (Bartholomew, 2012). This is classic Orthodox theology, rooted in reverence for the work of the Spirit. Writing on the sacraments (or 'mysteries' as, Orthodox call them), Bartholomew describes them as a way of relating to God and the world, 'whereby everything is received and shared as gifts of encounter and communion' (2008, pp. 154–5). I would argue that this is another way of articulating a sense of deep solidarity, in recognizing that 'Everything is created by God, embraced by God, and reconciled by God.' Bartholomew is clear that the sacraments do not work by magic but rather function 'mystically', in a 'silent manner, permeating the hearts and lives of those who choose to be open to the possibility of encounter with God'. This mystical openness to encounter with God sees, first, the sacrament of baptism as connected to the Spirit's brooding over the face of the world in Genesis with the renewal and sanctification of all creation, second, Chrismation as the 'seal of the Spirit' in 'all human beings, in all corners of the world, and in all elements of the universe', and third, the Eucharist as challenging 'individuals and communities to work for a just society, where basic food and water are plentiful for all and where everyone has enough'. This sacramental-mystical theology locates the sacraments from the moment of creation to its fulfilment, leading us from conversion to what the Orthodox call divination or *theosis* – whereby humanity is seen to take part in the Spirit's work of raising all of creation into the life of God, where we humans are called to 'realize the divine plan of healing and reconciliation throughout the world' and 'then the Spirit of God will transform this world into the kingdom of heaven, the fallen world into the new creation, and every activity into true life' (Bartholomew, 2008, p. 209).

The Namibian theologian Professor Paul John Isaak explores this Orthodox approach to the Spirit and the sacraments from a postcolonial perspective, recognizing that 'the liturgy is the participation in the great event of liberation from demonic powers', and therefore its continuation in life means 'a continuous liberation from the powers of evil', including 'all demonic structures of injustice, exploitation, agony and loneliness' creating 'real communion with persons in love' (2011, p. 244). This means that from a postcolonial perspective, mission means to go beyond and reject mission in service of the four 'Cs' of colonialism as I described above, but rather points us to 'God's reign of peace-making, reconciliation, healing as well as justice and ultimately salvation' (Isaak, 2011, p. 249).

Deep solidarity and the go-between Spirit

Above, I look at the Church of England as a case study to explore the exploitation of land and labour, considering moves towards liberation in theology and practice. Next, I will take a brief look at theologies from within the Church of England exploring this theme. So far I have reflected on theologies of the Holy Spirit as an approach to relationship transformation in terms of conversion and *theosis* in the direction of deep solidarity. Above I quote Rieger, who points towards Martin Buber's reflections on the dominical command: 'love your neighbour'. One of the most well-known reflections on the Holy Spirit from within the Church of England is bishop and former missionary John V. Taylor's 1972 book, *The Go-Between God*. Taylor draws extensively from Buber in this volume and turns to the Holy Spirit as the enabler of transformed relationship. With striking resemblance to Pope Francis and Anupama Ranawana's reflections on conversion, he writes:

> But what is this force which causes me to see in a way in which I have not seen? What makes a landscape or a person or an idea come to life for me and become a presence towards which I surrender myself? I recognize, I respond, I fall in love, I worship – yet it was not I who took the first step. In every such encounter there has been an anonymous third party who makes the introduction, acts as a go-between, makes two beings aware of each other, sets up a current of communication between them. (Taylor, 2021, pp. 18–19)

Christians name this go-between the 'Holy Spirit', the same Spirit that 'possessed and dominated the man Jesus Christ, making him the most aware and sensitive and open human being who ever lived' and 'fantastically aware of every person who crossed his path, especially the ones no one else noticed' (Taylor, 2021, pp. 18–19). Taylor's reflections on this renewed relationality in the Spirit are broad. He suggests that the 'same impulse' that leads Christians to 'healing ministries or the relief of the poor' must now send them into struggles against 'the titans of the age' (2021, p. 153). For Taylor, this is not rooted in a naive utopianism but rather 'the Christian's solidarity with mankind and his involvement in the human struggle has to be *kerygmatic*'. Our engagement in these struggles is a result of Jesus' ultimate victorious mastery of the powers – Christians must 'work for a juster, more humane order of society because we are the new humanity, inasmuch as the Go-Between Spirit makes us one with Christ' (2021, p. 153). While Taylor's 'Go-Between' encourages dialogue with other faiths and indeed with all others involved in struggles for a better tomorrow, he does not develop anything so materially focused or economically savvy as Rieger's 'deep solidarity'; indeed, he is more guarded about critiquing the way Christians and Christian theology have undergirded the capitalist and colonial projects that so clearly threaten our common humanity and our common home today.

As the British Pentecostal theologian Robert Beckford has argued, some theologies of the Spirit and transformation are anything but materially focused, more interested in personal transformation or 'private supernatural phenomena'. This weakness, affecting many different Christian traditions, must be addressed. Hughes also recognizes this in addressing how a hermeneutics of suspicion calls attention to the ways the Christian tradition has been 'infected with the interests and scars of class, race, gender, and personal psychological history', leading him to make the bold claim early in his book that abstract talk of 'human spiritual capacity' is worthless; rather, there is 'only the *materiality* of human existence and the movements of the Holy Spirit within it' (Hughes, 2008, p. 4; emphasis mine).

It is here, therefore, that I restate my claim that a renewed focus on the material is so important, both for the materiality of human existence Hughes highlights and, indeed, the Spirit's affinity with the materiality of creation and its raising into the life of God as the material of one 'all-embracing eucharist', for 'it characterizes the Spirit to rest upon matter' (Rogers, 2006, p. 69). Next I will close my argument by looking at two significant pieces of eucharistic liturgy in the Church of England's *Common Worship*, offering them as a challenge.

Deep solidarity and the double epiclesis

My argument in this chapter boils down to this: I have suggested that three of the liberation struggles of the twenty-first century are rooted in relationships with land and labour that are based on extraction, exploitation and so-called 'development', all linked to the inability to recognize the inherent dignity of God's creatures. I have suggested that one way to reflect theologically on this 'wound' is through a more materialist exploration of the work of the Holy Spirit in eucharistic conversion and *theosis* as a transformation of these unjust relationships in the direction of 'deep solidarity'. This then requires a pneumatology that goes beyond abstract notions of the transformation of individuals and even just interpersonal relationships, but that opens the hearts of people to all of God's material creation in a new way. I will offer closing remarks on this idea in looking at how the Church of England's use of a 'double epiclesis' in some of its Eucharistic Prayers might offer a challenge to the Church of England.

The Church of England's contemporary liturgy leaves room for a wide variety of practice, influenced to differing degrees by the Roman Catholic and Eastern Orthodox traditions. In all bar one of the approved Eucharist Prayers in our *Common Worship*, however, there is at least one prayer of 'epiclesis' invoking the Holy Spirit to bring the mysterious presence of Christ not only to the bread and wine but also upon the people. The Eucharistic Prayer I typically use on festal occasions (Prayer B) contains what is called a 'double' or 'split' epiclesis, where the invocation of the Spirit on the gifts and the people is separated either side of the words of institution ('This is my body'). A mix of western and eastern tradition, the words here are generative.

The epiclesis over the bread and wine is:

Lord, you are holy indeed, the source of all holiness;
grant that by the power of your Holy Spirit,
and according to your holy will,
these gifts of bread and wine
may be to us the body and blood of our Lord Jesus Christ.
(Archbishops' Council, 2000, p. 189)

These words 'may be to us' do not imply transubstantiation but rather the suggestion that our relationship to the bread and wine is changed now that Christ is mysteriously present. Reflecting on them has become important to me in my own journey. I came to realize, using these words as a place for reflection, that the gift of this eucharistic theology was that if I was able to come to accept Christ as mysteriously present in the bread and wine, according the due reverence this demands, maybe I could come to find Christ mysteriously present by the Spirit in the matter of all creation, as the Orthodox theology I quote above suggests. Indeed, my practice as a priest in preparing the table is to use traditional prayers giving thanks for bread, provided by God's goodness, which 'earth has given and human hands have made'. Here again we see that relationship between land and labour, and its transformation by the Spirit in the Eucharist, pointing to the greater transformation we who partake of that bread are called to participate in.

The second prayer of epiclesis says:

> Send the Holy Spirit on your people
> and gather into one in your kingdom
> all who share this one bread and one cup.
> (Archbishops' Council, 2000, p. 190)

This is an even clearer reminder that the Spirit's work in the Eucharist is not only to transform our relationship to the bread and wine, and Christ's mysterious presence in it, but also to transform our relationships with the human family. Although this is directed primarily at the relationships within the family of the church, a broader conception of what the Spirit is doing in the matter of all the world might lead us to recognize that all life forms on earth share the one bread and one cup of our common home. Indeed, should we fail to be 'gathered into one' in Christ's kingdom with all our created siblings, moving away from the relationships of land and labour exploitation that threaten our human existence and our earthly home, fields will no longer produce the grain, vineyards will no longer produce the grapes and human hands will no longer be able to produce the bread and wine for the eucharistic elements.

Our only hope, then, in the face of the existential threats to land and labour, is that an increasing proportion of the human family opens their hearts to the work of the one we Christians call the 'Holy Spirit', leading us to a deep solidarity where we organize and join in the work of the Spirit to liberate the land and labour together.

Conclusion: 'We whom the Spirit lights give light to the world'

I have spent much time in this chapter exposing the wound and beginning a theological reflection on how to treat it, which leaves little room to discuss praxis. But praxis, of course, properly belongs in the streets of parishes like the one I serve, searching out the 'poor and weak, the sick and lonely, and those who are oppressed and powerless' in places that the Church of England's ordinal for deacons describes as 'the forgotten corners of the world' (although one wonders, forgotten by whom exactly?!) (Archbishops' Council, 2007, p. 5).

I have suggested that material analysis in the context of neocolonial capitalism leads us to land and labour as the fulcrum of the liberation struggles of today, particularly class and labour struggles, decolonial struggles and the struggle to preserve our Mother Earth. I have argued that behind these struggles is a set of relationships based on extraction, exploitation and development, taking the Church of England as a case study of the material impact of these relationships. Finally, I have argued that it is the Spirit's work of conversion and *theosis* that calls forth the ongoing transformation of those relationships in the direction of liberation and deep solidarity. I close, therefore, with a few words from the closing prayer from the Church of England's order for the Holy Eucharist. I offer these words as a challenge to the Church of England and other churches complicit in the exploitation of land and labour, to respond to the Spirit. I offer them also as an encouragement to those who faithfully respond to the Spirit's still, small voice in the liberation struggles of today:

> All: May we who share Christ's body live his risen life;
> we who drink his cup bring life to others;
> we whom the Spirit lights give light to the world.
> (Archbishops' Council, 2000, p. 182)

I have explored practical ways for Christians and Christian communities to join in the Spirit's work of giving light and life to the world through day-to-day practices in the final chapter of my edited volume *Confounding the Mighty*, such as broad-based community organizing and living-wage campaigns, involvement in the trades union movement and developing worker cooperatives (2023, pp. 134–58). I lean also towards the Franciscans and the Diggers as examples of Spirited conversion towards land and labour liberation during the birth of capitalism in Europe.

However, returning to where I started, for now I offer the simple act of planting fruit trees in an area of post-industrial urban decay alongside comrades of all faiths and none, in the hope against all hope that one day we will enjoy their fruit while the Spirit keeps leading us to organize for liberation together. Borrowing from the faith tradition of my Muslim siblings, I take inspiration from the words of the Messenger of Allah (peace be upon him), 'Even if the resurrection were established upon one of you while he has in his hand a sapling, let him plant it.'

Veni Sancte Spiritus, pater pauperum, in labore requies, in aestu temperies, in fletu solatium. Amen.

References

Archbishops' Council of the Church of England, 2000, *Common Worship: Services and Prayers for the Church of England*, London: Church House Publishing.

Archbishops' Council of the Church of England, 2007, *Common Worship: Ordination Services*, London: Church House Publishing.

Bartholomew I., 2008, *Encountering the Mystery: Understanding Orthodox Christianity Today*, New York: Doubleday.

Bartholomew I., 2012, '"Global Responsibility and Ecological Sustainability", Closing Remarks', Istanbul.

Beckford, Robert, 2006, *Jesus Dub: Theology, Music and Social Change*, Oxford: Routledge.

Church Commissioners for England, 2023, 'Church Commissioners' Research into Historic Links to Transatlantic Chattel Slavery', London: Church Commissioners.

Cragoe, Matthew, 2016, 'The Church of England and the Enclosure of England's Open Fields – A Northamptonshire Case Study', *International Journal of Regional and Local History* 11(1), pp. 17–30.

'Enclosing the Land', n.d., *UK Parliament*, https://www.parliament.uk/about/living-heritage/transformingsociety/towncountry/landscape/overview/enclosingland/ (accessed 18.01.2024).

Hall, Sharon, 2022, 'Church Land and the Climate Crisis: A Call to Action', London: Operation Noah.

Hayes, Nick, 2020, *The Book of Trespass: Crossing the Lines that Divide Us*, London: Bloomsbury Publishing.

Hughes, Robert Davis, 2008, *Beloved Dust: Tides of the Spirit in the Christian Life*, New York: Continuum.

Isaak, Paul John, 2011, 'Mission as Praxis for Peace-Building, Healing, and Reconciliation: Critical Appraisal of the Praxis of CWM', in Desmond Van der Water (ed.), *Postcolonial Mission: Power and Partnership in World Christianity*, Upland, CA: Sopher Press.

Larner, Luke (ed.), 2023, *Confounding the Mighty: Stories of Church, Social Class and Solidarity*, London: SCM Press, ch. 1 and Conclusion.

Le Fanu, William Richard, 1921, *Queen Anne's Bounty: A Short Account of Its History and Work*, London: Macmillan and Co.

Malik, K., 2023, *Not So Black and White*, London: Hurst Press.

Marmot, M., Alexander, M., Allen, J., Egbutah, C., Goldblatt, P., Willis, S., 2022, *Reducing Health Inequalities in Luton: A Marmot Town*, London: Institute of Health Equity.

Oxford Centre for Global History, 2022, 'Enclosing the English Commons: Property, Productivity and the Making of Modern Capitalism', November, https://globalcapitalism.history.ox.ac.uk/files/case26-enclosingtheenglishcommonspdf# (accessed 27.01.2025).

Petrella, I., 2008, *Beyond Liberation Theology: A Polemic*, London: SCM Press.

Pope Francis, 2015, *Laudato Si': On Care for Our Common Home*, Huntington, IN: Our Sunday Visitor Pub.

Ranawana, Anupama, 2022, *A Liberation for the Earth: Climate, Race and Cross*, London: SCM Press.

Reddie, Anthony, 2019, *Theologising Brexit: A Liberationist and Postcolonial Critique*, Routledge New Critical Thinking in Religion, Theology, and Biblical Studies, London and New York: Routledge.

———, 2021, 'Panel on Theologising Brexit: A Liberationist and Post-Colonial Critique', Society for the Study of Theology Conference 2021.

Rieger, Jörg and Kwok, Pui-Lan, 2011, *Occupy Religion: Theology of the Multitude*, Lanham, MD: Rowman & Littlefield.

Rieger, J. (ed.), 2013, *Religion, Theology, and Class: Fresh Engagements after Long Silence*, New York: Palgrave Macmillan.

Rieger, J., 2022, *Theology in the Capitalocene: Ecology, Identity, Class, and Solidarity (Dispatches)*, Minneapolis, MN: Fortress Press.

Rogers, Eugene F., 2006, *After the Spirit: A Constructive Pneumatology from Resources Outside the West*, London: SCM Press.

Shrubsole, Guy, 2019, '"God's Acres": The Land Owned by the Church Commissioners', *Who Owns England?*, 4 November, https://whoownsengland.org/2019/11/04/gods-acres-the-land-owned-by-the-church-commissioners/ (accessed 27.01.2025).

Taylor, John V., 2021, *The Go-Between God: New Edition*, London: SCM Press.

UK Parliament, 2025, 'Enclosing the Land', https://www.parliament.uk/about/living-heritage/transformingsociety/towncountry/landscape/overview/enclosingland/ (accessed 17.02.2025).

Winstanley, Gerard, 1650, 'The Diggers' Song', reproduced at Counterfire, https://www.counterfire.org/article/the-diggers-song/ (accessed 18.01.2024).

Walker, Alison, 2023, 'Resisting the Building Project of Whiteness: A Theological Reflection on Land Ownership in the Church of England', *Studies in Christian Ethics* 37(1), November, https://doi.org/10.1177/09539468231216900.

PART 4

Specific Challenges

10

Postcolonial Reparation: Reading Fanon with Aquinas for Postcolonial Nations' New Humanity

HENDRAWAN WIJOYO

In 1804, Haiti became the first independent black republic in the western hemisphere after a successful uprising against French colonization. Unwilling to recognize Haiti's sovereignty, France sought compensation for the loss of its colony and enslaved workforce. Under the threat of reoccupation and international isolation, Haiti agreed to pay a massive sum to France. Haiti's indemnity payments strained its finances and political stability in its postcolonial period. The effects continue to haunt Haiti today. In our perverse world, victims become the party responsible for paying reparations.

Tragically, Haiti's story is not an exception. Today, most postcolonial nations' developments are still hampered by past colonization's ecological, social and economic scars.[1] Proper conception of reparation for colonization is crucial for decolonization, global growth and the survival of humans in the Capitalocene.[2] As Olúfẹ́mi Táíwò and Melanie Harris have argued, reparation also supports climate justice and prevents the reoccurrence of harm (Táíwò, 2022; Harris, 2017). Its absence hinders communities' survival and restoration process, both mentally and materially. Hence reparations need to cover both aspects. Material reparation can involve redistribution of land, monetary payments, free access to former colonists' public goods, restoration of ecological damages among other things. Immaterial reparations come in many forms: formal apology, mention of the wrongdoings in the educational curriculum of former colonists, postcolonial tribunal, committee for truth-telling and reconciliation and so on.

Unfortunately, reparation is often neither popular nor straightforward. Current societal arrangements still hang on apparatuses of colonization. Powerful parties in today's political constellations are people benefiting from past, present and future colonization (Sachs, 2021, p. xii). It is pervasive in contemporary global and local orders, even embedded in international laws (Miller, 2019). Any meaningful amendment to colonization will surely upset the current order. To make reparation more viable, decolonization disorders must be understood better and embraced willingly by more parties. Allies, especially powerful ones, can boost the reparation cause tremendously (Mullen and Darity, 2023).

In the spirit of making intelligible postcolonial reparation to Christian tradition, this chapter will set Thomas Aquinas as a dialogue partner for Franz Fanon.[3] The two are foundational figures in each tradition. Fanon's *The Wretched of the Earth* (2004) has been dubbed 'the Bible of decolonization' (Bhabha, 2004, p. xvi). Standing within the agonistic humanism of Black Atlantic, Fanon offers a helpful future orientation for reparation projects (Gilroy, 2019). Aquinas is a doctor of the Catholic Church and has influenced various Christian traditions. His works even shaped debates on the colonized people's humanity at the start of the colonization era. Synthesizing a wide range of Christian and non-Christian traditions, Aquinas provides excellent space to think theologically about reparation.

Reading them together, I argue that the Fanonian cause for reparation makes sense in Thomistic theology and works together in advancing the contemporary cause of reparation. To that end, I will first explore Fanon's interconnected ideas of the new humanity, violence and reparations in *The Wretched of the Earth*. This first section will unpack Fanon's complex, problematic but often misunderstood nature of violence. Second, I will expound on the relevance of Fanon's proposal to the contemporary challenges to fulfilling such reparations. Third, I will explain the implications of reading Aquinas together with Fanon on future-orientated reparations for postcolonial countries.

Forging postcolonial nations' future: reparation in the *Wretched of the Earth*

Colonial circumstance and path towards new humanity

The Wretched of the Earth (2004) is Fanon's diagnosis and prescription for colonized nations' maladies. Colonization has perverted humans into a compartmentalized order: the colonist on top and the colonized at the bottom. European colonists brought violence and dehumanization to the local populace, setting up a depraved order of colonialism (Fanon, 2004,

p. 3). They prop themselves up as a higher species by imposing western values and religion while denigrating the colonized people's culture and economy (pp. 4–9). Colonists vilify the colonized as the manifestation of evil (pp. 6, 182). Colonists validated their superiority with the spoils of the colony that adorned their opulent metropolis (pp. 2, 53–9). They act as if the colonized owe existence to them (p. 220). In reality, Fanon says, colonists are fat leeches:

> Europe is literally the creation of the Third World. The riches that are choking it are those plundered from the underdeveloped peoples. The ports of Holland, the docks in Bordeaux and Liverpool owe their importance to the trade and deportation of millions of slaves. (pp. 58–9)

The colonized are local repressed populations who have suffered long under the colonists' rule. They live in destitution because of colonial exploitation. Their identity as an animalistic colonized crowd is a fabricated one, made to subjugate them under colonization (pp. 2, 6). Contrary to colonists' imagination, the colonized are tacitly intelligent people ready to unleash their tense muscles and psyche violently (pp. 3, 5, 7, 8, 9, 16). They are ready to change their unjust lot in life, causing disorder to the colonial order (p. 2).

To break out of this compartmentalized humanity, Fanon says colonized nations must go through a decolonization process. It is a path towards a new humanity, a long and arduous journey. Decolonization entails the replacement of the colonists by the colonized subjects through a violent process (Fanon, 2004, pp. 1, 17). However, decolonization's *telos* lay beyond mere violence or expelling the colonizers (pp. 177ff.). Decolonizing means nation-building and economic prosperity for all formerly colonized people (pp. 179–80). His vision even includes the transformation of the colonists' nation into better societies (pp. 235–8). Hopefully, it will obliterate the compartmentalized human system, forging a new humanity for the colonized people (pp. 2, 50, 178, 236).

The role of violence on decolonial struggle: material liberation and anthropological rebirth

In *The Wretched of the Earth*, reparation is inseparable from violent decolonization. Fanon sees violence as an indispensable instrument to achieve two goals of colonized nations: anthropological rebirth and material liberation.[4]

First, decolonial violence aims to liberate colonized people's material conditions (Fanon, 2004, p. 35). Colonial governments are extractive machines propped up by violence and subjugation (pp. 235–8). Colonized subjects' well-being and future were never the concern of the colonial governments. Instead, colonists' daily jobs are crushing the colonized with violence, both physical and symbolic. Forced labour, looting, torture, rape and massacre are colonial governments' repertoire of physical violence. Symbolic forms of violence such as racial denigration, police forces, bugle calls, military parades and the flag flying remind the colonized that they are helpless under colonial subjugation (p. 16). Colonial violence permeates colonial rules so that metropoles can profit smoothly from the colony's land and blood. Colonial violence is a daily occurrence and normalized. Hence decolonial violence to liberate material conditions does not start violence; instead it aims to stop violence. The genealogy of violence must be traced to pervasive colonial violence. Fanon is pessimistic that the colonists will leave their colony without a fight. Colonized people who seek to end their predicament will face colonists' rifles' butts and napalm (p. 4). Colonists will not hesitate to slaughter herds of revolting beasts to preserve the exploitation of colonized people's land and labour (p. 47). Therefore colonized people must fight tooth and nail for every inch of the city and rural areas. Guerrilla warfare will often be the tactic of choice (p. 85). Decolonial material struggle speaks in the language of spears and rifles because colonists rarely leave without being forced to by someone or something. Unlike many colonized elites, rural people quickly realized the need to regain control over the cities and their agricultural land. Owning and managing their own land brings 'dignity and bread' to the people (p. 14, 112).[5] The dignity-generating potential of land repossession connects the first purpose of decolonial violence with the second, which will be explained below (p. 9). However, Fanon is clear that sovereignty over land is not enough. Material liberation also needs capital and technology (pp. 53, 57, 59). Here, colonized nations do not want to forget the stolen minerals, produce and labour that European states have robbed from them (p. 53). When they finally gave up and left the colonized nations, colonists took with them the extracted capital (pp. 54, 60). Forced to pull themselves up by the bootstrap, formerly colonized nations demanded reparations and aid (pp. 59, 61). In Fanon's words: 'What matters today, the issue which blocks the horizon, is the need for a redistribution of wealth. Humanity will have to address this question, no matter how devastating the consequences may be', hinting at the painful and challenging path such redistribution of wealth will be

(p. 55). This demand will require the European working class to side with the formerly colonized nations (p. 62).

Second, for Fanon, any meaningful future must involve remaking the colonized people's sense of self and society, something akin to anthropological rebirth. Under a colonial compartmentalized world, the reigning anthropology is Manichean (pp. 41, 50–1). 'European man' is the civilized and righteous *anthropos*, while colonized masses are vile and ignorant beasts that resemble *anthropos* but lower (pp. 14–15). It contorted colonized people's humanity. This Manichean anthropology is one of the colonial world's support systems. Other colonial support systems include colonially enforced values, cultures, religions, ethics, ontology and biology. They work in unison to fabricate colonial myths that the Caucasian species is leading, helping and civilizing other savage species through European noble conquest and colonization. Speaking in Hegelian terms, Fanon calls this the European spirit that legitimizes colonization (p. 237). This spirit must be annihilated. Colonial binary must be blown into pieces. The two-tiered *anthropos* is an evil invention. Humanity must be reinvented anew. Violence and nonviolent efforts are employed to annihilate the colonial world with all of its theoretical support systems. Non-violent ventures include political empowerment, nationwide education, equitable economic restructuring, societal unification, psychiatric therapy, agrarian reform, international diplomatic posturing, advocacy towards reparation and world peace (pp. 127–30, 138, 92–3, 100–2, 40–1, 60–1, 36, 55). The city intellectuals must encounter, teach and learn from the rural people, who are petrified but are the custodians of precolonial wisdom and culture (pp. 79, 88). Violence, however, plays a significant role in Fanon's anthropological rebirth. Due to the dehumanization that comes with colonial Manichean anthropology, physical and psychiatric tensions wreck the colonized person. In *Black Skin, White Masks*, he argues that these tensions are sociogenic, meaning they come from colonization's oppression (Fanon, 2008). Humiliation and destitution boil the colonized people's blood (Fanon, 2004, p. 17). Dance, possession and rituals are temporary vents for the violent steam (2004, pp. 19–20). Fanon does not see religions as answers either. Religions alienate human agency from changing colonial reality and absolve the colonists from their crimes since all bad things were decreed by God (2004, p. 18). As long as the oppressive colonial order exists, their mental-physical pressure will keep on mounting. Therefore, for Fanon, only decolonial violence cleanses colonized persons (2004, p. 51). In their violent resistance, the colonized will attack colonizers' strongholds, loot their opulence and occupy their places. The colonized will spill colonists' blood, proving once and for all that the Manichean myth is false. The colonized too can understand and change their predicament, even beating the colonists at their own game.[6] Moreover, when violence is rightly orientated towards liberation from colonization, it can remedy the disunity. Proper decolonial violence is national and totalizing. It integrates the fractured colonized people (2004, pp. 51, 83–84). In a decolonial war, Fanon observes that various groups of people who used to fall into the colonists' *divide et impera* strategy begin to reconcile with each other (2004, p. 44). Fanon claims that in such a condition, old resentment dies down. 'The villages witness a permanent display of spectacular generosity and disarming kindness, and an unquestioned determination to die for the "cause". All of this is reminiscent of a religious brotherhood, a church, or a mystical doctrine' (2004, p. 84). He says it restores their dignity, purging 'their inferiority complex, of their passive and despairing attitude. It emboldens them and restores their self-confidence' (2004, p. 51). Not all decolonial violence must be physical in nature. Symbolical violence like hoisting the national flag, singing the national anthem or speaking local languages also affirms colonized people's humanity. Cleansed from their dehumanization, decolonized people experience moral repair and can begin to work towards their Sartrean transcendence (2004, p. 46). Physical violence becomes metaphysical violence that slays the European spirit (Fanon, 2004, p. 34; Yountae, 2021).

Excursion on violence as redeeming humanity

In these parts of *The Wretched of the Earth*, Fanon advocates a manic call to the arms for overtly violent catharsis. Quoting Aimé Césaire, Fanon apparently sacralizes decolonial violence by utilizing the religious term of baptism (2004, pp. 46, 42). Fanon appropriates theological constructs to explain his soteriology, anthropology and ecclesiology. Decolonial violence redeems the colonized people from the sin of colonial Manichean anthropology into a new humanity that is united as new ecclesia (pp. 84, 96). From many Christian perspectives, this is an incomplete anthropology, deranged soteriology and misguided ecclesiology. Putting violence as the key redeeming and uniting agent, Fanon treads a path similar to Mikhail Bakunin's (Knight, 2012). Like Ludwig Feuerbach and Karl Marx, he underestimates the power of religion to humanize and unify people under oppression.

Fanon's sacralization of violence as the path towards humanity is problematic, especially because he wrote from the context of Algeria, which is part of the larger North and West Africa. These nations' historical memory is rich with resistance movements that started from religious convictions, especially Islam. Two astounding examples are Ahmadou Bamba and Emir Abd El-Kader. Bamba was a Sufi religious leader who led non-violent resistance against French colonialism (De Jong, 2022). He successfully improved his people's spiritual, mental, intellectual, political and material conditions. Well after his death, Bamba was feared and respected by the French colonial government and Senegalese people. Algeria's own history holds one of the best examples of religious power in uniting and humanizing people: El-Kader. He was a religious leader of the Sufi Qadiriyya tariqa. El-Kader led the armed resistance when the French colonial troops first invaded Algeria. Sufi spirituality was not tangential to his jihad campaign against the European invaders (Kiser, 2013; Marston, 2013). Instead, it was the key unifying and humanizing factor. Even French colonial authority deeply respected his smart battle tactics, upright moral conduct and pious diplomatic actions. With Bishop Antoine-Adolphe Dupuch, El-Kader ensured the people's and prisoners' safety. When the French government cheated him into imprisonment in France, he repeatedly expressed his forgiveness and positive trust that the French government would fulfil its promise. In the end, he amassed huge support among the French nobility, who pressed the government to release him from imprisonment. Even in his exile he defended Christians from the violent mob in the Damascus 1860 riot. In his life, Pope Pius IX, Abraham Lincoln and Napoleon III showered him with honours. Enemies and friends alike acknowledged him as a holy and noble man. Encountering El-Kader on the battlefield or in his residence, many Europeans recognized the humanity of this Arab man, which was often more humane than they were. Sufism's strong emphasis on the contemplation of God does not need to distract people from resistance movements against colonialism; instead, it can animate them (Muedini, 2015). Religions, in short, can unite and humanize colonized people to improve their psychological and material conditions. Fanon's dismissal of religions, including Islam and Christianity, is understandable because of the role that religions have played in colonialism worldwide, but perhaps a bit reductive. As we will see in the later part of the chapter below, in Christ, Christians can encounter true humanity that exhibits virtues of charity, hope, faith, justice, prudence, temperance and courage. Christ's ecclesia can, but does not have to, be an escapist and acquiescent society. Instead, it actively promotes the common good and justice. It is even ready to break conventional rules by inciting rebellion against tyrants, such as colonial governments, and enacting wealth retributions.[7] Yet all these actions must be governed by charity and prudence, not vengeance and manic bloodlust. Humans truly flourish as humans by contemplating God, not the blood of his oppressors. Only Christ's blood offers redemption, including redemption from perpetual violence, for he is the ultimate Girardian scapegoat (Girard, 1986).

Even outside Christianity, many disagree with Fanon's bloody path. Hannah Arendt, for example, sees violence as the death of politics (Bhabha, 2004, p. xxxvi). Judith Butler also expresses a similar concern about violence as a pure instrument. Butler sees weakness in Fanon's insistence that seeing self-creation cannot be separated from violence (Butler, 2008). Here, Homi Bhabha expresses a crucial point: decolonial violence is the colonized people's desperate means to overcome oppression and create the possibility of politics by and for the colonized people (Bhabha, 2004, p. xxiv). While violence during decolonization war might be unavoidable, after having achieved independence, postcolonial nations need to purge themselves from cycles of violence through truth-telling, judicial trial, reparation, reconciliation, cultivation of civic-democratic culture, and societal restructuration towards non-oppressive forms of life.

While Fanon's faith in violence as a key to humanization is mistaken, his proposal for the postcolonial world is bigger than it. A fair reading of *The Wretched of the Earth* must acknowledge that spilling blood is neither Fanonian only nor the end goal. The ultimate goal is forging a just, unified and stable life as an independent nation (Fanon, 2004, pp. 83–99). Fanon is not a vengeful sadist. He says: 'Hatred is not an agenda' (p. 89). Fanon gives no incitement for counter-genocide or terrorism in Europe as a vengeance. While Fanon embraces decolonial violence, he is not addicted to it. As a practising psychiatrist, Fanon fully realizes the price of violence to the psyche of resistance fighters, colonial victims and colonists. Analysing Fanonian violence, Lewis Gordon says that the colonial system and its dissolution make monsters out of us (Gordon, 2015, p. 124). The last chapter of *The Wretched of the Earth* reminds readers that Fanon helped both decolonial revolutionaries and European soldiers alike. Some of them are colonial troops who had tortured the colonized. In his clinic, Fanon treats them as humans. Hence his relationship to violence is complicated and should not be caricatured. He proposes measured violence, not merely spontaneous and anarchic violence (2004, pp. 92–5). Fanonian decolonial violence resembles a surgical scalpel rather than a blunt axe. For him, violence is a necessary evil to enable better ways of being in the world for the colonized people and the colonists. He denounces indiscriminate violence towards the colonists because, even among them, there are people sympathetic to the colonized's cause (p. 94). Muscular violence needs a purpose and guiding brains so that after the national liberation 'one no longer grabs a gun or a machete every time a colonist approaches' (pp. 95–6). Otherwise the children of revolution will not enjoy a new humanity but a new anarchy.

Fanonian forward-looking reparation: beyond overdetermining identities

Postcolonial countries achieve a new humanity not by imitating the bankrupt European ways of being human but by working with them to do colonial reparation (Fanon, 2004, p. 55; Wynter, 2003). By asking them to pay reparations, postcolonial nations do the right thing both to themselves and to their former colonizers. He says: 'Colonialism and imperialism have not settled their debt to us' and 'The riches which are choking [Europe] are those plundered from the underdeveloped peoples' (Fanon, 2004, p. 58). While the well-being of the formerly colonized nations does not solely depend on fair reparation, with their proper redistribution of wealth, formerly colonized people and their colonizers will be free to forge a better future for all of humanity (p. 55).[8]

Fanon's call in 1961 for reparation as part of the redistribution of wealth is still relevant today. In the Global South, many formerly colonized people still do not own land, capital or technology to realize their new humanity. As Fanon explains, colonialism returns to the formerly colonized people as neocolonialism (2004, pp. 27–8, 35, 99ff.). Neocolonization is spread by western countries and hegemonic non-western powers that have learned well from the West.[9] Ports are leased for decades; natural resources are extracted without benefiting local people; houses and farms are devoured by foreign investment into artificial scarcity; colonial discourses still dictate international laws; and enormous debts with oppressive interest rates still choke developing nations.[10] That is why it is important to acknowledge that colonialism has and is perpetrated also by non-western nations. Hence I will also use the Global North as another name to name these colonizing powers.

Despite its importance, one must reckon with Fanon's statement in *Black Skin, White Masks* before gleaning lessons from Fanonian reparation, which seems to contradict his argument in *The Wretched of the Earth*. In that earlier work, he says: 'I have neither the right nor the duty to claim reparation for the domestication of my ancestors. There is no Negro mission; there is no white burden' (Fanon, 2008, p. 178). How does *The Wretched of the Earth*'s call for reparation relate to *Black Skin, White Masks*' rejection of reparation? The confusion can be resolved by understanding *Black Skin, White Masks*' concern. There, he responds to a specific form of negritude movement by developing Jean-Paul Sartre's ideas (Sartre, 1995). Fanon does not want the colonized to disalienate themselves by refusing 'to accept the present as definitive' (Fanon, 2008, p. 176). The discovery and acknowledgement of the colonized's cultural past is something good. However, tangible material change is the most important thing (Fanon, 2004, p. 180). The past should not be a deterministic essence that dictates who the colonized should be (Fanon, 2008, pp. 175–6). A 'backward-looking stance' does not lead to a new humanity (or transcendence in Sartrean terms).[11] Instead, colonized people should be 'forward-looking' and focus on the present liberation of their fellow oppressed people.[12] In this context, Fanon refuses to seek reparation for his ancestors because 'reparation was about getting access to a site of freedom in which the body and the self are in conversation, a site free of the specters and ghosts of the past' (Verges, 1999). Fanon focuses on reparations that ensure future survival rather than reconciliation or repair for a past. Fanon sees any backward-looking stance as enslaving oneself to the past. It entails an essentialization of the colonized into the colonized *anthropos*, hindering anthropological rebirth and material liberation (2008, p. 175). 'Have I no other purpose on earth, then, but to avenge the Negro of the seventeenth century?' (p. 178). Instead, it is a call to give back the profit that European nations accrued from their colonies so that these new nations may achieve economic security, free to define their new humanity.

Fanonian forward-orientated reparations are helpful in untangling the contemporary conversation surrounding reparations. Scholarship on reparation has identified at least four common difficulties in realizing satisfactory reparation.[13] First, the identities of perpetrators who are responsible for making amends are obscured by time, death, economic transactions and colonial interests. People currently running European governments are not the people who decided to colonize the Third World brutally. Most slaveholders and plantation owners also have already died. The colonizers' descendants do benefit directly or indirectly from the colonization loot.[14] However, they do not merely passively receive such wealth. They feel they have managed or earned it through their labours inside valid legal frameworks. Furthermore, they neither choose to be born as colonizers' children nor condone their ancestors' acts.

When a country makes reparation, its citizens will inevitably bear some of the cost. Second, similar complications also arise in identifying the victims who deserve to receive the amends. Detractors of reparations question how far removed from the original crime descendants can be in order to justly receive compensation. Some demand biological markers as restrictive identification, like DNA, genealogy or blood quantum analysis (Ellinghaus, 2017). Many postcolonial countries' governments are unstable due to colonial haphazard border-making, inherited extractive economy and neocolonial influences. Some have split into two countries or more. Third, satisfactory reparation amounts, forms, laws and goals must be established. Although some formerly colonizing nations have expressed limited forms of verbal apology, many colonizers still refuse.[15] If verbal, sincere and comprehensive apologies are insufficient, what amount of money or material reparation will satisfy the past and current wrongdoings? Both reparation detractors and proponents underline the importance of not making it 'blood money' (Matache and Bhabha, 2021). Fourth, few colonizers are willing to do reparation. Some governments still refuse to teach their children the horror of their ancestors' wrongdoings. Years after independence and emancipation, the prevailing narrative in metropoles is that European nations civilized primitive rebellious subjects that they discovered alongside the empty lands.[16] Beset by the intricacy of their own politics and economic interests, reparation to former colonies is never widely popular among former colonizers.

Frantz Fanon has several things to say about these issues. First, as elucidated above, he envisions a postcolonial world where nations embody new humanity through anthropological and material liberation. While the anthropological liberation of postcolonial countries does not depend on colonizers' guilt-felt apology, these sincere expressions can confirm and edify postcolonial anthropological rebirth. Former colonizers must follow up their apology with material reparations because they still hold on to their former colonies' wealth. Western nations have benefited greatly from robbing the Global South. They have a responsibility to give back. All colonizers' properties need to be rethought in the light of their bloody source. The reparation amount is not measured by what has been lost but by an even more radical vision: redistribution of wealth (Fanon, 2004, p. 55). Those who have enjoyed or benefited from that wealth owe their entire lifestyle to the colonized nations. Fanon reminds contemporary reparation advocates and detractors that colonial stolen loot is choking the Global North (p. 59). By holding on to that wealth, they cling to colonial exploitative modes of living (p. 237). The working class of their nations will not slumber for ever (pp. 62, 237–9). Furthermore, depriving postcolonial people of their reparation will only prolong migration issues that keep the Global North awake at night (p. 61). These powder kegs should motivate the Global North to re-create itself into a new humanity alongside the Global South. Fanon claims that until postcolonized nations get all the necessary wealth, colonizers doom themselves (pp. 58–9).

Second, cautioning his readers from a fixation on the past, Fanon does not mention calculations of all stolen labour of his ancestors, kilograms of minerals stolen or cargo boxes of spices. Instead, for him, the goal of reparation is forward-looking: repossession of land, technologies and capital so that the postcolonial nations can prosper. Substantial improvement of material condition is Fanon's reparation target. The reparation amount should not mirror what was inflicted in the past but what is required for liberatory futures. Here, Fanon anticipates Táíwò's constructivist view of reparation (Táíwò, 2022; Mullen and Darity, 2023).[17] Reparation aims not to return postcolonial nations to recover imagined ancient glory but to propel them from their colonial facticity and achieve better futures. Fanon also counsels the contemporary postcolonial Global South that this transcendence should not follow the exploitative Manichean world of the Global North (2004, pp. 236, 237–8). He pictures this new world-making as spacious enough for all components of all nations, from urban to rural, from Third World nations to former colonial nations (2004, p. 129). In the Capitalocene, such world-making must reckon with the ecological disasters that western colonialism unleashed (Harris, 2017). Currently, climate impacts are borne unequally. Richer and stronger nations discuss various climate resilience plans while formerly colonized nations languish in poverty, struggling to survive against the rising sea and temperature. Wealth redistribution must address this.

Third, Fanon's complete rejection of essentializing people according to their race, class and social location also speaks to contemporary debates on deserving recipients of reparation. Seen from Fanonian texts, the blood quantum arrangement of the US government for American Indians is loathsome.[18] A Fanonian framework sees it as an essentialization of people into their biology. Recipient classification, such as blood quantum, repeats the Manichean anthropological binary from the colonialism playbook. Fanon eschews any restrictive and atomizing identity politics. One's biology, genealogy, census record, gender or sexuality should not imprison them.[19] The fact that someone is currently oppressed by colonialism and its vestiges should qualify them to receive support for transcendence. Hence Fanon's vision is more congenial to intersectional approaches. It seeks out common oppressions of various kinds of people inside postcolonial nations. The liberatory postcolonial agenda unifies people from all walks of life. Reparation then focuses on overcoming these oppressions for everyone's better living.

Fourth, Fanon's high regard for village assemblies (*djemaas* and palavers) is in sync with democratic and non-violent reparation processes (2004, pp. 11–2, 67–79). Echoing Kristen Mullen's recent suggestion, blue-ribbon commissions composed of sympathetic former colonizers and colonized can play key roles in achieving successful reparation (Mullen and Darity, 2023).[20] Truth and Reconciliation Commissions can help the healing process. Careful attention to actively listening to affected communities will prevent the reparation from devolving into merely blood money or, even worse, divisive financial disputes that rend former colonized people's social fabric.[21]

Finally, as An Yountae and Kameron Carter have argued, western colonialism stands on perverse theological grounds that justify the Manichean anthropologies (Yountae, 2021; Carter, 2008). The same theology still grips a sizeable population of the Global North. From the Fanonian perspective, it is imperative that iconoclastic efforts break such evil theology. The next section of this chapter will act as one such effort.

Reading Aquinas as colonized people

I will try to make sense of the postcolonial nations' quest for reparation by reading Thomas Aquinas from a postcolonial agenda. Hence from Aquinas' enormous theological architecture I will focus on areas where he diagnoses the perils of subjugated people and provides effective solutions to them. I will highlight two virtues in the relationship with postcolonial reparation: justice and charity. Justice is the moral virtue that demands one to render to everyone what they deserve. In this case, formerly colonizing nations and their descendants must make reparation to the colonized nation and its descendants. The second one is a theological virtue that enables us to love God as a friend and love anything that God loves. In the case of postcolonial reparation, it means sharing wealth and opportunity with the people from formerly colonized nations who are still suffering from the effects of colonization. Even if the direct perpetrators and victims have passed away, the predicament among the postcolonial nations for acts of charity still exists. I will situate the explanation of both virtues in Aquinas' larger framework of anthropology and its full flourishing. While some disagreements between Aquinas and Fanon will surely surface, I will argue that reparation is not only good for the colonized nations but necessary for faithful Christian living.

Material condition as necessary for virtue and blessedness

In Aquinas' *Summa Theologica* (*ST*), access to material things deeply relates to humans' quest to achieve their end. Humans' ultimate end is their happiness (*ST* I-II.5.3). They can only achieve perfect happiness through participating in God. A person's goal is to rest in union with God through their intellect because God is the ultimate goodness; God is happy by God's nature (*ST* I-II.3.2.ad. 1; 2.4.1). Perfection of this union is unattainable in this life because no one can fully experience or see God fully in this life (*ST* I.12.11). What they can do in this life is enjoy imperfect happiness by actively practising virtues, growing in imperfect contemplation of God and having imperfect communion with God (*ST* I-II.5.3; 181.4; II-II.23.ad. 1).

While perfect happiness is achievable without material possessions, humans need to use material goods to stay alive and enjoy imperfect happiness in this life (*ST* I-II.4.7). Aquinas says: 'External goods are required for the imperfect happiness open to us in this life, not that they lie at the heart of happiness, yet they are tools to serve happiness' (*ST* I-II.4.7). Material necessities enable humans to flourish into their full body, virtue, social, mental and contemplative potentials (*ST* I-II.4.5, 7; Lefebure, 2006). 'Ownership of them is required' so humans can develop and practise virtues (*ST* I-II.4.7). When cultivated and practised, these virtues reorient our passions and thoughts towards the right actions and contemplation of God.[22]

The human need for material things coincides with God's providential arrangement for them. God established as a natural law that humans should be able to use the world's goods for sustenance (*ST* II-II.66.7). Reflecting on Numbers 33.53–54, Aquinas says God wants humans to divide among themselves property into private holdings (*ST* I-II.105.2; Lefebure, 2006). Aquinas follows Augustine in that the division and apportionment of resources are not established by natural law but by human agreement (*ST* II-II.66.2). These agreements are embodied in positive laws written and upheld by rulers of this world. Agreeing with Aristotle, Aquinas mentions that without laws regulating possession, many states have been ruined. The laws must establish a just and loving order among humans' private ownership so everyone can benefit from the earth's resources (*ST* II-II.66.2.ad. 2; 66.7). Thus, in *ST* I-II.105.2, Aquinas asserts that laws should aim to divide equally according to the principle of justice (Num. 33.54). No one should monopolize resources or unreasonably bar others from using their property (*ST* II-II.66.2.ad. 2). When there is an imbalance of property, people with superabundance should share with people experiencing poverty. This is God's natural law (*ST* II-II.66.7). If it does not happen, the wealthy are not giving others what is due to them (*ST* II-II.66.7). This is injustice (*ST* II-II.66.5; II-II.58.1). Consequently, wealth injustice contradicts God's natural law that all humans should get proper nourishment from the earth (*ST* II-II.66.7).

Justice: functional and dysfunctional government

For Aquinas, all governments should rule according to this divine benevolent will. Hence kings and leaders must secure two kinds of justice: distributive and commutative (*ST* II-II.61.1; II-II.58.6-7). Distributive justice concerns what individuals should get from the community (*ST* II-II.61.3). Practically, leaders ensure access to abundant material goods for their subjects. Aquinas says these goods are crucial for virtuous conduct in his *De Regimine Principum* (*DRP*) (*DRP* XVI, in Dyson, 2002). They also should supply the people with internal safety, external security, unity and peace (*DRP* XVI). Commutative justice covers equal exchange between individuals. Theft, robbery, usury, defamation, fraud and violent assault breach commutative justice (*ST* II-II.61.3; 66.4). Any injury that disturbs commutative justice should be settled. Like many other church theologians, Aquinas contends that wealth can have moral valence.[23] Unjust accumulation morally taints the wealth in question. It contaminates the owners' lives, jeopardizing their virtues. Unjustly accrued wealth is unfit for withholding, giving or using. Here Aquinas gives theological grounds for Fanon's mysterious insistence that the stolen colonial riches are choking Europe (2004, pp. 58-9). For Aquinas, this unjustly accumulated and withheld wealth cannot even be used for donations to the church or as alms (*ST* II-II.32.7). Perpetrators must recompense the victims' loss until an equilibrium returns (*ST* II-II.61.3). In the contemporary case of postcolonial nations, this equilibrium has long gone and is difficult to calculate. Fanon's forward-looking reparation is more realistic. In fact, in Aquinas' letter to the Duchess of

Brabant, he acknowledges the inaccessibility of the past equilibrium. He says reparation must be returned to the rightful owner as restitution if tracking them is possible. If not, it should fund public goods (Aquinas, 'Letter to the Duchess of Brabant', in Dyson, 2002). If sovereigns do not uphold commutative justice, Aquinas says they are blameworthy and even responsible, to some extent, for paying reparation (*ST* II-II.61.3).

Aquinas cautions leaders who do not govern well: 'A tyrannical government is unjust because it is not directed to the common good' (*ST* II-II.42.2.ad. 3). They 'govern for the ruler's personal advantage to the people's harm' (*ST* II-II.42.2.ad. 3). Such tyrants bring peril to themselves and their people (*DRP* XI). The people are tacitly smart and know that they are getting the short end of the stick. They are eager to topple the hated tyrants who oppress them (*DRP* XI). Aquinas asserts that rebelling against tyrannical governments is not sedition. Instead, 'it is tyrants that are more guilty of sedition' because they breed discord and dissension among their subjects, robbing them of distributive goods (*ST* II-II.42.2.ad. 3; 61.3). Tyrants think they can rely on fear as mass control. Yet 'fear is a weak foundation' (*DRP* XI). There will be fearless or desperate subjects who are ready to fling themselves to the peril of death as long as the tyrant is gone (*DRP* VII, XI). Aquinas illustrates their pent-up anger as compressed water that will burst forth vigorously (*DRP* XI). Fanon's readers will easily recall the people's tense muscles that are ready to spring, slaying the colonists (Fanon, 2004, p. 16).

Aquinas, however, cautions the people. While unbearable tyrants should get what they deserve, some less oppressive tyrants should be tolerated (*DRP* VII). He is wary that an internal or external coup that topples the tyrant will simply become a new tyrant worse than their predecessor, perpetuating the oppressions (*DRP* VII). Rebellion's *telos* lay beyond merely expelling the tyrants. The goal is liberating the community and forging better living conditions. Therefore people should carefully consider the risks and benefits of seditions. Concerning the decision for the coup, Aquinas says the deliberation of a single individual is not enough. Aquinas suggests that public authorities should be consulted (*DRP* VII). The resulting disorder from the rebellion must not be so 'excessive that the people suffer more from it than from the tyrannical regime' (*ST* II-II.42.2.ad. 3). Here, echoes of Fanon's decolonial disorder to achieve better material conditions can be heard. Aquinas is notably more conscientious, though. He does not want to see a rebellion that hurts the people more than it helps.

At this point we can see that both Aquinas and Fanon want every person to have free access to good material conditions because it is crucial for their flourishing. Aquinas situates it in a larger frame of social, political, moral and spiritual flourishing, while Fanon focuses on psychological, social and political flourishing. Although Aquinas arguably has a more integral anthropological vision (Maritain, 1939), his view can relativize the importance of material condition in the name of spiritual reasons. It also opens doors to too easily yielding to corrupt and oppressive tyrants. Even worse, quoting Hosea 13.11 and Job 34.30, Aquinas put oppressed people's sin as the possible cause of endless tyrannical government (*DRP* VII). Such an argument is very conducive to transforming Christianity into perverse colonial theodicy: the gentile savage nations deserve European tyrannical colonial rules because they are sinners (Gutiérrez, 1987). Fanon's postcolonial insistence on humane material conditions can prevent perverse co-optations of Aquinas' view.

Charity: functional and dysfunctional wealth sharing

Accepting the Aristotelian distinction of ownership and usage, Aquinas believes material things should be owned and managed privately but aimed for the common interest (*ST* II-II.66.3; *ST* II-II.32.5.ad. 2). Wealth inequalities that will and have occurred do not refute the soundness of private property as a system. Disparity of wealth does not mean private wealth is illicit. Citing Basil the Great, Aquinas says that the rich have more, so they may learn to manage wealth well by sharing, and the poor may learn the virtue of patience (*ST* II-II.66.2.ad. 2). Humans should personally decide through virtue of prudence what and how to share with others in need (*ST* II-II.66.7). No one should lack anything they need because everyone should be generously eager to share their superfluous property (*ST* II-II.32.8). Generous sharing for common use should solve any problems that may arise from wealth inequality (*ST* II-II.66.3).

Generosity flows naturally from the chief virtue: charity. Charity is love but not ordinary human love. Charity is mutual loving between humans and God; every party wishes for what is good for others in a friendship. Without charity, no one can enjoy the salvation or eternal life that Christ's Passion has achieved for humankind (*ST* I-II.114.4; III.49.1). The object of charity covers not only God but also all other humans, both their bodies and souls (*ST* II-II.32.5). Charity demands corporal almsgiving to remedy others' miseries from lack of material sustenance.[24] Reflecting larger Christian traditions, Aquinas asserts that almsgiving is not unidirectional. Rather, by sharing their wealth with the destitute, almsgivers receive spiritual fruits, prayer and protection against evil tendencies (*ST* II-II.32.4). Hence, Thomist almsgiving is not a humanitarian donation but a reciprocal act of charity that builds friendship and edifies both parties (Bruni and Zamagni, 2007).

Among people in need of alms, one must prioritize giving to those with extreme needs, as in matters of life and death (*ST* II-II.32.4). Quoting Ambrose, Aquinas says refusing to feed people starving to death is killing them (*ST* II-II.32.5). When no one else can help, denying the destitute their alms constitutes a mortal sin. Matthew 25 links such actions with eternal punishment (*ST* II-II.32.5). Failure to do alms impedes charity and one's eternal life. Encounters with the destitute impinge on someone's claim to their own property, even the property they need to function and live decently. It pierces the perimeter of necessary possession, turning what is private into common.

In a perfect society, every person in need gets help. Moral tension ends at giving within means and beyond one's means. Justice is practised and charity is cherished. Unfortunately, no one lives in a perfect world. When someone is in severe destitution, people with excess wealth might either not be present to help or flatly refuse to give alms. While the first situation is understandable, the second reason contradicts justice and charity. Aquinas condemns people who are keeping private property that should be given to the impoverished. He tells them: 'You are committing as many injustices as there are things you could give away' (*ST* II-II.32.5.ad. 2). Describing uncharitable people, Aquinas says: 'Retaining what one owes another does the same sort of harm as taking something from another, and this is why unjustifiable taking must be held to include unjustifiable retention' (*ST* II-II.66.3.ad. 2). In other words, refusing to give alms without genuine ground is stealing from the poor who deserve to get the alms. Any unjustifiable withholding is theft.

Quasi-robbery as commutative justice against unjustified withholding

Expecting this to happen, Aquinas supplies further guidelines. When people witness a destitute person in need but without a means of help, they may take the property of others to aid the person in need (*ST* II-II.32.7.ad. 3). Aquinas quickly adds that consent of the property owner should be sought, if possible, and 'can be done without danger' (*ST* II-II.32.8.ad. 1). When no one is willing to help, the destitute themselves may take the property of others to preserve their lives (*ST*

II-II.32.7.ad. 3). For Aquinas, such taking is not properly speaking a theft/robbery (*ST* II-II.66.7). Inherent in the definition of stealing/robbery is the notion of injustice (*ST* II-II.66.4, 66.5). Justice is served when the destitute gets help. If they are left to die, injustice happens. Thus, in dire need, taking other people's property is not stealing (*ST* II-II.66.7). It is an act of commutative justice. Even if the taking is witnessed by and presumably is done with coercion towards the unwilling owner, Aquinas asserts that this is not robbery (*ST* II-II.66.4; 66.7). Necessity diminishes or erases all fault from the action (*ST* II-II.66.6.ad. 1; *ST* II-II.66.6.ad. 2).[25] Necessity is capable of transforming someone's private property into common property to be used by the people in need. This necessity exposes the society's failure to enact justice and charity in their human laws. Hence the natural laws take over (*ST* II-II.66.7). The real thieves and robbers are people with excess wealth who are unwilling to help the destitute (*ST* II-II.66.3.ad. 2). The quasi-stealing by the destitute person is restitution for the unjustly withheld wealth.

Considering all preceding arguments, Aquinas' words in II-II.32.7 succinctly describe the condition of private property in this imperfect world of his age: 'We can say that all riches are said to be of iniquity, that is, of inequality, because of their unequal distribution, one man being in need, another having too much' (*ST* II-II.32.7.ad. 1). Undistributed inequality is iniquity.

Aquinas with Fanon on reparation

Reading Fanon and Aquinas side by side from the perspectives of postcolonial nations, there are at least two frameworks for reparation advocacy. First, colonial governments are tyrannical regimes that trample distributive and commutative justice, making them bound to pay reparation to the postcolonial nations. Western colonial governments sought their metropoles' advantage without regard to colonized people's lives. Their dehumanizing and extractive political economy knew no virtues. As early as 1537, Pope Paul III published a papal bull reiterating that 'Native Americans were rational beings with souls whose lives and property should be protected' (Kiernan, 2007, as cited in Hofreiter, 2018). Yet in their avaricious lust they simply did not want to practise distributive justice for their colonial subjects (*ST* II-II.42.2.ad. 3; *DRP* XI, VII). Instead of providing goods, they committed treachery; fraud, theft, raping, kidnapping, forced labour and enslavement were rampant. Moreover, former colonial governments are responsible for recompense for failing to uphold commutative justice. As the party that claimed and acted as if they were the authorities of the colonized lands, they must recompense the colonial robbery that their settlers did under their watch (*ST* II-II.62.7). Spanish, Portuguese, French, British, German, Dutch and American empires treated American Indian, African and Asian people savagely, without charity, abusing them and their lands. These abhorrent colonial situations, unsurprisingly, resulted in armed rebellion. Hence, according to Aquinas and Fanon, a decolonial war against an unbearable tyrant's regime is an unfortunate but justified one. If orientated rightly, religions and cultures can galvanize humane and unified resistances. Violence might happen but should not be seen as redeeming, humanizing or uniting. After independence, the nationalization of colonizers' land and business is also justified when seen as forced reparation of colonial injustice (Aquinas, 'Letter', in Dyson, 2002). Here, Fanon's call for reparation of land and bread from the clutch of colonizers resembles Aquinas' defence of the Israelites' looting of the Egyptians (Fanon, 2004, p. 14; *ST* 66.5.ad. 1). Western colonial powers must apologize for what they have done, not to inflict white guilt but so that the work of repentance, reconciliation and forgiveness may truly start. Furthermore, the formerly colonizing governments must pay reparations. Wealth has moral valence. Without proper reparation, the colonial loot that animates their economies is tainting their moral, social, economic and spiritual life. Colonial reparations purge this filthy money by restituting commutative and distributive justice that colonizers have failed to uphold in the past. Otherwise, these spoils choke the former colonizers from virtuous lives.

Second, former colonizing western countries are responsible for sharing their wealth because charity demands corporal almsgiving. Indeed, the specific identities of recipients and givers might be murky, but the extreme need and wealth gap are clear. Even if western countries do not think that they are the direct perpetrators of colonialism, the fact is they have the financial power to help but withhold their wealth from colonized nations. This is unjustified withholding. People in postcolonial nations are dying from AIDS, lack of clean water and proper hygiene, while the West hoards treasures that they took by violence from the ancestors of these destitute souls. Reparation is the demand of justice. The world needs consistent wealth redistribution in the form of almsgiving. Each western country must prioritize doing reparation to struggling postcolonial countries with which they have a colonial past (*ST* II-II.32.9).

The amount of reparation is measured by the need to build postcolonial nations in the Capitalocene. The reparations must exceed the amount required to restore postcolonial nations to good living. This is because justice also demands reparation for non-material injuries and the breaking of peace among nations that colonial nations have inflicted on colonized people and their descendants (*ST* II-II.61.4; 62.2.ad. 3). Due to Aquinas' dependence on the Aristotelian framework, he mostly thinks reparation is about recovering past equilibrium. Counting stolen labour and every agricultural harvest during colonialism is impossible to get right. Here, postcolonial insights from Fanon can aid in widening Thomist vision. Reparation can focus instead on returning the commutative justice between formerly colonized and colonized nations.

Refusing to do reparation well will only exacerbate the world's problems. Forward-looking reparation must focus on helping postcolonial nations aim to forge a better future. For starters, some wealth and artefacts can be easily tracked and returned.[26] Debt can be cancelled. International scholarships should be dedicated to students from formerly colonized nations. Thomist reparation also must include climate justice because colonialism often entails wrecking the natural environment for profit (Táíwò, 2022). Reparations help the Global South withstand the effects of climate disasters that the Global North has caused. Otherwise the postcolonial nations cannot live well in their own land. The countries of the Global North should not be surprised if multitudes of people from postcolonial countries keep on coming to their land. Worse bewilderment happened centuries ago when the western colonizers burned, raped, looted and conquered the Global South. Hence the immigration policy of formerly colonizing nations should reflect their past wrongdoings.

Christian charity demands redistribution of wealth. This is not a humanitarian charity out of pity. This is their duty of love. Failure to do so means the leaders and people of the West are committing mortal sins, jeopardizing their blessedness and eternal life. If we take Matthew 25 and Thomism seriously, the West is queueing in the line of goats. No confession or repentance will matter until the reparation is paid (*ST* II-II.62.2). Fanon sums it up splendidly:

> The basic confrontation which seemed to be colonialism versus anti-colonialism, indeed capitalism versus socialism, is already losing its importance. What matters today, the issue that blocks the horizon, is the need for a redistribution of wealth. Humanity will have to address this question, no matter how devastating the consequences may be. (Fanon, 2004)

Like Fanon, Aquinas is adamant: undistributed inequality is iniquity.

Notes

1 The current structures of neocolonialism continue to suffocate the so-called developing countries. It is imperative to stop it and make reparations for these exploitative patterns. The same urgency also applies to the case of reparation for the enslavement of millions of African and African American people in the Americas. Various colonial dispossession that befell indigenous people of the Americas, Australia and New Zealand also must be addressed. However, due to space restrictions, this chapter will focus on reparation for past colonization between western and postcolonial nations. Because of the many similarities between these reparation cases, readers interested in related reparations might also benefit from this discussion.

2 'Capitalocene' refers to the current world's epoch in which capitalism significantly leaves ruinous impacts on the earth's ecosystems. Seeing the world this way highlights how economic systems driven by profit and accumulation have contributed to social injustice, ecological degradation and suppression of other ways of being. For a deeper exploration of it from a theological perspective, see Joerg Rieger, 2022, *Theology in the Capitalocene: Ecology, Identity, Class, and Solidarity*, Minneapolis, MN: Fortress Press, pp. 197–9.

3 Writing a dialogical paper between Aquinas and Fanon might sound like an oxymoron. The former is a western Christian thinker whose theologies are part and parcel of western, especially Catholic, empires. The latter is a champion of decolonization who rejects any western colonial metaphysics, keenly annihilating colonization with violence. In spite of their differences, this chapter will seek to find intersections of interests among them. See different but complementary arguments for the relevancy of Thomism in post/decolonial discourse in Callum Scott, 2019, 'The Decolonial Aquinas? Discerning Epistemic Worth for Aquinas in the Decolonial Academy', *South African Journal of Philosophy* 38(1), pp. 40–54; David Lantigua, 2015, 'The Freedom of the Gospel: Aquinas, Subversive Natural Law, and the Spanish Wars of Religion', *Modern Theology* 31(2), pp. 312–37.

4 'Anthropological rebirth' is a term that I propose, not one that Fanon used.

5 Bhabha also read Fanon in a similar way; cf. Bhabha, 2004, p. xi.

6 Fanon, 2004, pp. 16, 44. Fanon thinks that by being able to drive out the colonists, the colonized reasserted their intelligence, strength, fortitude, wisdom, mercy and kindness beyond the vile *anthropos* of colonial myth.

7 See the exploration of Thomas Aquinas' *ST* II-II.42.2.ad. 3 and 61.3 below.

8 Important as it is, formerly colonized people are not at the mercy of their former colonizers' reparation. Through various forms of solidarity economy, formerly colonized people can flourish even without proper reparation: see Nembhard, 2014; Mohammad Hatta, 1957, *The Co-operative Movement in Indonesia*, Ithaca, NY: Cornell University, pp. 29–35.

9 I of course do not mean to forget eastern nations' historic empires and colonization. Ancient Chinese empires have been the historic hegemonic power in East Asia and Indochina. Beyond them, the Mongol Empire, the Ottoman Sultanate and the Japanese Empire were colonizing powers. However, few are as dehumanizing and totalizing as the European empires' colonization.

10 See, for example, Makhura Rapanyane, 2021, 'Neocolonialism and New Imperialism: Unpacking the Real Story of China's Africa Engagement in Angola,

Kenya, and Zambia', *Journal of African Foreign Affairs* 8(3); Hilary Beckles, 2021, *How Britain Underdeveloped the Caribbean: A Reparation Response to Europe's Legacy of Plunder and Poverty*, Jamaica: University of the West Indies Press.

11 Fanon, 2008, pp. 175ff. On forward and backward orientation, see Chris Buck, 2004, p. 124.

12 'I am not a prisoner of history. I should not seek there for the meaning of my destiny. I should constantly remind myself that the real leap consists in introducing invention into existence. In the world through which I travel, I am endlessly creating myself' (Fanon, 2008, p. 179).

13 These four obstacles are my condensation of several reparation proposals and success stories. See them in Jacqueline Bhabha, Margareta Matache and Caroline Elkins (eds), 2021, *Time for Reparations: A Global Perspective*, Philadelphia, PA: University of Pennsylvania; Lenzerini, 2008.

14 Descendants of plantation owners and government officials might still inherit wealth extracted from the colony. These are direct beneficiaries of colonization loot. Low- and middle-class people in colonizing countries might have no direct ownership of the loot but indirectly through a higher quality of life, richer national economy and stronger social safety net.

15 See, for example, French relationships with African countries under its sphere of monetary influence in Pérez, 2022, pp. 851–87 and Sylla, 2021, pp. 32–49.

16 See, for example, Susan Slyomovics, 2021, p. 203.

17 It is interesting to note that Táíwò neither uses nor quotes Fanon at all in his reparation book, yet he arrived at a very similar conclusion.

18 The blood quantum policy is a criterion for deciding eligibility for tribal membership and benefits within Native American communities. This policy quantifies an individual's Native American ancestry as a percentage, often requiring a specific fraction, such as one-quarter or one-eighth. While intended to establish a connection between individuals and their indigenous heritage, the blood quantum policy is arbitrary, divisive and destructive. See Doerfler, 2017, pp. 41–7; Ashleigh Lussenden, 2023, 'Blood Quantum and the Ever-Tightening Chokehold on Tribal Citizenship: The Reproductive Justice Implications of Blood Quantum Requirements', *California Law Review* 111, pp. 287–324.

19 Cultures and races are not eternal or permanent structures. Colonial realities caused colonists and colonized to be transformed. Identities are floating and negotiated under the colonial power dynamics. Basing reparation on such concepts only reinforces its deadly grip on the contemporary world. Essentialist approaches that do not recognize this creolization are incompatible with Fanon's new humanity. See Gilroy, 1993.

20 Mullen and Darity (2023) take this lesson from the post-Second World War Japanese American reparation effort. Independent reparation commissions with diverse, highly regarded experts and national figures raise the acceptance level of reparation efforts.

21 See Immler, 2021, pp. 161, 164–7, where Nicole Immler noticed the communal nature of colonization wounds and their healing process during her study of the Netherlands' reparation to decolonization war victims in Indonesia. Lack of communication and social sensitivity in the court proceedings caused conflicts to arise from the distribution of the reparation in the victims' community. In the end, victims are doubly wounded.

22 On passions, affections and souls in *ST*, see Robert Miner, 2009, *Thomas Aquinas on the Passions: A Study of* Summa Theologiae, *1a2ae 22–48*, Cambridge: Cambridge University; Thomas Dixon, 2003, *From Passion to Emotions: The Creation of a Secular Psychological Category*, Cambridge: Cambridge University.

23 See Bruni and Zamagni, 2007.

24 If a spiritual or moral defect is the problem, one should do the spiritual almsgiving (admonishment, rebuke etc.). See divisions of almsgiving according to the misery in *ST* II-II.32.2.

25 Whose properties should be the priority targets of restitution? If the destitute have options, they should take it from wealthier people rather than those in danger of poverty. Impoverishing another person to preserve oneself is passing on the destitution problem. Among the more affluent, people who unjustly withhold their wealth from almsgiving should be the preferred target. Those who actively impoverish others but escape human laws should be the highest priority. Be it avaricious businessmen who exploit the labourers or corrupt politicians, restitution is ripe for such people. They are the worst thieves of society, those whom Aquinas says are guilty of peculation. According to him, it is a mortal sin that deserves the death penalty by authorities. See *ST* II-II.66.6.ad. 2.

26 The contemporary French government's audacity in its colonial pride can be witnessed in its prolonged rejection of returning the colonial archives to Algeria. See how they make bargaining chips out of Algerian people's historical record in Slyomovics, 2021.

References

Aquinas, T., *Summa Theologica (ST)*.
Bhabha, H., 2004, 'Foreword', in F. Fanon, *The Wretched of the Earth*, trans. Richard Philcox, New York: Grove.
Bruni, L. and Zamagni, S., 2007, *Civil Economy: Efficiency, Equity, and Public Happiness*, Bern: Peter Lang.
Buck, C., 2004, 'Sartre, Fanon, and the Case for Slavery Reparations', *Sartre Studies International* 10(2), pp. 123–38.
Butler, J., 2008, 'Violence, Nonviolence: Sartre on Fanon', in J. Judaken (ed.), *Race after Sartre: Antiracism, Africana Existentialism, Postcolonialism*, New York: University of New York, pp. 211–32.
Carter, K., 2008, *Race: A Theological Account*, Oxford: Oxford University Press.
De Jong, F., 2022, *Decolonizing Heritage: Time to Repair in Senegal*, Cambridge: Cambridge University Press.
Doerfler, J., 2017, '"We aren't like Dogs": Battling Blood Quantum', *Wasafiri* 32(2), pp. 41–7.
Dyson, R. W. (ed.), 2002, *Aquinas: Political Writings*, Cambridge: Cambridge University Press.
Ellinghaus, K., 2017, *Blood Will Tell: Native Americans and Assimilation Policy*, Lincoln: University of Nebraska.
Fanon, F., 2004, *The Wretched of the Earth*, trans. Richard Philcox, New York: Grove.

Fanon, F., 2008, *Black Skin, White Masks*, trans. Charles Markmann, London: Pluto.
Gilroy, P., 1993, *The Black Atlantic: Modernity and Double Consciousness*, Cambridge: Harvard University Press.
——— 2019, 'Never Again: Refusing Race and Salvaging the Human', 2019 Holberg Lecture, Bergen, Norway.
Girard, R., 1986, *The Scapegoat*, Baltimore, MD: Johns Hopkins University Press.
Gordon, L., 2015, *What Fanon Said: A Philosophical Introduction to His Life and Thought*, New York: Fordham University Press.
Gutiérrez, G., 1987, *On Job: God-Talk and the Suffering of the Innocent*, Maryknoll, NY: Orbis Books.
Harris, M., 2017, *Ecowomanism: African American Women and Earth-Honoring Faiths*, Maryknoll, NY: Orbis Books.
Harris, M. L., 2017, 'Ecowomanism and Ecological Reparations', in J. Hart (ed.), *The Wiley Blackwell Companion to Religion and Ecology*, Hoboken: Wiley & Sons, pp. 195–202.
Hofreiter, C., 2018, *Making Sense of Old Testament Genocide: Christian Interpretations of Herem Passages*, Oxford: Oxford University Press.
Immler, N., 2021, 'Colonial History at Court: Legal Decisions and their Social Dilemmas', in J. Bhabha, M. Matache and C. Elkins (eds), *Time for Reparations: A Global Perspective*, Philadelphia, PA: University of Pennsylvania Press, pp. 153–68.
Kiernan, B., 2007, *Blood and Soil: A World History of Genocide and Extermination from Sparta to Darfur*, New Haven, CT: Yale University Press.
Kiser, J., 2013, *Commander of the Faithful: The Life and Times of Emir Abd El-Kader (1808–1883)*, New York: Monkfish.
Knight, R., 2012, 'Anti-colonial Anarchism, or Anarchistic Anti-Colonialism: The Similarities in the Revolutionary Theories of Frantz Fanon and Mikhail Bakunin', *Theory in Action* 5(4), pp. 82–92.
Lantigua, D., 2015, 'The Freedom of the Gospel: Aquinas, Subversive Natural Law, and the Spanish Wars of Religion', *Modern Theology* 31(2), pp. 312–37.
Lefebure, M., 2006, 'Appendix 2', in Thomas Aquinas, *Summa Theologiae: Volume 38, Injustice: 2a2ae. 63–79*, Cambridge: Cambridge University Press.
Lenzerini, F., 2008, *Reparations for Indigenous Peoples: International and Comparative Perspectives*, Oxford: Oxford University Press.
Makhura, R., 2021, 'Neocolonialism and New Imperialism: Unpacking the Real Story of China's Africa Engagement in Angola, Kenya, and Zambia', *Journal of African Foreign Affairs* 8(3), pp. 89–112.
Maritain, J., 1939, 'Integral Humanism and the Crisis of Modern Times', *The Review of Politics* 1(1), pp. 1–17.
Marston, E., 2013, *The Compassionate Warrior: Abd El-Kader of Algeria*, Bloomington, IN: Wisdom Tales.
Matache, M. and Bhabha, J., 2021, 'The Roma Case for Reparations', in J. Bhabha, M. Matache and C. Elkins (eds), *Time for Reparations: A Global Perspective*, Philadelphia, PA: University of Pennsylvania, pp. 253–71.
Miller, R., 2019, 'The Doctrine of Discovery: The International Law of Colonialism', *The Indigenous People's Journal of Law, Culture, and Resistance* 5(1), pp. 35–42.

Muedini, F., 2015, 'Sufism and Anti-Colonial Violent Resistance Movements: The Qadiriyya and Sanussi Orders in Algeria and Libya', *Open Theology* 1(1), pp. 134–45.

Mullen, K. and Darity, W., 2023, 'Learning from Past Experiences with Reparations', in W. Darity, K. Mullen, L. Hubbard (eds), *The Black Reparations Project: A Handbook for Racial Justice*, Berkeley, CA: University of California, pp. 111–37.

Nembhard, J., 2014, *Collective Courage: A History of African American Cooperative Economic Thought and Practice*, University Park, PA: Pennsylvania State University.

Pérez, F. J., 2022, 'An Enduring Neocolonial Alliance: A History of the CFA Franc', *The American Journal of Economics and Sociology* 81(5), pp. 851–87.

Sachs, A., 2021, 'Foreword', in J. Bhabha, M. Matache and C. Elkins (eds), *Time for Reparations: A Global Perspective*, Philadelphia, PA: University of Pennsylvania.

Sartre, J. P., 1995, *Anti-Semite and Jew: An Exploration of the Etiology of Hate*, trans. G. J. Becker, New York: Schocken.

Slyomovics, S., 2021, 'Repairing Colonial Symmetry: Algerian Archive Restitution as Reparation for Crimes of Colonialism?', in J. Bhabha, M. Matache and C. Elkins (eds), *Time for Reparations: A Global Perspective*, Philadelphia, PA: University of Pennsylvania, pp. 201–18.

Sylla, N. S., 2021, 'Fighting Monetary Colonialism in Francophone Africa: Samir Amin's Contribution', *Review of African Political Economy* 48(167), pp. 32–49.

Táíwò, O., 2022, *Reconsidering Reparations*, Oxford: Oxford University Press.

Verges, F., 1999, '"I am not the Slave of Slavery": The Politics of Reparation in (French) Postslavery Communities', in A. Alessandrini (ed.), *Frantz Fanon: Critical Perspectives*, London: Routledge, pp. 258–75.

Wynter, S., 2003, 'Unsettling the Coloniality of Being/Power/Truth/Freedom: Towards the Human, After Man, Its Overrepresentation – An Argument', *CR: The New Centennial Review* 3(3), pp. 257-337.

Yountae, A., 2021, 'On Violence and Redemption: Fanon and Colonial Theodicy', in E. Craig and A. Yountae (eds), *Beyond Man: Race, Coloniality, and Philosophy of Religion*, Durham, NC: Duke University Press, pp. 204–25.

11

Freedom of Religion and Expression of Faith for Incarcerated LGBTI+ People in Brazil

HELOISA MELINO AND
FERNANDO LANNES FERNANDES

Introduction

This chapter presents findings of a research project focusing on LGBTI+ people deprived of liberty in Brazil.[1] The project was a collaborative effort between UNIperiferias and Observatório de Favelas (both from Brazil) and the University of Dundee (Scotland). Financial support was provided by the Scottish Funding Council and Global Challenges Research Funding (United Kingdom). This project complemented two other studies conducted in India (Ghosh et al., 2020) and the United Kingdom (Fernandes, Kaufmann and Kaufmann, 2021), all led by the University of Dundee, with the aim of comprehending the experiences of LGBTI+ individuals within prison systems and fostering international dialogue. The inaugural step in this direction was the 1st International Seminar on LGBTI+ People Deprived of Liberty, held in Rio de Janeiro in 2019.

The primary objective of the project was to contribute to the growing interest in the issue of LGBTI+ individuals in detention, both in terms of academic research and the development of national and international policy frameworks. Given the emerging interest in this subject, our aim was to explore it from a decolonial and intersectional perspective, considering critical aspects such as race and territorial stigma within the Brazilian context. Importantly, we recognized the need to approach this sensitive topic with a strong commitment to a human rights agenda, aiming to support the work of human rights defenders and inclusive religious organizations. Throughout the project, we observed that organizations working on prisoner rights often lack the capacity or understanding to address issues related to the LGBTI+ population, while most LGBTI+ organizations typically lack comprehensive knowledge of prisoner rights. Consequently, the project played a crucial role in fostering collaboration between these two fields of work and increasing their collective impact. This became the central objective of the project, evolving through continuous dialogue with civil society organizations. Strengthening the critical mass of civil society advocacy groups is paramount in the Brazilian context, as these groups have historically driven progressive agendas by proposing legislative and policy changes. Their work has become particularly vital in recent years, as LGBTI+ and prisoner rights have faced threats due to the rise of anti-human rights narratives in Brazilian politics.

As for religion, we learned that the support provided by these institutions is both vital and sometimes problematic. Interviewees with lived experience in the Brazilian prison system emphasize that religious gatherings inside the prison were sometimes their only chance to have comfort. The support from religious leaders was the only human contact with people from outside jail, especially for those whose family ties had been cut off when they were out(ed) as LGBTI+. On the other hand, we heard testimonies about questionable practices that appear to be of an abusive and violating nature, involving micro-aggressions, coercion and 'blackmail' of inmates into gathering in their meetings, converting to their religion and even serving as 'examples' for being freed from the 'sin' of homosexuality. This scenario, as we got to know, happens inside and outside prisons, with the administration of 'passage houses' for those who were just released from prison and had/have nowhere else to go.

Certainly there are criticisms that must be made of the support system of LGBTI+ people being offered mainly by Christian churches, especially the neo-Pentecostal ones. However, the importance of their work should not be lost from sight. In the same way, there is a bigger critique to be made: the lack of support from the state for those who are being kept from liberty and in their custody – therefore, their sole responsibility.

In this chapter we seek to bring the current scenario of the prison system in Brazil, made known by our research. Beside that, we seek to reflect on the above matters, which we find crucial for understanding this reality and for proposing public policies for changing the precarity in which people live in Brazilian prisons.

The invisibility of certain contentious human rights issues has hindered the advancement of a more progressive policy environment in Brazil. The lack of systematic and reliable information about LGBTI+ populations[2] within the prison system not only perpetuates their invisibility but also obscures the violations of their rights. Efforts have been made, especially since Brazil's adoption of the Optional Protocol to the United Nations Convention against Torture (OPCAT), to systematically monitor human rights violations within the prison system through preventive and anti-torture mechanisms. Civil society organizations, inclusive religious ones, have played a significant role in including the LGBTI+ agenda in this monitoring process. Our research contributes to these efforts by increasing the visibility of these issues and providing evidence to support the development of improved policies and practices that promote and protect the human rights of LGBTI+ individuals in detention.

Theoretical-conceptual considerations

The research project adopted an intersectional and decolonial analysis to examine the experiences of LGBTI+ individuals in prison. Intersectionality recognizes that gender identity and sexual orientation intersect with multiple systems of oppression and domination, such as economic, social, cultural, racial and ethnic factors (Crenshaw, 1989). It emphasizes the importance of understanding and addressing the unique vulnerabilities and marginalization faced by different groups within the LGBTI+ community.

The study was guided by the principles of the pedagogy of *convivência*/coexistence and the paradigm of *potência*/strength. The pedagogy of *convivência*/coexistence promotes horizontal lines of dialogue in society to challenge intolerance and discrimination. It is based on the principle of conviviality, where differences coexist and groups are open to learning from each other through a decolonized and ecologically aware perspective. This pedagogy provides a framework for bridging gaps and overcoming challenges imposed by dominant epistemologies, socio-political systems, and cultural norms rooted in intolerance and discrimination. To enable pedagogies of *convivência*/coexistence, it is necessary to recognize peripheral epistemologies and acknowledge the strength of marginalized groups. Strength of the peripheries refers to the combination of forces emerging from peripheral practices that challenge established forms of meaning and agency in the world. It represents an alternative to oppressive practices within a new philosophical and epistemological perspective. The project recognizes and upholds the voices, practices and knowledge produced by peripheral groups as part of a dialogue that affirms their right to live and coexist.

Therefore, we engaged in an open dialogue with LGBTI+ communities, public agents and individuals involved in the promotion and defence of human rights within prisons and for LGBTI+ individuals. We adopted a horizontal and culturally sensitive approach to build relationships and engage in dialogue with people from diverse backgrounds who are connected by the intersection of prison and LGBTI+ issues. We therefore recognize and value the social, identity and political expressions of marginalized groups, including those who are or have been deprived of their liberty and LGBTI+ individuals. Also, we aimed to confront the dehumanization of these groups and acknowledge their creative strength as a guiding principle in the pursuit of human dignity.

Colonial legacy also needs to be considered as shaping social inequalities. Therefore, we acknowledge the presence of social domination in the formation of social and political institutions throughout history (Quijano and Wallerstein, 1992; Quijano, 1999, 2000a, 2000b, 2007). We perceive the influence of structural racism and sexism in Brazilian society, and also of cis-heterosexuality in shaping the structures we live in (Lugones, 2007).

We consider crucial the historical processes that have contributed to the stigmatization and dehumanization of marginalized groups, including black people, individuals from lower socio-economic backgrounds and LGBTI+ people. This dehumanization reinforces narratives of hate and practices of violence, many of which persist within institutions, including the criminal justice system, where rights violations, abuse and neglect are prevalent.

Brazil's socio-political conjecture

The situation of LGBTI+ people in Brazilian prisons is influenced by broader societal discrimination and human rights violations against LGBTI+ populations. LGBTIphobia presents challenges in interpersonal relationships and within institutions that perpetuate discrimination. The prison system must address systemic LGBTIphobia, which is intertwined with structural issues in the criminal justice system. Historical factors such as poverty criminalization, structural racism, gender norms and institutional violence contribute to these challenges. Public policies have been implemented to protect LGBTI+ rights, starting with the National Human Rights Program II in 2002 and the 'Brazil Without Homophobia – Program to Combat Violence and Discrimination against GLBT and Promote Homosexual Citizenship', from 2004.

However, the effectiveness of these mechanisms remains limited due to societal LGBTIphobia. Marginalized groups, including black people, indigenous communities and those living in poverty, face intersecting forms of discrimination. The socio-political climate in Brazil reinforces the stigmatization and dehumanization of LGBTI+ people, particularly of trans people, along with other marginalized groups. The rise of conservatism has endangered their human rights, leading to violence and inequalities.

Black people are disproportionately represented in the prison system[3] and face police violence in marginalized areas (Human Rights Watch, 2021; Amnesty International, 2021; FBSP, 2021).Within LGBTI+ populations, there are individuals who face specific forms of violence due to the intersection of their race, sexual orientation, and gender identity and expression. Data on LGBTI+ populations is limited, but civil society organizations have worked to document violence against LGBTI+ individuals, especially transexual individuals who are often victims of lethal violence (Borges, 2019; Benevides et al., 2020; Feffermann et al., 2018; Picanço, 2019; Amnesty International, 2021; FBSP, 2021).

In comparison to other countries in the world that publish data of this nature, Brazil has the highest number of killings of LGBTI+ people (ILGA, 2017), especially of trans people and transvestites (TGEU, 2020), and 78% of trans people who were victims of lethal violence were black (ANTRA, 2021). These statistics reflect an institutional culture that perpetuates exploitation, erasure and criminalization. Understanding the vulnerabilities and human rights violations faced by LGBTI+ people in prisons requires considering multiple factors, including gender identity, sexual orientation, origin and skin colour, which contribute to structural inequalities in Brazilian society.

Rights, policies and regulations related to LGBTI+ people deprived of liberty

The criminalization and pathologization of homosexuality and transsexuality in Brazil have deep historical roots that have influenced the development of laws and policies affecting LGBTI+ populations. Throughout history, LGBTI+ individuals have faced stigmatization and criminal prosecution, dating back to the colonization process (Facchini, 2005; Green and Polito, 2006; Trevisan, 2011). This historical legacy, coupled with the erasure of LGBTI+ people in official state data, has serious consequences, including a lack of understanding of their specific needs, the violence they endure and the necessary measures to address these violations. It also hinders the effective development and implementation of public policies to assist and protect vulnerable LGBTI+ individuals.

Activists and social movements have fought for recognition and the acknowledgement of diverse ways of living, pressuring the state to recognize the existence of such individuals. While existing regulations encompass principles of equality and non-discrimination, they do not guarantee equality in society or eliminate discrimination.[4] They also fail to dismantle historical barriers that impede access to fundamental rights, such as the right to life, integrity and human dignity (Melino, 2020).

In Brazil's legal system, rights are typically codified in laws and codes, with jurisprudence serving as a secondary source of rights. However, critical perspectives on human rights recognize that rights are dynamic processes and provisional outcomes of ongoing struggles to reduce inequality and ensure access to resources for a more equitable society (Herrera Flores, 2008; Melino, 2017). Recognizing rights is essential, but it is just one stage in the ongoing fight for broader access to basic needs and legal goods for all individuals.

Brazil has regulations aimed at recognizing the unique experiences of LGBTI+ people in prisons and the need to protect them. However, our research indicated that these regulations have not been effectively implemented in practice.

Particularities of the challenges of LGBTI+ populations: structural, institutional and domestic violence

Before addressing issues regarding religious freedom in Brazilian prisons, it is our understanding that we should set the scenario in which LGBTI+ populations live in these institutions. In this way, we hope to assist readers in understanding why addressing the particularities of the experience of LGBTI+ people in prison is necessary.

In the interviews we conducted, incarceration was often referred to as institutional violence towards people who are the most susceptible to structural violence in Brazilian society. It was pointed out that the chances of imprisonment are significantly higher for people who live in favelas or on peripheries, are black or poor. LGBTIphobia was also highlighted as a structural and institutional violence that aggravates the risk of imprisonment, especially when interacting with race, territory and social class.

This structural and institutional violence against LGBTI+ people is aggravated by domestic violence they suffer when sexual orientation, gender identity and expression diverging from the cis-heteronormative expectation is perceived by family members or is declared. For the people interviewed, those families are usually the first place of dehumanization and naturalization of psychological, emotional, patrimonial and, in many cases, physical and sexual violence against LGBTI+ people. Often, this pattern of behaviour leads to LGBTI+ people being evicted from their family home or forced to leave.

> People, they are in domestic violence from their family, because of their relatives, the violence they suffer from LGBTphobia in the family. Or they are homeless, living on the streets. Or they are in shelters where they also suffer from violence. Or in a precarious housing situation, paying rent in very precarious places ... This bond already doesn't exists out here, this family bond for LGBTI+ people already doesn't exist out here. This bond is already broken because of LGBTphobia. So when you are in the prison system you ask, of course, to get in touch [with them]. Now you figure, a family that has already abandoned you because you are LGBTI+, imagine, because you are LGBT and now you are a convict, imprisoned. So, imagine that, the issue gets worse, so it's even more abandonment. (Sofia)

Many of them are still very young when these family breakdowns happen, which seriously jeopardizes their access to education, the job market and housing. Therefore, they often end up in precarious housing situations, or being homeless. Needing to earn money to survive and to support themselves, some end up getting involved in illicit activities, such as drug trafficking, or with activities associated with high stigma, such as prostitution. They take on high-risk positions, such as working in the street, for low payments, with greater exposure to violence and arbitrariness from the police.

> When I was 12, I was raped. At 13 I had my child. At the age of 16, I was kicked out of the house and started collecting cardboard on the streets of [city]. When I was around 17 to 18 years old I met the night of [city]. I started to be the bouncer of nightclubs, brothels in [city], with sex workers. I can say that it was there where I learned a lot about life and unfortunately, but fortunately, which is what makes me [Marcos] today, I started dealing. I was considered one of the biggest drug dealers in the city ... but at one point in my life I lost everything.

> And I became a homeless person and a crack user. I lived on the street for three years, going through the worst situations, sleeping a lot on the floor, and one of the best foods on the street, for me, was sour food. (Marcos)

It was also highlighted that even when LGBTI+ people do not go through family abandonment, the more their gender expression is non-conforming with the social norm, the greater their difficulties in entering the labour market can be. This is usually the case for butch lesbian or bisexual cisgender women and for transmasculine people.

The criminalization of LGBTI+ people just for being who they are was highlighted in the interviews as an aggravating factor for the risk of imprisonment. This institutional posture was referred to as a greater possibility of arbitrariness and abuse from the police, as well as greater austerity from magistrates in criminal proceedings in which LGBTI+ people appear as defendants or accused. Less chance of defence and more severe penalties will be part of these judicial processes, leading to over-representation of LGBTI+ people in prison, often being improperly imprisoned.

> There is a parallel universe, in which almost everyone is *entendida* [understand themselves as not cis-heterosexual]. They are even called with masculine names, the ones that want to. There are codes. I'm telling you, women's jails are almost entirely filled with lesbians. They are treated by masculine names, there is no questioning on that, there is no questioning ... it's not only 50%, it's not only half, it's the majority in jail. I have been working inside the system for [over ten years], almost all of them are lesbians and there are a lot of trans men or *caminhão* [butch/dykes, but here interviewee also refers to transmasculine people], so this quota ... I would love to conduct research, it must be around 30% or 40% [of trans men or transmasculine people]. So they, for instance, if you are a girlfriend, woman from the man ... there they say it like this, they say *my husband, my man*, they say it like this, this politically correct here, outside, is one thing, reality in there is another ... *Roberto, João*, and it is a trans person, that doesn't even know what *trans* means ... if you call them *trans*, they will even think you are calling them names. They perceive themselves like this, they say they are *sapato* [butch/dyke], it's the man, ready and over. (Paola)

Violations in relation to LGBTI+ people in Brazilian prisons

In the interviews we conducted, we heard many reports on violations of rights and human dignity to which incarcerated populations are subjected. Many of the reported violations of rights pointed to the excessive precariousness of prisons, resulting from the state's insufficiency in fulfilling its constitutional obligations towards the most basic needs. Inefficient access to water, whether for bathing or drinking; provision of food with low nutritional value, little variety, suspicious appearance, bad odour and often sourness, leading many people in prison to excessive losses of weight and endangering their health; precariousness of the supply of material for personal hygiene; violence from security agents who practise torture and direct inhumane, cruel and degrading treatment of inmates, even when they have health issues; non-compliance with daily sunbathing norms; difficulty in entering education programmes, professional training and job vacancies; lack of access to healthcare, with uncommitted health professionals who conduct inhumane treatments, and lack of any sort of medication, even those of daily and continued use – these are some of the violations that affect all people deprived of liberty.

Besides all those violations, LGBTI+ people are subjected to other abuses motivated by hate, prejudice and disrespect of their gender identities and expressions, or of their sexuality, as one of our interviewees described:

> 'Do you want to be a man? Hold on.' And they begin to beat you. All the time, when they are torturing people, *dykes/butches*, they always say this 'Don't you want to be a man? So you're going to get beaten like a man.' Unfortunately, this is very common inside. There are some situations that *dykes/butches* have to endure further. (Tereza)

According to the interviews, those acts of violence are way more directed towards black *dykes/butches* and black transmasculine people or trans men. It is considered by the prison staff that, due to the colour of their skin and to their gender expression, associated to masculinity, they can better put up with pain.

> They think way further before beating up white people. That's not because the amount of black men and women is greater. No way. [Black people] are the ones chosen for the distribution of punishment, for them to suffer more. The black body inside [jails] are seeing the same

way they're seeing here, outside ... they associate physical resistance to your colour. The black body must put up with everything. (Tereza)

That violence and discrimination enhances their vulnerability and aggravates the obstacles to the capacity in accessing scarce resources within the prison system.

We will now bring summarized results of violations of human rights and dignity that were mostly highlighted during the interviews we conducted.

Prison facility structures are binary, cis-heteronormative and reinforce gender patterns

[Miguel] is a trans man, he never had any doubts. So, he had thousands of women, hooked up with them, and so on. And he fell in love with the chief from the jail there which, by his narrative is a masculine woman, got it? He says *she is an actual dyke*. He differentiates himself. He also considers himself as dyke, but a dyke who is a man, and differentiates her, who is an actual dyke, that is, a strong, fierce woman, masculine. How both handled masculine values, the masculine performance, a huge fuss was created when they showed up holding hands in jail. Because, heteronormative as the jail is, two masculines can't be together, for that weakens the masculine. Masculine can only act upon and perform as the dominance to the feminine. So, two 'men' together are faggots. *What the fuck?!* The jail fell. So, both, in the same situation, in the same context, but one identified herself as a masculine woman, which, by what he narrated, the closer to that, which is a *caminhoneira* [a dyke/butch], and the other, which is him, that is a man, who has nothing of a *caminhoneira*. (Alexandre)

In Brazil, there are principles of non-discrimination in regulations relating to the justice and prison system, including the treatment that should be given to LGBTI+ people in the justice system, in direct or indirect public administration bodies and even, specifically, to LGBTI+ people in the deprivation of liberty.[5] However, prison normativity is based on the presumption of people as cisgender and heterosexual, which is recognized as cis-heteronormativity. This is also the pattern in which all state institutions function. A symptom of that cis-heteronormativity is the lack of a census to present a reliable look at the LGBTI+ population in the prison system. These people, by and large, are treated as if they do not exist. Lack of census was highlighted by many of the people we interviewed as a difficult factor for mapping these populations, as well as for monitoring their living conditions in prison.

Despite current regulations determining respect for the social name,[6] disrespect was signalled in the vast majority of interviews we conducted. There are reports of agents who respect the social or 'common' name, but they are a minority. Even they only respect the social name within the units, but every time there is any summons to court, visit or healthcare, the registration/civic name is used. It was reported to us that the Penitentiary Identification System (SIPEN)[7] does not respect social identity and social names.

Mischaracterization of gender identity and expression due to the lack of access to hormone therapy and the imposition of dress and conduct codes was also very present in the interviews we conducted. This happens when non-feminized women, non-masculinized men or trans people are required to meet standards of behaviour and clothing considered appropriate ('correct') in the feminine or masculine patterns of gender.

In addition to disrespect for the social name, even in medical reports and psychological assessments, the mischaracterization of the gender identity of trans people due to the lack of access to hormone therapy was widely highlighted as a violation in the field of health considered as primary healthcare. It was reported that the interruption of this treatment for people who were already undergoing it causes great discomfort and detachment of the trans person in relation to their own image, which can cause or accentuate dysphoria. It is expected that the state guarantees that there is no interruption, but for this it is necessary to ensure follow-up with a specialized endocrinologist, with care being carried out from the start of their time in prison, so that hormone therapy can be done in a safe and healthy way.

Issues concerning the right to freedom of religion for LGBTI+ people in Brazilian prisons

Ensuring religious freedom is one of the fundamental rights listed in Article 5 of the Brazilian Federal Constitution; therefore, religious organizations generally have greater ease of entry into the prison system.

We heard testimonies that these organizations routinely bring supplies, personal hygiene materials, carry out leisure activities and provide emotional and spiritual support, especially for people who identify with the religious types that work in the system. According to the interviews, most religious organizations that access the prison are Christian – Evangelical or Catholic. It was pointed out by some people interviewed that prison administrations tend to privilege access to Evangelical Christian organizations.

There were many reports of the importance of the presence of intramural religious organizations. During the research we learned about an Umbanda[8] religious organization that has authorization to enter to provide religious assistance. They are considered to have a highly relevant role in women's units, which was reported to be recognized and valued by people who defend human rights, by people who have been in prison and by people who are employees and directors of the units where this organization operates. We heard about Christian ministers who welcome LGBTI+ people in prison, sometimes being the only outside contact they had. Some interviewees pointed out that, even when the people inside did not identify with Christianity, they used to attend services or Masses to participate in some activity outside of their routine, to have contact with people different from those they are used to interacting with daily, to access material inputs – which are generally distributed to assistants. Some people, even though they did not have a religious identity, liked to be there simply to listen to the messages given.

On the other hand, we also heard reports of human rights violations by Christian representatives, which ranged from asking internal people to simulate miracles in cults, to acting with lesbophobia and transphobia towards lesbian and bisexual women and trans men. There were reports of some pastors of Evangelical churches causing great psychological suffering, due to which some lesbian women felt convinced that they needed to stop having relationships with other women in order not to live in 'sin' and achieve new lives upon leaving prison. Other reports included women victims of domestic violence being led to think that the violence carried out against them was their fault, for they were 'sinners'.

Despite the contradictions that may exist in these relationships with Christian entities, it is necessary to recognize that the work done by these religious organizations has an effective role in reducing suffering in prison for many people inside. Just as there are cases of violations of rights and human dignity, there are also many reports of Christian leaders who do their work in a committed and compassionate way with solidarity. There are even religious organizations that work alongside social movements and human rights organizations, seeking to exert political influence for the improvement of prison structures and work in the prison system; such is the case of the *Pastorais Carcerárias* (Prison Ministry/Pastoral Work).[9]

Challenges when leaving incarceration

When I got out of prison, I realized that I had developed a feeling of persecution, I developed OCD without realizing it, because I lived in real dumps. The first day, when I left for good, I wasn't coming back, I was only on parole, it was the first time I went out for a home visit. And I remember I went to the market with my sister in the morning, my sister went to pick me up in *Bangu*, I left and walked around that city of prisons there. My sister was at the gate, I got in the car, we went to the market. I was extremely happy, but at the same time, very dizzy. I had a physical space situation, with spatial dimension. My sister would go by the side of the cars, I would shrink back, I didn't think there was any room. I had totally lost track of space. I entered the market, I thought that everyone was already aware that I was just out of jail. People were looking at me. I said: *Sister, everyone noticed that I got out of jail, let's go.* I was hit with a few freaks, like that, but over time I got over it. For crossing the streets too. I would stand and wait for people to move. When they moved, I moved. Because it seems like a silly thing, but I had a little trouble on differentiating the red light and the green light. I had this little difficulty, and I didn't know how many steps I had to take to be across the street. I was afraid it would take too long to cross. I had these issues. I wrote down the cars that were behind me. I would drive and start noting down the licence plates. I thought that DESIPE [Penal System Department] was tracing my steps. There were times when I thought it was the police. (Tereza)

We also heard that passing through prison creates mental illness, which continues even after leaving prison. Some of the people we interviewed highlighted the importance of being able to undergo therapy, having family support, or having found some civil society organization that would welcome them, because the period of incarceration left sequelae that needed attention.

At least in the state of Rio de Janeiro, where the research was mainly conducted, Houses of Passage for former convicts that are led by religious authorities seem not always to respect LGBTI+ identity, sexual orientation and expression. We heard testimonies about the work of religious organizations that act as Houses of Passage for people who have recently been released from prison, which provide temporary shelter and help in seeking entry into the job market. About these houses, there were reports of solidarity, highlighting the importance of these spaces, but also of violation of rights, especially for LGBTI+ people who, in many cases, need to hide their gender identity or sexual orientation to stay in these places and receive the assistance offered.

It was also pointed out that some therapeutic communities, which are places for people with mental health issues, and alcohol and other substances abuse, were not always places of care. This is supported by the Brazilian Federal Council of Psychology's National Report on Therapeutic Communities, which pointed out that many of those communities do not address gender identity and sexual orientation matters. It was even noted that some of them conduct what is known as 'gay cure', which is the enforcement of cis-heteronormative patterns of behaviour to 'correct' homosexuality and/or transsexuality (Conselho Federal de Psicologia et al., 2018).

The main challenges in getting out of prison were related to obtaining income to access food and housing, which was identified as particularly difficult for LGBTI+ people who have, in their history, family breakdowns. In the case of trans, lesbian and gay or bisexual people with non-binary gender expression (non-feminized women, non-masculine men), access to the labour market was already difficult before the incarceration experience. When they go through prison, many of them still end up moving away from their extended families or even losing ties, which makes the process of resuming their lives even more difficult, after conditional or definitive release. And their situation is aggravated by the stigma of having passed through the prison, which accompanies them from then on.

Final considerations

In Brazil, the data we have on LGBTI+ people (whether about violence against them or from other angles) is extremely scarce. When any data is available, the methodology of production of this data is not always unquestionable, especially because there are very few efforts from public agencies in assuring reliable data. It is, in fact, as if LGBTI+ do not exist, or their lives do not matter.

The research we conducted about LGBTI+ people in deprivation of liberty is one of only a few in Brazil. And we had very little funding for our work. Our report has a lot of data, but we could not do much more than frame the scenario. We could not work in prisons, for example, which narrows the reach of the research. We interviewed LGBTI+ people who experienced incarceration, human rights defenders who work with LGBT human rights and with the prison system, and we came to know that the interface that connects those two areas is very little worked on.

Religious leaders are some of the very few people who can go into Brazilian prisons with ease, and most of them are fundamentalist Christians. Living in prison in Brazil is very harsh; the system is beyond overcrowded, with the vast majority of people who are incarcerated being black and poor people, from favelas and the peripheries of Brazil. LGBTI+ people who are incarcerated have the same background, and beyond that they also have dealt with domestic violence from their family members, who more than often kick them out of their homes when they are still very young.

Faith plays a significant role in prisons, not only for people to know that they are not alone, and they can live 'better' lives, but also because religious leaderships provide personal items, such as toilet paper, pads for women, medication, glasses and so on. All that should be provided by the state but is not. Since most of those leaders who get into prisons are fundamentalist Christians, LGBTI+ people are often 'blackmailed' into being 'cured' and becoming cisgender or heterosexual, hearing they must 'abandon a life of sin to improve their lives'. We discovered that there is only one leader from African-Brazilian religions who visits prisons, and she works in women's units in Rio de Janeiro.[10]

This fundamentalist Christian 'blackmailing' LGBTI+ people to be 'cured'/'healed' from transsexuality or homosexuality happens in jail and outside jail as well. We researched shelters that receive people who are just out of prison and need urgent assistance, and most of them are also led by fundamentalist Christians. And the same goes for therapeutic communities, as shown by the Federal Council of Psychology from Brazil. We must add that both Houses of Passage (or shelters) and therapeutic communities are funded by the state, the so-called laic state.

The paradigms of *potência das periferias* (strength of the peripheries) and the pedagogy of *convivência* (coexistence) help us think about how to build models of care for LGBTI+ people who have been incarcerated. We firmly believe in the possibility of building alliances among progressive religious groups, human rights defenders and LGBTI+ people who were formerly incarcerated. Organizations that are active are certainly capable of integrating these populations. However, for that to happen, a different theological approach is necessary, especially one that highlights the importance of solidarity, humanity, love, affection and faith in the pursuit of a better world in which diversity of forms of living is measured by its true strength.

Notes

1 https://revistaperiferias.org/wp-content/uploads/2023/04/lgbts-em-privacao-de-liberdade.pdf (accessed 21.01.2025).

2 We chose to refer to LGBTI+ populations in the plural, as we recognize the multiplicity of populations to which this acronym refers.

3 Penitentiary Information System (InfoPen, 2019) compared to the National Household Survey from Brazilian Institute of Geography and Statistics (IBGE, in Portuguese), shows that, while black people represent 53% of the Brazilian population, they represent over two-thirds of the Brazilian prison system's population (Infopen, 2019; IBGE, 2019).

4 Only jurisprudence transformed into Binding Precedents* or decisions of some specific actions of the Federal Supreme Court have normative force equivalent to laws – even so, those decisions are susceptible to be modified by judicial or legislative procedures, which are much less rigorous than those required for legislative changes.

*'Binding precedent' (*Súmula vinculante*) is a constitutional mechanism for standardizing the jurisprudence of the Federal Supreme Court that has normative force to the Judiciary, as well as on all direct and indirect public administration, in federal, state and municipal spheres.

5 We will address them when matters arise in this chapter.

6 Articles 5, 6 from Resolution 348/2020 by the National Council of Justice (CNJ); Article 2 from Resolution 558/2015 from Rio de Janeiro's Penitentiary Administration Office (SEAP-RJ); Article 2, XVII from Brazil's LGBT National Health Policy (*Política Nacional de Saúde LGBT*). Besides, nominal calling is listed as one of the rights of the arrested person, according to Article 41, XI from Law 7,210/84 (Criminal Enforcement Law – *Lei de Execução Penal*), which read combined and coherently with Article 3 from the Brazilian Federal Constitution, must be extended to trans people, resulting in them being called by their social name, when they do not have their birth record rectified.

7 This is also contrary to what is stated in Rio de Janeiro's Decree 4,065, from 8 July 2011, which asserts the right to use social names for trans people, in public administration organs from the state.

8 Umbanda is a Brazilian religion of African origin.

9 Their work can be further known at https://carceraria.org.br/ (accessed 31.10.2023).

10 Here we are referring to Mãe Flavia Pinto, from Casa do Perdão. You can get to know her work further at https://www.instagram.com/maeflaviapinto/ and https://www.instagram.com/casadoperdao/ (accessed 31.10.2023).

References

Amnesty International, 2021, *Amnesty International Report 2020/21: The State of the World's Human Rights*, https://www.amnesty.org/en/documents/pol10/3202/2021/en/ (accessed 27.02.2025).

Associação Nacional de Travestis e Transexuais do Brasil (ANTRA), 2021, 'Dossiê dos assassinatos e da violência contra travestis e transexuais brasileiras em 2020',

Editora Expressão Popular, https://antrabrasil.files.wordpress.com/2021/01/dossie-trans-2021-29jan2021.pdf (accessed 21.01.2025).

Benevides, B. et al., 2020, 'Não existe cadeia humanizada: Estudo sobre a população LGBTI+ em privação de liberdade', *Associação Brasileira de Lésbicas, Gays, Bissexuais, Trans e Travestis* (ABGLT), https://antrabrasil.org/wp-content/uploads/2020/12/nao-existe-cadeia-humanizada-nf.pdf.

Borges, J., 2019, *Encarceramento em massa*, São Paulo: Editora Jandaíra.

Crenshaw, Kimberle, 1989, 'Demarginalizing the Intersection of Race and Sex: A Black Feminist Critique of Antidiscrimination Doctrine, Feminist Theory and Antiracist Politics', *University of Chicago Legal Forum*, 1989(1) http://chicagounbound.uchicago.edu/uclf/vol1989/iss1/ (accessed 21.01.2025).

Conselho Federal de Psicologia et al., 2018, *Relatório da Inspeção Nacional em Comunidades Terapêuticas – 2017*, Brasília DF: CFP.

Facchini, R., 2005, *Sopa de Letrinhas? Movimento homossexual e produção de identidades coletivas nos anos 90*, São Paulo: Garamond Universitária.

Feffermann, M. et al., 2018, 'Interfaces do Genocídio no Brasil: raça, gênero e classe. Temas em Saúde Coletiva nº 25', *Instituto de Saúde*, http://www.saude.sp.gov.br/resources/instituto-de-saude/homepage/pdfs/temassaudecoletiva25.pdf.

Fernandes, F. L., Kaufmann, B. and Kaufmann, K., 2021, 'LGBT+ People in Prisons: Experiences in England and Scotland' (Full Report), University of Dundee, https://discovery.dundee.ac.uk/files/56478375/LGBT_People_in_Prisons_Full_Report_09_FEB_21_WEB.pdf (accessed 21.01.2025).

Fernandes, Silva and Barbosa, J. 2018, 'The Paradigm of Potency and the Pedagogy of Coexistence', *Revista Periferias*, https://revistaperiferias.org/en/materia/the-paradigm-of-power-and-the-pedagogy-of-coexistence/ (accessed 21.01.2025).

Fórum Brasileiro de Segurança Pública (FBSP), 2021, *Anuário Brasileiro de Segurança Pública*, 15th edn, https://forumseguranca.org.br/anuario-brasileiro-seguranca-publica/ (accessed 21.01.2025).

Ghosh, A., Dhanuka, M., Bourothu, S., Fernandes, F. L., Singh, N. and Kumar, C., 2020, 'Lost Identity: Transgender Persons Inside Indian Prisons', Commonwealth Human Rights Initiative, https://discovery.dundee.ac.uk/ws/portalfiles/portal/55098109/160637717 1Lost_Identity_Transgender_Persons_in_Indian_Prisons.pdf (accessed 21.01.2025).

Green, J. N. and Polito, R., 2006, *Frescos Trópicos: Fontes sobre homossexualidade masculina no Brasil (1870–1980)*, Rio de Janeiro: José Olympio.

Herrera Flores, J., 2008, *La reinvención de los derechos humanos*, Sevilla: Atrapasueños, http://www.derechoshumanos.unlp.edu.ar/assets/files/documentos/la-reinvencion-de-los-derechos-humanos.pdf (accessed 21.01.2025).

Human Rights Watch, 2021, 'World Report 2020: Brazil Events of 2020', https://www.hrw.org/world-report/2021/country-chapters/brazil (accessed 21.01.2025).

Instituto Brasileiro de Geografia e Estatísticas (IBGE), 2019, 'Pesquisa Nacional por Amostra de Domicílios Contínua', https://sidra.ibge.gov.br/tabela/6408 (accessed 21.01.2025).

International Lesbian and Gay Association (ILGA), 2017, 'State-Sponsored Homophobia – A World Survey of Sexual Orientation Laws: Criminalisation, Protection and Recognition', 12th edition, http://ilga.org/downloads/2017/ILGA_State_Sponsored_Homophobia_2017_WEB.pdf (accessed 21.01.2025).

Lugones, M., 2007, 'Heterosexualism and the Colonial/Modern Gender System', *Hypatia* 22(1), pp. 186–209.
Melino, H., 2017, *Potência das ruas: Direito, linguagens e emancipação: processos de luta e o potencial transformador dos movimentos sociais*, Rio de Janeiro: Editora Multifoco.
Melino, H., 2020, 'Descolonialidade do poder, do saber e do ser: Propostas epistemológicas para as Ciências Sociais e Jurídicas, a partir da alegria das sabedorias populares brasileiras', PhD thesis (Law), 189f., Universidade Federal do Rio de Janeiro (UFRJ), https://www.academia.edu/62717463/Descolonialidade_do_poder_do_saber_e_do_ser_Propostas_epistemol%C3%B3gicas_para_as_Ci%C3%AAncias_Sociais_e_Jur%C3%ADdicas_a_partir_da_alegria_das_sabedorias_populares_brasileiras (accessed 21.01.2025).
Penitentiary Information System (Infopen), 2019, 'National Penitentiary Department Information System', Brazil's Ministry of Justice – National Penitentiary Department,https://www.gov.br/depen/pt-br/sisdepen/mais-informacoes/relatorios-infopen/relatorios-analiticos/br/brasil-dez-2019.pdf (accessed 21.01.2025).
Picanço, L. B., 2019, 'Brazil's Mass Incarceration Policy has not Stopped Crime', *Wilson Center – Brazil Institute*, https://www.wilsoncenter.org/blog-post/brazils-mass-incarceration-policy-has-not-stopped-crime (accessed 21.01.2025).
Quijano, A., 1999, 'Coloniality of Power and its Institutions', Symposium on Colonialidad del poder y sus ámbitos sociales, Binghamton University: Binghamton and New York, 22–24 April.
Quijano, A., 2000a, 'Coloniality of Power, Eurocentrism, and Latin America', *Nepantla* 1(3), pp. 533–80.
Quijano, A., 2000b, 'Colonialidad del poder y clasificación social', *Journal of World Systems Research* 6(2), pp. 342–86.
Quijano, A., 2007, 'Coloniality and Modernity/Rationality', *Cultural Studies* 21(2), pp. 168–78, http://dx.doi.org/10.1080/09502380601164353.
Quijano, A. and Wallerstein, I., 1992, 'Americanity as a Concept, or The Americas in the Modern World-System', *International Social Sciences Journal* 134, pp. 549–57. Paris: UNESCO.
Transgender Europe (TGEU), 2020, 'Trans murder monitoring', *Transrespect*, https://transrespect.org/en/map/trans-murder-monitoring/ (accessed 21.01.2025).
Trevisan, J. S., 2011, *Devassos no Paraíso: a homossexualidade no Brasil, da colônia à atualidade*, 8th edn, Rio de Janeiro: Record.

12

Can the Subaltern Code? AI Ethics and Liberation Theology

MATTHEW ELMORE

AI ethics, liberation theology and subalternity

In 2016, a team of German researchers built an AI model to detect malignant skin lesions. To train it, they used over 100,000 images – most of which featured white skin (Dutchen, 2019). If the model had been deployed to serve a region like mine in North Carolina, it would have led to a massive underdiagnosis of patients with darker pigmentation, worsening an existing disparity in care. Examples like this form a central concern of AI ethics, a field that has grown rapidly to examine numerous sectors of industry and government, yielding an already sizable literature in less than a decade. Algorithmic bias affects decisions about who gets a job, who receives a loan, who is insured, who is arrested and who gets a longer prison sentence – to name just a few conspicuous issues. In general, to quote Kate Crawford, AI has a documented 'white guy problem', negatively impacting every group outside that one dominant category (Crawford, 2016).

As a relatively young discourse, AI ethics is still pluripotent, meaning it could still develop many forms of attention and concern. My aim in this article is to suggest a form of attention not yet deeply considered, an approach inspired by liberation theology. I want to situate its virtues in a dialogue between Marxist and Catholic thought, offering insights from their cross-pollination to the field of AI ethics. Understandably, some have questioned whether such a cross-pollination is possible; liberation theology has itself been a subject of great scrutiny in Catholic teaching. While it arose from the experience of Catholic theologians in the Global South, its Marxian class analysis provoked immediate worries about an atheist vision of freedom and social action (Ratzinger, 1984). To some extent, those worries have subsided since the fall of the iron curtain, but the need for a clear analysis of power remains. This chapter seeks to meet that need by looking at the dynamics of technological power in the post-Cold War era – dynamics that continue to eclipse a preferential option for the poor. In my view, the best instincts of liberation theology arise not from Marxist materialism but from Christian reflection; which is to say that the best elements of Marxist critique bear witness to a deeper wellspring of justice, care and communion. With those elements of analysis, we can better understand the problem of algorithmic bias and take steps to deconstruct its underpinnings. And with a love transcending classical Marxism, we can set about repairing the breaches of justice that continue to afflict the marginalized.

The *Catechism of the Catholic Church* defines the common good as 'the sum total of social conditions which allow people, either as groups or as individuals, to reach their fulfillment more fully and more easily' (*Catechism*, 1995, §1906). No group is to be exploited and silenced for the sake of another group. That's the principle I have in view as I consider my topic, and for me it carries the inflection of Gustavo Gutiérrez, who insisted that true spirituality first entails conversion *to* the oppressed, not *of* the oppressed. In his words: 'Conversion means a radical transformation of ourselves; it means thinking, feeling, and living as Christ – present in exploited and alienated persons' (Gutiérrez, 1988, p. 118). Arguably, the conversion *of* the oppressed occurs in the form of liberation, as we find in the book of Exodus. A culture of liberation brings joy to those who receive it, including those converted from deceptive self-interest and the will to power. Liberation is not lawless but loving, participating in the care of God for one's neighbour.

Bearing that in mind, I want to show how AI can tend to silence and exploit people who face precarity in the Global South. The harms of algorithmic bias certainly reach beyond the United States – but that is not the main point. Algorithmic bias remains symptomatic of an older logic still expressed in projects of massive data gathering, a logic that began in Europe and expanded to its colonies (Wiggins and Jones, 2023, pp. 50–3). Gayatri Spivak, in her landmark essay 'Can the Subaltern Speak?', famously wrote that the strategies of European power had disqualified the local and traditional knowledge of colonized communities (Spivak, 1993). Spivak was among the first to point out that unless the colonized could make themselves intelligible to the legal, political and economic frameworks of Europe, they had no official voice, no recognizable agency in the hegemonic system of the known world. Her essay is now more than three decades old but it remains as salient as ever. While not an orthodox treatment of Marxism, it owes an intellectual debt to Marx and, as we'll see, Spivak's thinking follows the moral arc of conversion recognized by theologians like Gutiérrez.

I would like to extend Spivak's analysis to the present day, looking at the development and deployment of artificial intelligence in postcolonial settings. Instead of asking if the subaltern can speak, I want to ask if the subaltern can *code*, which is only a slight modification of Spivak's original question. To keep to the point, I'll set aside debates about the exact definition of subalternity, but a few remarks are in order. First, the subaltern subject exists at the bottom of all social strata, having no access to lines of social mobility. Second, subalternity is not exactly the same as being oppressed. One can belong to an oppressed class without being subaltern, though the subaltern subject is always oppressed. Third, western academic privilege is often dislocated from the subaltern situation but it puts a burden of responsibility on the shoulders of academics – especially those of us who read theorists like Spivak. So to expand on her question in her own words: 'What must the elite do to watch out for the continuing construction of the subaltern?' (Spivak, 1993, p. 90). By 'elite' I take her to mean the intellectually privileged – those of us with academic credentials and the weighty symbolic capital amassed by our various forms of expertise. What must *we* do to watch out for the construction of subalternity? This, I believe, is the primary question for AI ethics, taking us beyond mere questions of algorithmic bias. The question has to do with the global ubiquity of algorithms and, more precisely, with the forms of life left unsupported by the development of algorithmic rationality.

AI safety and hegemony

I want to note right away that commitments to 'AI safety' can obscure the question Spivak has prompted me to ask. Using concepts like 'existential risk', key opinion leaders tend to promote dystopian worries about machines outsmarting 'us' – not only taking jobs but bypassing human decisions in high-stakes arenas like nuclear warfare and virus research. If AI goes rogue, they argue, or if it falls into the wrong hands, we could face a major global catastrophe: maybe not a nuclear holocaust or another pandemic, but something else, some unexpected crisis on the same order of magnitude (Center for AI Safety, 2023). Such concerns are broadly shared by prominent figures in the tech industry, many of whom recently agreed to enhance their safety protocols in dialogues with government officials. Noteworthy as their efforts are, they overshadow more pressing matters of injustice, matters long obscured by the legacy of colonial power in the Global South.

The tragic irony is twofold: AI has in fact led to a growing job market in places like Nairobi, where data enrichment workers are hired to make AI safe and ethical. Recent investigative reports have shown that a very human, low-wage labour force played a crucial role in training the content algorithms of Facebook and ChatGPT. Among corporate contractors was Sama, a California-based firm that brands itself as protecting 'the soul of AI'. Recruiting workers from Kenyan slums and informal settlements, Sama has publicly touted its efforts to lift locals from poverty. Its workers, all the while, have faced precarious conditions in more ways than one. Earning less than $2 per hour, those who trained ChatGPT received small bonuses for exposing themselves to the most harmful content on the internet. Their livelihood, in other words, depended on graphic depictions of self-harm, murder and sexual violence, which they tagged to set up guardrails for the outputs of the system. In the name of safety and ethics, workers suffered harm. And while many reported symptoms of psychological trauma, their cries were effectively muted until public interest in ChatGPT prompted journalists to uncover its backstory (Perrigo, 2023).

When *Time* magazine first exposed the company's working conditions, one employee described the job as 'a kind of mental torture' that left workers with no way out. 'Sometimes I feel like I want to resign', the worker said. 'But then I ask myself: what will my baby eat?' (Perrigo, 2022). Attempts to unionize have been met with strategic layoffs, as another worker recalled, describing events from 2019 when workers threatened to strike: 'They made sure by firing some people that this will not happen again. It feels like modern slavery, like neo-colonialism.' Still, Sama markets its product as 'ethical AI', promising to fight harmful bias with the production of enriched data. So here we have a sense of the stakes. Data-centred techniques do not provide a rich enough framework for the pursuit of justice. AI ethics needs to re-centre its priorities, and it can take the line of approach drawn out by liberation theology and subaltern studies.

It's true that Nairobian data workers do in fact possess a form of social mobility, albeit a narrow and conscripted one. They escape subalternity in so far as they can make themselves employable, even if the danger of subalternity limits and shapes their choices. Meanwhile, subalternity is the unavoidable byproduct of AI elsewhere in the Global South. A clear example occurs in the agricultural sector of India, where farmers have been systematically uprooted from traditional small-scale methods, compelled instead to adopt big data systems enforced by philanthropists, government agencies and tech industry partners. Burdened by unpaid loans for large equipment, farmers deal with crop failures from climate change – a crisis compounded by the expense of genetically modified, pesticide-resistant seeds. Left without economic options or political agency, they find themselves moving down the social strata, from oppressed precarity to subalternity.

I will return to the plight of Indian farmers shortly, but my point for the moment is this: in both cases, human agency is restricted by a hegemonic interest in algorithms. Kenyan data workers play a part in training those algorithms, while Indian farmers are subject to their implementation. The algorithms in question may differ but they represent the same hegemonic logic, the same formation of databased labour in the Global South.

Neoliberal data power

A wider analytical frame will clarify the problem I wish to address. We live in a bewildering new evolution of the information age, a mode of political economy yet to be named. Shoshana Zuboff calls it 'surveillance capitalism', noting how our online behaviour is tracked and manipulated for the sale of targeted ads (Zuboff, 2019). Yanis Varoufakis goes further, calling our economic paradigm 'techno-feudalism' (Varoufakis, 2021). Whatever we call it, today's informatic logic fosters an impression that the whole of reality is codable. Everything from fashion trends to relationships, from travel routes to sleep patterns, must take on the primary form of data. In the 1980s, Donna Haraway described the underpinning logic of our age as *'the translation of the world into a problem of coding*, a search for a common language in which all resistance to instrumental control disappears and all heterogeneity can be submitted to disassembly, reassembly, investment and exchange' (Haraway, 2016, p. 34; emphasis original). The main reason, arguably, is money, which may seem a bold statement until we consider the economic groundwork laid at the time of Haraway's writing. The social scientist Jathan Sadowski observes that under neoliberal governance, finance capital is borderless. Its transnational pathways allow for the capture, flow and accumulation of data in a globalized private sector running beyond the gaze of national governments – and often through collaborations with them. In other words, 'a company could collect the personal information of Americans, store the data in Taiwan, and sell it in Europe' (Sadowski,

2019). The data firm is everywhere, profiting from exchanges everywhere, and many state officials count that as a good thing. Carl Bildt, the former Prime Minister of Sweden, said in a piece for the *Financial Times* that 'barriers against the free flow of data are, in effect, barriers against trade' (Bildt, 2015). Data, as others have said, is the new oil.

A decade ago, Eric Schmidt observed that cyberspace is a realm 'not truly bound by terrestrial laws' (Schmidt and Cohen, 2014, p. 3). Schmidt, who acted as Google's chief executive from 2001 to 2011, oversaw the company's expansion after the World Trade Center fell. The timing of his statement was uncanny; Edward Snowden had just blown the whistle on the National Security Administration, revealing a network of state–market relations that took shape during Schmidt's tenure at Google. When the threat of terrorism was at its peak, US officials justified a secret extension of emergency power, reaching deep into the private sector to collect user data from the nation's largest tech companies. The first paid agreement took place between the NSA and Microsoft in 2007. Yahoo, Google and Facebook soon followed, and they were later joined by others including Verizon, YouTube and Apple. The government programme behind it all, known as PRISM, built a composite profile of every user, mapping subjects on to a grid of their social networks, their physical locations and their online habits. The technique resembled contact tracing in epidemiology, monitoring the population for symptoms of extremism to prevent its spread. Government contractors like Snowden had access to all the raw data, making use of a search function modelled by Google. Even if some information was classified, no technical barriers were put in place; the contractor in the cubicle was functionally above the law (Snowden, 2013). When Snowden finally alerted journalists to the situation, the story was reported as an overreach of governmental power (Greenwald and MacAskill, 2013). But by that time the NSA had become a governmental shell where private-sector workers monitored private-sector data. The tech business had developed a suite of new capacities in a well-funded state of exception (Fung, 2013).

Recounting all this, I am aware that public concern over these matters drifts habitually to the nightmare of an Orwellian superstate. But despite having reasons for that nightmare, we live in the future of a different 1984. As Ronald Reagan himself promised at the New York Stock Exchange in 1985, state deregulation has allowed commercial markets to reach their 'full potential' across the globe (Associated Press, 1985). The neoliberal nexus permits an oligopoly of market actors to create, sell and exploit vast mines of population data. They represent what Michael Hardt and Antonio Negri describe as the 'pinnacle of world command', transforming the dynamics of modern democracy – and not only in terms of privacy rights (Hardt and Negri, 2001, p. 310). Boycotting, once a core tactic of the Civil Rights Movement, no longer functions to bring about substantial change because civil society can no longer mediate between the forces of capital and the state. One needs only to consider the scale of a boycott that would disempower a global firm like Amazon or Google: it borders on the impossible. The data market has created a system of subject formation that goes beneath and beyond the optics of a government by the people, because in the new regime, people are users before they are citizens. And as the activist Vandana Shiva puts it: 'A "user" is a consumer without choice in the digital empire' (Shiva, 2020, p. 180).

Shiva's statement, born of her solidarity with Indian farmers, returns us to the subaltern question. For many regions of the world, our data-based economy results in a process that the moral philosopher Miranda Fricker identifies as 'epistemic injustice' (Fricker, 2007). In Shiva's words: 'It assumes there are "experts" with "objective" knowledge, who are separate from, and superior to, ordinary men, women, peasants, workers, and experts of other knowledge traditions' (Shiva, 2020, p. 41). That mindset, a problem Shiva calls 'the mechanical mind', has only gained momentum in what Crawford calls 'the Great Houses of AI', which are 'explicitly attempting to capture the planet in a computationally legible form' (Crawford, 2021, pp. 11, 21).

With the commercial launch of Google – its Earth, its maps, its intensive profiling of user behaviour – the mechanical mind ascended to a new level of informatic power. Many of its aims, to be fair, were altruistic; it granted unparalleled access to a tremendous archive, supplying users with impressive tools for searching, translating and navigating the world. But its architecture, like a mansion built on a graveyard, is continually haunted by the spectre of harmful bias. The mechanical mind promises to create a world of rationally organized knowledge, a world of accessible resources; its promise, however, cannot transcend its cultural parameters, its profit models or its rankings of valuable information. As a consequence, it cloaks a brutal underside, endangering any form of life beyond its codability structure.

The political economy of oversight

Not long ago the MIT professor Alex Pentland suggested that big data can bring us closer to synoptic control over the real world. 'If we had a "god's eye," an all-seeing view,' he said, 'then we could potentially arrive at a true understanding of how society works and take steps to fix our problems' (Pentland, 2014, p. 11). The call for a god's-eye view – a post-Babel litany of the same old ambition – is a founding myth of the modern subconscious. Images of a single, informatic language have risen from a strong desire to solve any number of problems, and we ought to ask what that means for the construction of subalternity.

Microsoft India recently signed a contract to develop a 'digital ecosystem for agriculture' (DACFW, Government of India, 2021). As part of an effort to clean up India's land records, the company will act as a ministry of state, sending representatives to some 100 villages for the personal and financial information of farmers. The project, layered on to an 'Agristack' of databased technologies, will let the government calculate subsidies at 'an almost individual level', according to one ministry secretary. When asked why Microsoft was chosen for the task, the secretary said: 'We simply do not have the means to collect and analyse what is in all probability petabytes of big data. Microsoft does' (Saha, 2021).

Microsoft, in fact, could analyse the data using the architecture of ChatGPT, thanks to a new partnership with OpenAI. If that occurs, the exploitation of Kenyan data workers will have taken place directly upstream of Indian farmers, as if in a separate building on the same factory grounds. Capitalizing on their labour, Microsoft will build its capacity to 'search the haystack by the time you've finished saying "needle"', to borrow an expression from Ted Chiang (2019, p. 187). The needle, in this case, will not merely present itself as a dataset. Suppose an official wants to see a report on a precinct, comparing its farmers' earnings with their crop yields, measuring those figures against other regions. The query will generate a full executive summary, complete with risk predictions and subsidy recommendations. And the entire program, running outside the official borders of political representation, will cohere with the mapmaking strategies first imposed by colonial governments. As James Scott points out in *Seeing Like a State*, modern European designs for local agriculture have always been 'calculated to make the terrain, its products and its workforce more legible – and hence manipulable – from above and from the center' (Scott, 1998, p. 2). The same mentality will gain efficiency through a partnership between two Great Houses of AI, meaning that the 'centre' will have morphed into a syndicate, a network of corporations contracting with public agencies to carve out a share in the global harvest and milling of data.

The problem can be summarized as follows: the mechanical mind, whether colonial or neocolonial, implies conditions of oversight in two senses of the term – it governs populations while remaining unaware of what it cannot see. Traditional Indian farmers, whose local knowledge is unreadable to the power nexus, now find themselves bereft on land they often sharecrop under the watch of farming conglomerates. With many farmers sinking into unpayable debt, hundreds of thousands have taken the only exit they can find – by taking their own lives. The exact count, as if by some morose irony, is hard to know; one article estimates the number of farmer suicides at 30 per day (Kaur, 2022). Artificial intelligence will probably do more to exacerbate than to heal the cause of their misery because it will not be attuned to their voices but to values aligned with computable solutions. The problem exceeds the customary framing of algorithmic bias, which many technologists would like to correct by adjusting model parameters or including more representative data. A crisis like this will not subside as AI builds more comprehensive datasets, producing ever more granular readouts of individual lives. Data-focused refinements cannot remedy the subaltern condition because subalternity is a byproduct of the mechanical mind, which always looks for solutions from above.

Neither will the crisis diminish as a result of non-profit initiatives enmeshed in the same paradigm. Take for example the Gates Foundation, chaired by the tech billionaire whose philanthropy ties itself to commercial enterprise at the largest of scales. In addition to financing vaccination efforts and drug research, Bill Gates and his foundation have invested in seed patents and databased farming methods, purporting to solve global food shortages while confirming that they see the world in giant data models. Because of the grant money they provide to groups like Monsanto-Bayer and Microsoft India, the Gates Foundation is yet another expression of synoptic power, constructing a subject-forming gaze beyond and through state mechanisms. Their financial model sets the agendas of researchers and policymakers worldwide, steering priorities towards computable solutions at a massive scale. Of course, none of that implies ill will on the part of Gates; it means he represents a new iteration of high modern optimism, blithely following the logic of colonial technocracy. Regarding the situation, Vandana Shiva does not mince words:

Gates has created global alliances to impose top-down analysis and prescriptions for health problems. He gives money to define the problems, and then he uses his influence and money to impose the solutions. And in the process, he gets richer. His 'funding' results in an erasure of democracy and biodiversity, of nature and culture. His 'philanthropy' is not just philanthrocapitalism; it is philanthroimperialism. (Shiva, 2020, p. 205)

In short, the promise of a God's-eye view carries tremendous weight but it places a burden of disparate measure on people from local cultures who see the world another way. If AI ethics is to distinguish itself from the mechanical mind – staying appropriately critical, alert to the risk of being a mere annex of the industry – it needs insights from elsewhere. At the same time it needs to articulate a vision of hope and repair; critique holds no meaning if repair is impossible. The point is not to denounce every algorithm as fundamentally violent. To do so would be as ignorant as claiming that big data can provide answers to every social ill. An algorithm is simply a tool of thought, a set of instructions used to solve a problem. AI ethics, in its general bearing, should therefore work to assess and change the meta-algorithm, the cultural set of instructions encoded in the collection and use of data. Clearly that work entails a collective movement towards new incentives, empowering developers from low-income countries to work closely with their communities, crafting research ideas from the bottom up. But the greatest contribution of AI ethics will be to insist that life is irreducible to coding – and that coding, finally, is surpassed by life as it is.

The moral arc of conversion

My discussion so far has introduced AI ethics as a field primarily concerned with biased algorithms. I suggested at the outset that liberation theology and subaltern studies can offer the field a new line of approach, deepening the same concern while exposing the underpinning problem. To exemplify the problem, I looked at the situation of Kenyan data workers and Indian farmers, whose labour is exploited by the same industrial complex, their hardships obscured by a linkwork of neoliberal data power. I have applied an openly Marxist analytic to the problem but I have yet to fulfil my initial commitment – to show how my perspective integrates with Catholic moral thought, informing an AI ethics for the common good.

I now come to the title question: 'Can the subaltern code?' Unequivocally, Spivak would say 'no', because the subaltern subject cannot speak in the codified language of the dominant system. A core task for AI ethics, then, is to embrace two ideas that Spivak herself advocates. First, we should welcome the ongoing pursuit of intelligence in what she calls 'silenced areas', a process she sees unfolding in disciplines like anthropology, political science, history and sociology (Spivak, 1993, p. 91). To Spivak's list we can add her own areas of literature, philosophy and the arts. What we need is a diversified translation of knowledge, a hybrid field where numerous methods of trained perception can reveal their insights. But we should be mindful of a caveat: such efforts may, in the long run, inadvertently align with the work of imperialist subject formation, mixing epistemic violence with the advancement of learning. Inevitably the anthropologist will apply a grid, a code, to make the subject legible to a defined discourse. So the boundaries of the field must remain loose, even as its moral imperative attains greater clarity. Our true task, in Spivak's words, involves 'learning to learn from below' – not merely studying but deeply internalizing what the subaltern has to say (Spivak, 2004). The subaltern *can* speak in his or her own language.

When Gutiérrez called for a similar practice in the 1970s he was met with resistance from fellow clergy, many of whom believed he was following Marx more than Christ. To them the voices of Latin American revolutionaries were theologically incoherent and wayward, even dangerous. But Gutiérrez saw that the structures of pastoral power had not afforded the people a language fitting their circumstances:

> If they are not always able to express in appropriate terms the profound reasons for their commitment, it is because the theology in which they were formed – and which they share with other Christians – has not produced the categories necessary to express this option, which seeks to respond creatively to the new demands of the Gospel and of the oppressed and exploited people of this continent. But in their commitments, and even in their attempts to explain them, there is a greater understanding of the faith, greater faith, and greater fidelity to the Lord than in the 'orthodox' doctrine (some prefer to call it by this name) of reputable Christian circles. (Gutiérrez, 1988, p. 117)

Speaking to Christians on behalf of those who claimed the same identity, Gutiérrez indicated that the oppressed were incoherent only if the dominant discourse held sway. His statement evoked a problem we might call theo-colonial intelligibility, its implications being no less political and economic than theological. He was aware, furthermore, that the problem had to do with the doctrinal formation of subjects. On one side, the problem was exhibited by the poor, who were left without a clear theological option for their own liberation; on the other, it was demonstrated by Christians, whose theological priorities were ill-suited to hearing the poor in their own words. Gutiérrez therefore championed conversion, the very doctrine marshalled to bring subjects into conformity. Drawing upon it deliberately, he recognized its undercurrents as both subversive and unitive, capable of 'bringing to the surface unknown or forgotten aspects of Christian life' (Gutiérrez, 1988, p. 117). In just a few sentences he explained what I take to be the heart of his project:

> A spirituality of liberation will center on a *conversion* to the neighbor, the oppressed person, the exploited social class, the despised ethnic group, the dominated country. Our conversion to the Lord implies this conversion to the neighbor. Evangelical conversion is indeed the touchstone of all spirituality. Conversion means a radical transformation of ourselves; it means thinking, feeling, and living as Christ – present in exploited and alienated persons. To be converted is to commit oneself to the process of the liberation of the poor and oppressed, to commit oneself lucidly, realistically, and concretely. It means to commit oneself not only generously, but also with an analysis of the situation and a strategy of action. To be converted is to know and experience the fact that, contrary to the laws of physics, we can stand straight, according to the Gospel, only when our center of gravity is outside ourselves. (Gutiérrez, 1988, p. 118; emphasis original)

For me, his words indeed bring up many forgotten aspects of Christian life. His statement uniquely resonates with the origins of hospital care, established in the fourth century by St Basil as a preferential option for the poor. Basil's fellow bishop, Gregory of Nazianzus, wrote a fundraising speech urging the same manner of conversion upon his wealthy audience. In Gregory's view, prosperous Christians were failing to respond to the sick and poor, a failure he diagnosed as a misperception of their own well-being. His argument followed the logic of St Paul: when one member suffers, the whole body suffers (1 Cor. 12.26). 'You should revere him who endured wounds and frailty for your sakes,' said Gregory, 'and you will show your reverence if you are kind and compassionate to the one who is a member of Christ' (Gregory, 2003, p. 69).

Oneness was the main idea, and it sprang from the gospel text where Christ self-identifies with the hungry, the sick, the stranger and the prisoner (Matt. 25.35–36). Invoking it, Gregory promoted a shift in consciousness like the one Gutiérrez championed centuries later. It was a conversion from the centre to the margins – or better put, a conversion to a new sense of the centre, where Christ truly is. God was incarnate in the needy. The rich, in turn, were to recognize their own need, becoming one with God in the poor. While other religions of the day sought followers among the healthy and wealthy, the ministry of Christ had instituted a new option, a new ethic that Gregory impressed upon his audience (Larchet, 2002, p. 82). The hospital was to announce a redistribution of power, a radical form of hospitality expressed in solidarity with the afflicted. It was to upend the dynamics of Roman culture, because the rich were not to think of themselves as extending a magnanimous upper hand, playing only the part of host; they were guests, bringing gifts to the one who welcomed them into the kingdom of God. 'While we may,' said Gregory, 'let us visit Christ, let us clothe Christ, let us welcome Christ, let us honor Christ' (Gregory, 2003, pp. 70–1). He then concluded with the following appeal: 'Let us offer to him through the poor who are today downtrodden, so that when we depart this world they may receive us into the eternal habitations in Christ himself, our Lord, to whom be glory forever' (Gregory, 2003, p. 71). The incarnation occurred, so to speak, in the destitute neighbour, who signified a conversion of power manifesting in the shared well-being of eternal life.

The ontology of data

Gregory's vision rested in a frame of mind very different from dialectical materialism – which, despite what Marx imagined, cannot come to rest. While the industrial age indeed gave rise to the struggle of workers against conditions of ownership and domination, it has not led to a classless social order. Many theorists over the decades have repeated that point, from Sartre in the 1960s to Hardt and Negri more recently. 'Capitalism can always escape into the future', as the cultural theorist Byung-Chul Han puts it: 'Accordingly, industrial capitalism has now *mutated* into neoliberalism and financial capitalism, which are implementing a post-industrial, immaterial mode of production – instead of turning into communism' (Han, 2017, p. 5; emphasis original).

Marxism advanced a materialist option for the poor, aiming to emancipate labour from the bourgeois system of religious power. But workers in its wake now participate in a global economy of data, which, as Han points out, 'represents a new kind of *transcendence*' (Han, 2017, p. 7;

emphasis original). To be sure, the immaterial transcendence of data remains bound to industrial processes like rare earth extraction, microchip production and the operation of server farms. But materiality in the digital age has brought about a new formation of our religious instincts – a point Han strengthens with a notable comparison:

> Smartphones represent *digital* devotion – indeed they are the *devotional objects of the Digital*, period. As a subjectivation-apparatus, the smartphone works like a rosary ... *Like* is the digital *Amen*. When we click *Like*, we are bowing down to the order of domination. The smartphone is not just an effective surveillance apparatus; it is also a mobile confessional. Facebook is the church – the global synagogue (literally, 'assembly') of the Digital. (Han, 2017, p. 12; emphases original)

Hyperbolic as it is, Han's metaphor suggests that modern progress has not emancipated people from religion. It has converted people into users, creating a new opiate for the masses, constructing a transcendent power to organize a new set of global devotional practices. Emancipatory work thus requires us to see beyond the modern transcendence apparatus, even as it requires us to admit that freedom from transcendence is a mirage. If we take both requirements into account, the virtues of liberation theology are clear: they present us with a mode of contemplative action beyond the pitfalls of both Marxism and consumer capitalism. In the words of Gutiérrez:

> Where oppression and human liberation seem to make God irrelevant – a God filtered by our longtime indifference to these problems – there must blossom faith and hope in him who came to root out injustice and to offer, in an unforeseen way, total liberation. (Gutiérrez, 1988, p. 118)

The unforeseen event, occurring beyond the gaze of statistical averages, was the incarnation of God.

Through centuries of reflection, that unexpected possibility gave birth to institutions like the first hospital, which nourished its own set of devotional practices to God and the poor. We would do well to contemplate the ground on which those practices rested. Before I turn finally to the field of AI ethics, my wish is to reset the context of the entire discourse. What is AI when data is not, in fact, the transcendent power of the world?

Gregory's speech on love for the poor, though perhaps catalogued today as an esoteric piece of Christian history, is a touchstone of western thought. It continued to gather influence when Maximus the Confessor, almost three centuries later, developed its most profound metaphysical insight: the Logos of God was revealed as One and many, the universal Good in many logoi. Maximus painted a picture that, in its initial outline, appears to be a simple Neoplatonic gloss of what we find in Genesis: the Word of God has spoken words, calling different kinds of being into the created order. From all eternity, says Maximus, the Logos 'contained within himself the pre-existing logoi of created beings. When, in his good will, he formed out of nothing the substance of the visible and invisible worlds, he did so on the basis of these logoi' (Maximus, 2014, p. 95). Nuancing the picture, Maximus goes on to include the virtues among the logoi. Wisdom and justice, for example, find their essence in the one Logos of God. The picture therefore expands beyond a simple taxonomy of species, though it does not yet stray from the tradition of Plato, who likewise defined the virtues as universal ideals.

However – and here is where Maximus breaks new ground – the logoi also occur at the level of individuality (Maximus, 2014, p. 97). Every particular being is a word of God, spoken uniquely in history, known for ever in the Word. The nature of God is to love the particular, which is why particulars exist. It is also why the divine Logos made himself one with all things through his own particular humanity. In his advent as a man, the Word became one flesh with the life of every creature.

Against the tendency to separate the transcendent from the particular, Maximus understood that the two realms are one in Christ, who inaugurates a new reading of everything. The incarnation does not stand apart from other events but draws people and times together. Hence the ministry of Christ begins when he announces the fulfillment of a prophetic hope: he has come to proclaim good news to the poor, to set the oppressed free (Luke 4.18). He celebrates the Exodus of Israel beyond the house of Israel, as when he frees an outcast Gentile from a legion of oppressive spirits. He explains the meaning of love with a story about a good Samaritan, a half-breed who outpaced the religious elite, and he says that whoever cares for the least of society will effectively care for him. Finally, when observing the feast of Israel's liberation, the Passover, he commemorates it as the sharing of his very body. His incarnation is to be an ongoing event, accomplished in particular movements of communion and care. As Maximus puts it: 'The Logos of God, who is God, wills always and in all things to achieve the mystery of his embodiment' (Maximus, 2014, p. 107). A man who loves his neighbour thus incarnates the One who joins all things together; simultaneously, he loves the One who incarnates himself in the hungry, the sick, the stranger, and the prisoner. These many types of Christ, these many logoi, bring about the embodiment of God.

How does that image affect the commonplaces of western philosophy? How does it transform prior notions of materiality, relationality and personhood? More to the point, what does it imply for the status of the poor and the alienated – and what does it mean for us today, as we respond to modern technologies of power?

Universality, intelligence and incarnation

Spivak trusts in the concept of difference over oneness, and for good reason. No two people, no two groups are exactly the same (Spivak, 1996, pp. 17–25). Under the heading of oneness, sameness represents oppression, making subjects intelligible to centralized mechanisms of control. But a theology of liberation brings forth another conception. What we have uncovered, by tracing a line of thought from Gutiérrez back to Gregory and Maximus, is a vision of the One born to Jewish peasants under Roman occupation. He was born, no less, during a time of imperial data gathering, a census that displaced his family to such an extent that he was born outside, among livestock. In the world known by Christian reflection, the Logos joins the masses of people whose agency is restricted by the designs of global power. And from that very subject position he initiates a form of life unanticipated by those designs. His life on earth is a new conception of the universal, a conception from below, realized by loving the One in one's neighbour.

Compelled by that vision, Maximus unified multiple strands of the Greek intellectual heritage, even reaching beyond the Greeks to the Asian East, carving a deep channel where many tributaries flowed together with ease. Yet the heralding of Christ as Logos was more than a synthesis of ideas; it was a new method of listening to others. It restructured the hierarchies that once demoted whole classes of people to unimportant silence. Moreover, it converted philosophical attention from the realm of immaterial forms, casting new light on the materiality of God. As Gutiérrez understood, the incarnation makes a temple from the whole of nature, from the whole of material history: 'The "pro-fane," that which is located outside the temple, no longer exists' (Gutiérrez, 1988, p. 110). The incarnation simultaneously opens a perceptual horizon beyond the bounds of a crudely material dialectic; it presents what Maximus calls 'the marvelous mixture of opposites – God incarnated by means of the virtues' (Maximus, 2014, p. 3). That image reveals another option, a course of action participating not only in material struggle but in the risen life of Christ, ultimately undefeated by the designs of earthly power.

Turning, then, to the field of AI ethics, what forms of insight does liberation theology offer? The first is metaphysical. Instead of a giant data model representing the world and its populations, the One and the many are conceived in the unfolding mystery of God's embodiment. The mystery is inaccessible from above because a true God's-eye view is manifest in receptive encounters with the alienated. A second insight follows. Rather than merely creating AI protocols to mitigate bias and enhance safety, the moral task is to embark on a journey of self-transformation. Spivak thus advocates for an openness to forms of coherence beyond our established frameworks of knowing. 'We must make place for logic not just as the property of Europe', she urges. 'We must make place to see how it is held within other kinds of thick and rich knowledge systems' (Spivak, 2004). Her exhortation conveys the presence of a universality (the Logos, we might even say) known from below, in the diverse excellences of human nature, exceeding any single field or form of knowledge.

'The universal', to quote the womanist theologian Emilie Townes, 'is created in the creolization of discourses, not in the austere terrain of monochromatic abstract conceptualizations spuming from the fantastic hegemonic imagination' (Townes, 2006, p. 38). Her remark follows Paul Gilroy, who wrote about 'the inescapable hybridity and inter-mixture of ideas' in the Atlantic world (Gilroy, 1993, p. xi). Gilroy insisted that the consciousness of European traders and settlers never sealed itself from the Africans they enslaved. Against the racial fantasy of a pure national identity, he argued that there was 'another, more difficult option: the theorization of creolization, métissage, mestizaje, and hybridity' (Gilroy, 1993, p. 2). From the confluence of cultural streams, new expressions of life emerge, crafting innovative cultural forms that change human subjectivity in a relentless pursuit of flourishing.

In this light, AI ethics can hope to transcend the realm of *artificial* intelligence; it can become an exploration of *multiple forms* of intelligence, opening lines of discourse beyond artificially imposed codability structures. By adopting such an approach, AI ethics may incite a profound shift, disrupting hegemonic interest by reshaping the very trajectory of what intelligence means. The point is not to deplatform algorithms. The point is to relativize them, showing that algorithmic rationality is not a pure and universal truth; it is but one language among many – or really a sector of language, a specialized grammar developed in various linguistic suburbs of the modern West (see Wittgenstein, 2009, para. 18).

Of course, the modern suburbs of codability reflect a pattern that now extends across the entire landscape. (One can imagine superhighways and power grids as entailments of its existence.) But despite the changes arising from the coded networks of modernity, human language has always been – and should be – mixed. This, after all, is what the Logos revealed by transforming the paradigms of Greek thought, fulfilling Hebrew Scripture in unexpected ways. The Christian celebration of Pentecost is the exact counterpoint of Babel: a God's-eye view received and multiplied from below in the gift of many languages and cultures.

Building from these insights, an ethical vision for AI calls for a shift towards hybrid knowing, emerging in collaborative, community-based practices that weave AI into a broader pursuit of intelligence. Recognizing that AI may not always benefit communities, developers need to assess their project ideas at the ground level, embracing Spivak's principle of 'learning to learn from below'. Furthermore, they need to explore alternative business models like cooperatives, redefining shareholder interest in terms of the common good. They may yet foster an environment where AI projects can be critically examined, indeed shaped, by the knowledge of people often marginalized by technological change. Such an approach not only counters the hegemony of the mechanical mind; it distinguishes between the superficial aims of bias management and the deeper goal of equity, distributing benefits wisely by integrating justice into the very purpose of model design.

But most importantly, the promise of AI ethics should always be to demonstrate how life, in all its richness and complexity, transcends the logic of a coded world. Coding, at its best, is a partial account of life, and it must support rather than supplant the varied tapestry of human experience – especially where life is silenced by the interests of power. Along those lines we can find a guiding light in the work of liberation theology and subaltern studies. Technologies born of the human intellect – be they linguistic, manual, industrial or digital – are never aloof and remote. They are deeply embedded in the difficulty and festivity of the human condition, which is where Christ said we would find him. The divine Logos invites us to reflect on him in the material conditions of the disenfranchised, incarnating wisdom and justice in whatever we create. As artificers of a plural intelligence, our challenge is to limit and thereby infuse the political economy of data with the truth beyond calculation: love.

References

Associated Press, 1985, 'Reagan Opens Day at NYSE, says he'll "Turn the Bull Loose"', *LA Times*, 28 March.
Bildt, Carl, 2015, 'EU Should Resist the Urge to Rig the Rules of Cyberspace', *Financial Times*, 3 May, https://www.ft.com/content/5d626a4e-f182-11e4-88b0-00144feab7de (accessed 27.01.2025).
Catechism of the Catholic Church, 1995, New York: Doubleday.
Center for AI Safety, 2023, 'AI Extinction Press Release', 30 May, https://www.safe.ai/press-release (accessed 27.01.2025).
Chiang, Ted, 2019, 'The Truth of Fact, the Truth of Feeling', in *Exhalation: Stories*, New York: Vintage.
Crawford, Kate, 2016, 'Artificial Intelligence's White Guy Problem', *New York Times*, 26 June, https://www.nytimes.com/2016/06/26/opinion/sunday/artificial-intelligences-white-guy-problem.html (accessed 27.01.2025).
Crawford, Kate, 2021, *Atlas of AI*, New Haven, CT: Yale University Press.
Department of Agriculture and Farmer Welfare (DACFW), Government of India, 2021, 'Standard Operating Procedure (SOP) for verifying Farmer's Database (100 Villages)', https://drive.google.com/file/d/146TcaGm1BGjpJxsXbWoMK2iGHiEkR5fn/view (accessed 31.01.2024).
Dutchen, Stephanie, 2019, 'The Importance of Nuance: Artificial Intelligence may seem Objective, but it's Subject to Human Biases', *Harvard Medicine*, Winter, https://magazine.hms.harvard.edu/articles/importance-nuance (accessed 27.01.2025).
Fricker, Miranda, 2007, *Epistemic Injustice: Power and the Ethics of Knowing*, Cambridge: Cambridge University Press.
Fung, Brian, 2013, 'The NSA Paid Silicon Valley Millions to Spy on Taxpayers', *Washington Post*, 23 August, https://www.washingtonpost.com/news/the-switch/wp/2013/08/23/the-nsa-paid-google-and-facebook-millions-to-spy-on-taxpayers/ (accessed 27.01.2025).
Gilroy, Paul, 1993, *The Black Atlantic: Modernity and Double Consciousness*, London: Verso.
Greenwald, Glenn and MacAskill, Ewen, 2013, 'NSA Program Taps in to User Data of Apple, Google and Others', *The Guardian*, 7 June, https://www.theguardian.com/world/2013/jun/06/us-tech-giants-nsa-data (accessed 27.01.2025).
Gregory of Nazianzus, 2003, 'Oration 14', in trans. Martha Vinson, *Select Orations*, Washington, DC: Catholic University Press.
Gutiérrez, Gustavo, 1988, *A Theology of Liberation*, trans. Sister Caridad Inda and John Eagleson, Maryknoll, NY: Orbis Books.
Han, Byung-Chul, 2017, *Psychopolitics: Neoliberalism and New Technologies of Power*, trans. Eric Butler, London: Verso.
Haraway, Donna, 2016, 'A Cyborg Manifesto', in *Manifestly Haraway*, Minneapolis, MN: University of Minnesota Press.
Hardt, Michael and Negri, Antonio, 2001, *Empire*, Cambridge, MA: Harvard University Press.
Kaur, Gunisha, 2022, 'The Country where 30 Farmers Die Each Day', *CNN*, 17 March, https://www.cnn.com/2022/03/17/opinions/india-farmer-suicide-agriculture-reform-kaur/index.html (accessed 27.01.2025).

Larchet, Jean-Claude, 2002, *The Theology of Illness*, trans. John and Michael Breck, Crestwood, NY: St Vladimir's Seminary Press.
Maximus the Confessor, 2014, *On the Difficulties of the Church Fathers*, Vol. I, trans. Nicholas Constas, Cambridge, MA: Harvard University Press.
Pentland, Alex, 2014, *Social Physics: How Good Ideas Spread – The Lessons from a New Science*, New York: Penguin.
Perrigo, Billy, 2022, 'Inside Facebook's African Sweatshop', *Time Magazine*, 17 February, https://time.com/6147458/facebook-africa-content-moderation-employee-treatment/ (accessed 27.01.2025).
Perrigo, Billy, 2023, 'Exclusive: OpenAI Used Kenyan Workers on Less than $2 Per Hour to Make ChatGPT Less Toxic', *Time*, 18 January, https://time.com/6247678/openai-chatgpt-kenya-workers/ (accessed 27.01.2025).
Ratzinger, Joseph, 1984, 'Instruction on Certain Aspects of the "Theology of Liberation"', *The Vatican*, https://www.vatican.va/roman_curia/congregations/cfaith/documents/rc_con_cfaith_doc_19840806_theology-liberation_en.html (accessed 27.01.2025).
Sadowski, Jathan, 2019, 'When Data is Capital: Datafication, Accumulation, and Extraction', *Big Data & Society* 6(1), January.
Saha, Sashwata, 2021, 'Why Microsoft's Role in Digitizing India's Land Records is Worrying Farmer Groups', *Newslaundry*, 2 June, https://www.newslaundry.com/2021/06/02/why-microsofts-role-in-digitising-indias-land-records-is-worrying-farmer-groups (accessed 27.01.2025).
Schmidt, Eric and Cohen, Jared, 2014, *The New Digital Age: Transforming Nations, Businesses, and Our Lives*, New York: Vintage.
Scott, James C., 1998, *Seeing Like a State: How Certain Schemes to Improve the Human Condition Have Failed*, New Haven, CT: Yale University Press.
Shiva, Vandana with Shiva, Kartikey, 2020, *Oneness vs. the 1%: Shattering Illusions, Seeding Freedom*, White River Junction, VT: Chelsea Green Publishing.
Snowden, Edward, 2013, 'Edward Snowden: NSA Whistleblower Answers Questions', *The Guardian*, 17 June, https://www.theguardian.com/world/2013/jun/17/edward-snowden-nsa-files-whistleblower#block-51bf2e06e4b03725b2ebf323 (accessed 27.01.2025).
Spivak, Guyatri, 1993, 'Can the Subaltern Speak?', in Patrick Williams and Laura Chrisman (eds), *Colonial Discourse and Post-Colonial Theory: A Reader*, New York: Columbia University Press, pp. 67–111.
——, 1996, 'Bonding in Difference: Interview with Alfred Arteaga', *The Spivak Reader: Selected Works of Gayatri Chakravorty Spivak*, New York: Routledge.
——, 2004, 'The Trajectory of the Subaltern in My Work, Lecture at the University of California, September', YouTube video posted 8 February 2008, https://www.youtube.com/watch?v=2ZHH4ALRFHw (accessed 27.01.2025).
Townes, Emilie, 2006, *Womanist Ethics and the Cultural Production of Evil*, New York: Palgrave Macmillan.
Varoufakis, Yanis, 2021, 'Techno-Feudalism is Taking Over', *Project Syndicate*, 28 June, https://www.project-syndicate.org/commentary/techno-feudalism-replacing-market-capitalism-by-yanis-varoufakis-2021-06 (accessed 27.01.2025).
Wiggins, Chris and Jones, Matthew L., 2023, *How Data Happened: A History from the Age of Reason to the Age of Algorithms*, New York: W.W. Norton.
Wittgenstein, Ludwig, 2009, *Philosophical Investigations*, trans. G. E. M. Anscombe, Oxford: Blackwell.

Zuboff, Shoshana, 2019, *The Age of Surveillance Capitalism: The Fight for a Human Future at the New Frontier of Power*, New York: Public Affairs.

Further reading

AI ethics and AI safety

Broussard, Meredith, 2023, *More than a Glitch: Confronting Race, Gender, and Ability Bias in Tech*, Cambridge, MA: MIT Press.
Criado-Perez, Caroline, 2019, *Invisible Women: Data Bias in a World Designed for Men*, New York: Abrams.
Eubanks, Virginia, 2017, *Automating Inequality: How High-Tech Tools Profile, Police, and Punish the Poor*, New York: St Martin's Press.
Future of Life Institute, 2023, 'Pause Giant AI Experiments: An Open Letter', https://futureoflife.org/open-letter/pause-giant-ai-experiments/ (accessed 27.01.2025).
Lanier, Jaron, 2013, *Who Owns the Future*, New York: Simon & Schuster.
Noble, Safia, 2018, *Algorithms of Oppression: How Search Engines Reinforce Racism*, New York: New York University Press.
O'Neil, Cathy, 2016, *Weapons of Math Destruction: How Big Data Increases Inequality and Threatens Democracy*, New York: Crown.
Ord, Toby, 2020, *The Precipice: Existential Risk and the Future of Humanity*, New York: Hachette.
Tiku, Nitasha, 2023, 'How Elite Schools Like Stanford Became Fixated on the AI Apocalypse', *Washington Post*, 5 July, https://www.washingtonpost.com/technology/2023/07/05/ai-apocalypse-college-students/ (accessed 27.01.2025).
The White House, 2023, 'Fact Sheet: Biden-Harris Administration Secures Voluntary Commitments from Leading Artificial Intelligence Companies to Manage the Risks Posed by AI', 21 July, https://bidenwhitehouse.archives.gov/briefing-room/statements-releases/2023/09/12/fact-sheet-biden-harris-administration-secures-voluntary-commitments-from-eight-additional-artificial-intelligence-companies-to-manage-the-risks-posed-by-ai/ (accessed 19.04.2025).

Catholic engagements

Danielou, Jean, 1951, 'Sacred History and Marxist History', *The Review of Politics* 3(4), October, pp. 503–13.
Dussel, Enrique, 1992, 'Liberation Theology and Marxism', *Rethinking Marxism* 5(3), October, pp. 50–74.
Gaudet, Matthew J., Herzfeld, Noreen, Scherz, Paul and Wales, Jordan J. (eds), 2024, *Encountering Artificial Intelligence: Ethical and Anthropological Investigations*, Eugene, OR: Pickwick.
Pontifical Academy for Life, 2020, 'The Rome Call for AI Ethics', *The Vatican*, https://www.romecall.org/wp-content/uploads/2022/03/RomeCall_Paper_web.pdf.

Other topics covered

Aschoff, Nicole, 2019, 'Tech Billionaires Think SimCity is Real Life', *Jacobin*, 22 May, https://jacobin.com/2019/05/future-cities-tech-giants-alphabet-toronto (accessed 27.01.2025).

Elmore, Matthew, 2022, 'The First Hospital and the Construction of Leprosy', *Dialog* 61(2), pp. 107–11.

Internet Freedom Foundation, 2020, 'Save Our Privacy: A Public Explainer for Feedback on the Agristack', 4 December, https://drive.google.com/file/d/1XC7EyKRQy6VzvvYJ2cswBuoirW8gWGvE/view?ref=static.internetfreedom.in (accessed 27.01.2025).

Sartre, Jean-Paul, 1968, *Search for a Method*, trans. Hazel E. Barnes, New York: Washington Square Press.

Tiwary, Deeptiman, 2014, 'NDA, UPA Failed to Curb Farmer Suicides', *The Times of India*, 3 August, https://timesofindia.indiatimes.com/india/NDA-UPA-failed-to-curb-farmer-suicides/articleshow/39501676.cms (accessed 27.01.2025).

Index of Names and Subjects

Abuiyada, R. 37, 38
Acosta, Alberto 130
AF Consult (now AF Poyry) 95
Africa
  AI ethics 232, 245
  enslavement xiv, 149, 164, 165, 169, 245
  wider discussion 31, 190–1, 206n1
agonistic humanism 186
agriculture and farming
  AI ethics 232–3, 236
  Ao-Naga women 114–15
  genetically modified (GM) crops 79–80, 233
  Jhum 91–2, 94–5, 96, 97, 98
  wider discussion 8, 58, 132, 166
  see also land enclosure
AI (artificial intelligence) ethics 229–46
  liberation theology 229–30, 239–46
  Marxist/material analysis 229–31, 239, 241–2, 244–5, 246
  mechanical mind 235, 237–8, 246
  subalternity 230–3, 237, 239, 244, 245, 246
air pollution 158, 159
Akuno, Kali 22
alcohol use 94, 224

Algeria 190–1, 208n26
Ambrose 202
American Baptist Missionaries 108, 109–11
Anacin, C. J. 67
anthropological rebirth 187, 189–90, 194, 195
Antillean people 38
anti-trafficking paradigm 28, 30, 32, 39–45, 47
Ao, Revd L. Kijung 109
Ao Baptist Arogo Mungdang (ABAM) 119
Ao-Naga people 103–20
  decision-making 103, 105, 113, 115, 117, 118, 120n2
  education 103–11, 114, 117–19
  women 4, 103–4, 105–8, 109, 110, 111–20
apartheid 18–19
Aquinas, Thomas
  De Regimine Principum 199–201, 203
  introduction to 186, 197–8
  'Letter to the Duchess of Brabant' 199–200
  Summa Theologica 198–205
Arab people 8, 16–18, 191
Árbenz, President Jacobo 12
Arendt, Hannah 192
Argentina 100
Aristotle 198, 201, 205

Arju (boys' dormitory) 104–5, 107–8
Armas, Castilla 12
Armed Forces Special Powers Act (India) 95
artificial intelligence *see* AI (artificial intelligence) ethics
Asia 31, 40, 88–9
Assam Education Board 110
atepzung 98–100
Australia 206n1

Bakunin, Mikhail 190
Bamba, Ahmadou 191
Baptist Christianity 108, 109–11, 151
Barber, Keith 80
Bartholomew, Patriarch 173, 174–5
Basil the Great, Saint 201, 240
Beaudoin, Tom 81
Beckford, Robert 177
Bellesa, Mauro 138
Bello, Walden 60
Benjamin, Walter 137
Bevins, Vincent 10
Bhabha, Homi 67, 192
Bhagwan, James 76–7
Bildt, Carl 234
black people
  Antilleans 38
  Brazil's favelas 146, 148, 149
  Brazil's LGBTI+ prison population 215, 216, 219–20, 225
  reparations 185, 194
  UK 158, 170
blood quantum policy 196
bodies/embodiment 138, 139–40, 144, 149, 162
bonded labour 169

botantes 59, 65–6, 69
Brazil
  Christianity 150–7, 212, 222, 225
  demographics 150, 151
  history of 146, 148–9, 152
  mining 129
  see also favelas
Brazil's LGBTI+ prison population 211–25
  human rights 211–13, 214–16, 219–22, 225
  race and racism 215, 216, 219–20, 225
  religion 212, 221–2, 225
  violence 215, 216–17, 222, 225
Brexit 159, 170
Britain *see* United Kingdom (UK)
British Empire 166, 170
British Mandate (1918–45) 15–17, 18, 19
Brown, Marie Alohalani 84
Brumadinho Dam 129
Buber, Martin 176
Butler, Judith 192

Cabnal, L. 138
Cáceres, Berta 129
Câmara, Dom Helder 152–3
Canudos War 146, 149
capitalism
  developmental theory influenced by 37, 44–5
  introduction to xiv–xvii
  religion coopted by 144–5, 149–50, 152, 189
  see also extractivism
Capitalocene 162, 185, 196, 204
Carey, William 87
Carter, Kameron 197
Casado, J. 129

INDEX OF NAMES AND SUBJECTS

Casas, Bartolomé de las xiii
Catechism of the Catholic Church 230
Catholic Action 13, 14
Catholic Church 15, 150–3, 163, 178, 186, 229–30
Central America 12–15
Césaire, Aimé 146, 190
charity, reparations context 192, 197, 201–2, 203, 204
ChatGPT 232, 236
Chiang, Ted 236
Chomsky, Aviva 14
Christianity
  Ao-Naga people 103, 108, 109–11
  Brazil 150–7, 212, 222, 225
  fascism, relationship with 49–50
  frugality 81–2
  further mentions xvi, 20, 43, 46
  humanizing role 191–2
  Northeast India Massif 97
  Palestine 16–17
  Philippines 60
  prosperity gospel 35, 63–4, 69, 150, 156
  see also Aquinas, Thomas; Catholic Church; Church of England; Eastern Orthodox Christianity; *Itneg* community
church buildings 63, 65
Churches and Mining movement 137
church leaders 63, 68, 97, 119
Church of England
  Holy Spirit 159–60, 176–8
  land enclosure 165–8, 170, 171–2
  material analysis 159, 162, 171–2, 177–8

CIA (Central Intelligence Agency, USA) 12
Civil Rights Movement 235
Clark, Dr Edwin Winter 109, 110–11
Clark, Mary Mead 109
Clark Memorial Higher Secondary School 109–10, 118
Clark Theological College 111, 118
class
  AI ethics 229, 241
  Brazil 147, 216
  land enclosure 165–8, 171–2
  plantation labour economics 169–70
  UK 158, 159, 160, 161, 162
class solidarity 17, 18, 22
climate change 36, 162, 169, 196, 205, 233
climate justice 185, 205
Coal India Ltd. 93
Coatsworth, John 12
coexistence, pedagogy of 213, 225
Colectivo de Miradas 138–9
colonialism, definitions 128, 186–7
coloniality, definition 60–1
colonization, definition 164
common good 82, 173, 191, 200, 202, 230, 246, *see also* good life/well-being
common lands 165–6, 167, 168
communion 173–5, 177–9, 230, 243
communism 3, 7, 10, 12, 14, 18, 152–3, 167
commutative justice 199, 200, 202–4, 205

conflict resolution 105, 113, 117, 120
conversion 173, 174, 175, 230, 240-1
Cooperative Business Incubation Program (Indonesia) 11
Cooperative Jackson 21-2, 23
Co-operative Law no. 25/1992 (Indonesia) 10
cooperatives 3-23
 AI ethics 246
 Ao-Naga women 115
 Central America 13-15
 definitions 3-5
 Indonesia 6-11
 Palestine 16-20
 statistics 6, 19
 USA 20-2
cooperative work, *Itneg* community 57, 65-70
Cordillera 57-9, 61, 67
coups d'état 10, 12, 14-15, 200
Covid-19 44-5, 77, 94
craft traditions 80, 96-8, 113-16, 119
Cragoe, Matthew 166-7
Crawford, Kate 229, 235
Credit Suisse Global Wealth Report (2021) 44

dams 94-5, 127, 129
Das, Debjyoti 92
Davis, Ellen 79
decent work 31-2, 41, 50
 definition 30-1
decision-making processes
 Ao-Naga people 103, 105, 113, 115, 117, 118, 120n2
 Itneg community 66, 68
 Pacific region 74, 79
 wider discussion 4, 41, 139, 197

deep solidarity 48-9, 173-9
dehumanization
 Brazil's LGBTI+ prison population 214, 217
 further mentions 4, 84, 164, 168-9
 reparations 186-7, 189-90, 203
 of women 46-7, 104
De La Torre, Miguel 83
development
 definitions 33, 60-1, 88, 90, 130-2
 Itneg conceptualization of 58-9, 61
 Itneg theology of 62-9
Dibang Multipurpose Project 94-5
Diggers 167
dignity
 Ao-Naga women 106
 Brazil's favelas 146, 147, 148, 149, 152, 153-7
 Brazil's LGBTI+ prison population 214, 215, 219-22
 class 162
 extractivism 164, 177
 feminist liberation theology 46-7
 reparations 188, 190
distributive justice 199, 203, 204
divide-and-conquer strategies xv, xviii, 16, 190
Djukurnã, Shirley 127
domestic violence 217, 222, 225
Down, Revd W. F. 109
drug trafficking 154, 217-18
drug use 94, 224
Dulles brothers (John Foster and Allen) 12
Dupuch, Bishop Antoine-Adolphe 191

Dutch East India Company 6

Eastern Orthodox Christianity 173, 174–5, 178
eco-feminism 138–40
ecological justice 83, 164
ecology *see* land and labour
economic growth, measurement options 34
economic justice 21, 46
education
  Ao-Naga people 103–11, 114, 117–19
  Brazil 152, 154, 219
  wider discussion 8, 33, 34, 60, 76
Einstein, Albert 75
El-Kader, Emir Abd 191
El Salvador 15
embodiment *see* bodies/embodiment
England 128, 165, *see also* Church of England; United Kingdom (UK)
enslavement
  Africa xiv, 149, 164, 165, 169, 245
  AI ethics 232, 245
  favelas, formation of 146, 148, 149
  reparations 185, 187, 188, 194, 203
  transatlantic slave trade 164, 165, 168, 169, 171
  see also human trafficking
environmental damage
  climate change 36, 162, 169, 196, 205, 233
  Latin America, extractivism 127, 129–30, 132, 133
  pollution 129, 158, 159

environmental stewardship 163, 166
Esack, Farid 18–19
Eucharist 173–5, 177–9
Europe 186–7, 189, 230, 245
European Commission 30
Evangelical Christianity 14, 150–1, 153, 156, 222
extractivism
  AI ethics 242
  cooperatives, as response 12, 22
  land enclosure in England 166, 167
  Latin America xiv, 127–30, 133, 137–40, 144, 149
  Northeast India Massif 92–5
  Pacific region 78
  reparations 188, 194, 195, 203
  theology of 127–8, 130–8, 164

Facebook 232, 234, 242
Fanon, Frantz
  Black Skin, White Masks 38, 189, 193–4
  interpreted *via* Aquinas 200–1
  nations 89, 187, 190, 192, 195–6
  reparations 187, 188, 193–7, 204, 205
  The Wretched of the Earth 186–93, 194
farming *see* agriculture and farming
fascism 49–50
favelas
  Brazil's LGBTI+ prison population 216, 225
  description of 144, 145–50
  liberation theology 150–7
Fazl Ali College 118

Federal Council of Psychology 224, 225
feminism
  Ao-Naga women 105, 112, 117
  human trafficking, approaches to 31, 42, 44, 46–7
  Itneg community, study of 57, 66, 67, 71n8
  Latin America 138–40
  Northeast India Massif 96
Fiji 74, 77
forced labour 188
forests 93, 94
France 5, 38, 185, 187, 191, 208n26
Francis of Assisi, Saint 173, 174
Francis, Pope
  Laudato Si' 163, 166, 173, 174
  mining 137
Franklin, Benjamin 75
Fraser, John 79
Freire, P. 48
Fricker, Miranda 235
frugality 81–3, 84

ganap 59, 65–6, 69
Gates, Bill 237–8
gender xv, xvi, 33, 36–7, 66, see also men; women
gender identity 213, 215, 217–18, 219–21, 224
genetically modified (GM) crops 79–80, 233
Gilroy, Paul 245
glebe land 167–8
Global Challenges Research Funding (UK) 211
Gómez, M. 130, 139–40
Gonçalves, C. W. 129
good life/well-being
  atepzung 98–100

common good 82, 173, 191, 200, 202, 230, 246
extractivism 133
Fanon 188, 193
Itneg community 59, 63–5, 68–70
material analysis 159, 162
Google 234, 235
Gordon, Lewis 192
Graeber, David 6
Grande, Rutilio 15
Great Commission 170
Gregory of Nazianzus 240–1, 242–3
Gross Domestic Product (GDP) 34
Guatemala 12–15
Gudynas, Eduardo 133–4, 136, 137–8
Guerrilla Army of the Poor (EGP) 14
Gutiérrez, Gustavo 13, 45–6, 230–1, 239–40, 242

Haifa 17
Haiti 185
Han, Byung-Chul 241–2
happiness 88, 89–91, 95, 96, 98, 198
Haraway, Donna 233
Hardt, Michael 234–5, 241
Harris, Melanie 185
Harrison, K. David 83
Hatta, Mohammed 7–8, 10
Havea, Jione 76
Hayes, Nick 166, 168
health care access
  Brazil 148, 152, 219, 221, 224
  UK 159, 161
  wider discussion 14, 36, 41, 80–1, 114

INDEX OF NAMES AND SUBJECTS

Henkel-Rieger, Rosemarie 47–9
Heritage Publishing House (HPH) 118
Hinkelammert, F. 133
Holy Spirit 159–60, 174–9
homelessness 217–18, 224
Honduras 129
hooks, bell 100
Houses of Passage 212, 223–4, 225
Hughes, Robert Davis 174, 177
Human Development Index (HDI) 34
humanism 186
humanity/humanization 187, 189–96, 198, 243, 246
human rights
  Brazil's LGBTI+ prison population 211–13, 214–16, 219–22, 225
  further mentions 15, 18, 21
  marginalized women 32, 37, 103
human trafficking
  anti-trafficking paradigm 28, 30, 32, 39–45, 47
  definition 39
  women's experiences 28–32, 39–44, 47, 50
hybridity 67, 245–6
hydro-electric projects 94–5, 129

identity politics xvi, 161, 162, 196, *see also* gender identity
Igreja do Caminho (Church of the Caminho) 156
Imkongliba Memorial Civil Hospital 118
immaterial reparations 185, 195
Immler, Nicole 207n21
Immoral Trafficking (Prevention) Act (India) 41
imprisonment *see* Brazil's LGBTI+ prison population
Impur Mission Training School 109
incarnation 241–6
India
  AI ethics 232–3, 236
  human trafficking 28, 39, 40, 41, 43, 44
  LGBTI+ prison population 211
  see also Ao-Naga people; Northeast India Massif
indigenous knowledge
  Ao-Naga people 104–8, 113, 115, 116, 119
  atepzung 98–100
  extractivism's impact on 128, 139
  further mentions 88, 189
  pre-development 'wrappings' 131–2
  subalternity 230–3, 237, 239, 244, 245, 246
  time, conceptualizations of 75–84
  see also Itneg community
individual self-interest 81–2, 98, 152, *see also* private property
Indonesia 6–11, 207n21
Indonesian Cooperative Council 7
industrialization 4, 36, 87, 145–6, 166, 241
informal economy
  wider discussion xvi–xvii, 11, 44
  women 29, 30–1, 39–42, 46, 49–50
informal housing *see* favelas
institutional violence 216–17
intelligence, redefinition 245

Intergovernmental Panel on
  Climate Change (IPCC) 36
International Cooperative
  Alliance (ICA) 5, 19
International Court of Justice 18,
  19
International Labour
  Organization (ILO) 30, 45
Isaak, Paul John 175
Islam 6–10, 15–16, 20, 158, 180,
  191
Islamophobia 158
Israel 18–19, 23n5
Israeli Communist Party 17
Itneg community 57–70
  development, conceptualization
    of 58–9, 61
  good life/well-being 59, 63–5,
    68–70
  theology of development 62–9
  women's ministry 57, 65–70
Ixil people, Guatemala 13, 14–15

Jesuits 15
Jesus Christ 154, 176, 178–9, *see
  also* incarnation
Jewish people, in Palestine 15–18
Jhum 91–2, 94–5, 96, 97, 98
John Paul II, Pope 173
Jorhat Mission School 109
Jubilee Memorial College 118
justice
  AI ethics 230, 232, 235, 243
  conversion 173, 174
  Holy Spirit 175, 176
  material analysis 160–3, 171
  see also climate justice;
    commutative justice; ecological
    justice; economic justice;
    reparations; restorative justice;
    social justice

Kempadoo, Kamala 43, 44
Kenya 232, 236
Kharsing, Agnes 94
knowledge *see* indigenous
  knowledge; marginalized
  knowledge
Korten, David 34
Kreider, Alan 20
Kwok, Pui-Lan 174

land and labour 159–65, 168–73,
  177–8
Land Conflict Watch 93
land enclosure 165–8, 170, 171–2
The Land of Despair Sprouts with
  Hope (*Ard el-Ya's*) 20
land ownership 12, 128, 163–4,
  188
Latai, Latu 78
Latin America
  extractivism xiv, 127–30, 133,
    137–40
  history of 130, 144, 146, 239
  informal economy xvii, 31
  liberation theology xiii, 138–40,
    153, 160
Laudato Si' 163, 166, 173, 174
LGBTI+ people *see* Brazil's
  LGBTI+ prison population
LGBTIphobia 214–15, 216–17,
  222
liberation theology
  AI ethics 229–30, 239–46
  atepzung 99–100
  Central and Latin America xiii,
    12, 13, 15, 138–40, 150–7, 160
  deep solidarity 48–9, 173–9
  definition 13
  further mentions 20, 88, 170
  human trafficking, approaches
    to 32, 45–6, 48–9, 50

Itneg community 64–5, 66, 68
  and material analysis 160–2
Logos of God 243–4, 246
London 146, 149, 158
London Missionary Society (LMS) 78
Look East Policy (later Act East Policy) 94
Lugones, M. 67
Luton 158

Maldonado-Torres, Nelson 61
Malik, Bela 91–2
Malik, Kenan 169
Manichean anthropology 189–90, 196, 197
Maoism 94–5
marginalized knowledge 32–3, 37–9, 42–3, 45–9, 51, *see also* indigenous knowledge
Mariana Dam 127, 129
Mari, Naiq 20
Marxism
  AI ethics 229–31, 239, 241–2
  cooperatives 5, 10
Marx, Karl xvii, 134
Mātauranga Māori 80
material analysis
  AI ethics 230, 241–2, 244–5, 246
  land and labour 159–63, 171–3, 177–8
material conditions, Aquinas 198, 200–2
material liberation 187–90, 194
material reparations 185, 195
Maximus the Confessor 243, 244
Mayangnokcha Higher Secondary School 118
Mbembe, Achille 81
McLaren, Brian 81

McNally, David 44
mechanical mind 235, 237–8, 246
Mejía Victores, Óscar Humberto 15
men
  Ao-Naga 103, 104–5, 107–8, 111–12, 117–18
  further mentions 28, 40
mental health 223, 224
Meyer, Matt 22
Michaud, Jean 88–9, 98
Microsoft 234, 236, 237
middle class xiv, 16, 81, 160, 194
migration 29–32, 39–43, 45, 49–50, 196, 205
militarization 94–5, 96, 136
mining
  Latin America 127, 128–30, 133, 137
  Northeast India Massif 92–4
  Pacific region 78
  wider discussion 134–5, 136, 242
Miranda, Moema 132, 137
modern slavery 39, 232
Mokokchung Bible School 111
Mokokchung district 96–8, 109–10, 118
money, link to time 75–6, 77
Montt, General Efraín Rios 14–15
mothers 65, 66, 80, 100, 154
motugā'afa, definition 74
Mullen, Kristen 197
murder 130, 155, 188, 215, 232
Muslimat Mandiri cooperative 11

Naga Customary Law 120n2
Nagaland 96–8, *see also* Ao-Naga people

Nagaland Legislative Assembly 119
Nairobi 232
Nangwaya, Ajamu 22
Naqvi, Syed 9
National Human Rights Program II (Brazil) 214
National Security Administration (USA) 234
nations
 Fanon 89, 187, 190, 192, 195–6
 national solidarity 17
 reparations 89, 185, 187, 190, 192, 195–6, 204
 vs. universality 245
Native Americans xiv, 196, 203
natural law 198–9, 203
Ndlovu, M. 61
Negri, Antonio 234–5, 241
neocolonialism, overview 193
neo-Pentecostal churches 212
Netherlands 187, 207n21
new humanity 187, 189–90, 193–6
New Zealand 206n1
Northamptonshire 166
North Eastern Coalfield (NEC) 93
Northeast India Massif 89, 91–100, *see also* Ao-Naga people

Observatório de Favelas 211
Occupy Wall Street movement xvi, 174
OpenAI 236
Operation Noah 171
Optional Protocol to the United Nations Convention against Torture (OPCAT) 213

Ortega, M. 67
Osman-Elasha, Balgis 36–7
Oxford Centre for Global History 165–6

Pacific region 74–85
Pakistan 23n2
Palestine 15–20
Palestine Communist Party 18
pansayaatan/panpiyaan/pan-amayan (good life) 59, 63–5, 68–70
Pantjasila 7
Pappé, Ilan 16–18
passage houses 212, 223–4, 225
Pastorais Carcerárias 222
Paul III, Pope 203
Payeras, Mario 14
Pentecostal Christianity 62, 150, 151, 177, 212
Pentland, Alex 236
Perrine, Revd S. A. 109
Petrella, Ivan 160, 161, 162
Philippines 57, 59–61, *see also Itneg* community
plantations 94, 169–70, 194
Plato 243
pneumatology 159–60, 174–9
poverty
 AI ethics 230, 232, 240–1
 Brazil's favelas 144, 147, 152, 153, 154–6
 Brazil's LGBTI+ prison population 214, 216, 225
 definitions 46
 further mentions 92, 161, 199
 primitiveness 91–2, 96, 195, *see also* 'savage'/colonialized other
PRISM 234
prisons *see* Brazil's LGBTI+ prison population

private property 165–6, 198–9, 201, 202–3
prosperity gospel 35, 63–4, 69, 150, 156
prostitution/sex work 28, 29, 39–44, 47, 217
Protestant work ethic 78

Queen Anne's Bounty 168, 170, 171
Quijano, Anibal 60–1
Qur'an 9

race and racism
  apartheid 18–19
  Brazil's demographic density 150
  Brazil's favelas 146, 148, 149, 152
  Brazil's LGBTI+ prison population 214, 215, 216, 219–20, 225
  further mentions xv, xvi, 16, 21, 30, 229
  marginalized knowledge 30, 32, 38, 43
  plantation labour economics 169–70
  UK 158, 170
  white supremacy 43–4, 50, 161, 165, 168–72, 229
  see also enslavement
Rahim, Roesli 7–8, 10
Rah, Soong-Chan 82
rainforests 93, 94
Ranawana, Anupama 163–4, 173, 174
Reagan, President Ronald 14, 234
Reddie, Anthony 170
religion
  Brazil's LGBTI+ prison population 212, 221–2, 225

humanizing role 190–2
religious fundamentalism 18, 153, 225
reparations
  Aquinas 197–8, 200, 204, 205
  contemporary debates 194–5
  Fanon 187, 188, 193–7, 204, 205
  Fanon and Aquinas 186, 203–5
  material and immaterial 185, 195
repatriarchalisation 139–40
reproductive labour xvii, 30, 80, 160
restorative justice 117–18
Revolutionary Organization of Armed People (ORPA) 14
Rieger, Joerg
  Capitalocene 162
  deep solidarity 48–9, 173–4
  wider discussion 30, 35, 47, 75, 81, 165
Rio de Janeiro 144, 145–7, 148, 149, 223, 225
Roman Catholic Church 15, 150–3, 163, 178, 186, 229–30
Romero, Archbishop Oscar 15
Roughan, John 76

Sadowski, Jathan 233
Sama 232
Samoa 74–5, 78–83
sanitation 152, 204, 219
São Sebastião Crusade 152
Sarekat Dagang Islam (later Sarekat Islam) 8
Sartori, Vitor Bartoletti 135
Sartre, Jean-Paul 190, 194, 241
Sassen, Saskia 29, 41
'savage'/colonialized other 87, 89, 189, 201

Schleiermacher, Friedrich xiii
Schmidt, Eric 234
Scott, James 236
Scottish Funding Council 211
Senegal 191
sex trafficking 28, 29, 39–44, 47
sexual orientation 213, 215, 217–18, 219, 224
sexual violence 37, 188, 217, 232
Shiva, Vandana 235, 237–8
Shrubsole, Guy 171
slums 146–7, 149
smartphones 242
Smith, Adam 80
Snowden, Edward 234
social justice 9–10, 13, 34, 154–7, 159
solidarity
  AI ethics 241
  atepzung 100
  Brazil's LGBTI+ prison population 222, 225
  cooperatives 17, 18, 19, 21, 22
  deep solidarity 48–9, 173–9
  human trafficking, approaches to 42–3, 45, 47–51
  introduction to xvi, xvii, xviii, xix
  Itneg community 63, 70
  Pacific region/frugality 81–2
  Palestine 17, 18, 19
Solomon Islands 76
Southeast Asian Massif 88
Southeastern Center for Cooperative Development 20–1
South Sea Company 168
Spain 59, 128, 130
Spirit 159–60, 174–9
Spivak, Gayatri 230–1, 239, 244, 245, 246

stigma 30–1, 40, 152, 214–15, 217, 224
structural violence 216–17
student unions 43
subalternity 230–3, 237, 239, 244, 245, 246, *see also* indigenous knowledge; marginalized knowledge
Sufism 191
suicide 155, 237
Sukarnho 7
Sung, Jung Mo 154–5
Sustainable Development Goals (SDGs) 35
Sweden 234
symbolic violence 188, 190

Táíwò, Olúfémi 185, 196
Taylor, John V. 176–7
tea plantations 94
technology 62, 64, 116, 233, *see also* AI (artificial intelligence) ethics
theological education, Ao-Naga people 110–11, 118
theology of development, *Itneg* community 62–9
theology of extractivism 127–8, 130–8, 164
theosis 174–5
Thomas Aquinas *see* Aquinas, Thomas
time, Pacific region conceptualizations of 75–84
tithes 167–8
torture 96, 188, 192, 213, 219
tourism 96
Townes, Emilie 245
trade unions 17–18, 50, 180, 232
transatlantic slave trade 164, 165, 168, 169, 171

INDEX OF NAMES AND SUBJECTS

Truman, President Harry 90
Truth and Reconciliation Commissions 197
Tsuki (girls' dormitory) 104, 105–8
Turner, Sarah 98

Uili, Afereti 79
Ul-Haq, Mahbub 34
Umbanda 222
Unger village, Mokokchung district, Nagaland 96–8
UNIperiferias 211
United Fruit Company (now Chiquita) 12
United Kingdom (UK)
  class 158, 159, 160, 161, 162
  race and racism 158, 170
  wider discussion 5, 78, 187, 211
  see also British Mandate (1918–45); Church of England; England; London
United Nations 6, 34, 147
United States of America (USA)
  American Baptist Missionaries 108, 109–11
  cooperatives 20–2, 23
  foreign policy 10, 12–13, 14, 15, 19, 60
  inequalities 35
  liberation theology 160
  race and racism xv, 21, 196
University of Dundee 211

Vaai, Upolu 76
vagrancy 169
Vale do Rio Doce 129
Van Schendel, Willem 89
Varoufakis, Yannis 233
Veenhoven, Ruth 89–90

violence
  AI ethics 232, 238
  Brazil's LGBTI+ prison population 215, 216–17, 222, 225
  murder 130, 155, 188, 215, 232
  reparations 186–93, 200, 204
Vision 2020 93, 95

Walker, Alison 171–2
Walker, Andrew et al. 11
water pollution 129, 159
water supplies
  Asia 69, 92, 93
  Brazil 129, 152, 219
  further mentions 36, 204
wealth redistribution 188, 192, 193, 195–6, 205
weaving 80, 96–8, 114–15
well-being see good life/well-being
Wesley, John 81–2
white supremacy 43–4, 50, 161, 165, 168–72, 229
Winstanley, Gerard 167–8
women
  Ao-Naga 4, 103–4, 105–8, 109, 110, 111–20
  extractivism's impact on 138–40
  human trafficking, experiences of 28–32, 39–44, 47, 50
  informal economy 29, 30–1, 39–42, 46, 49–50
  Itneg ministry roles 57, 65–70
  marginalized knowledge 32, 37, 42–3, 45–9
  mothers 65, 66, 80, 100, 154
  Northeast India Massif 95–8
  reproductive labour xvii, 30, 80, 160

wider discussion xviii, 11, 36–7, 45
worker cooperatives 5, 8, 11, 16–18, 20–3, 180
working class
 Church of England 159, 160, 162
 race and racism 161, 165, 169–70
 reparations 189, 194, 196
 wider discussion 10, 16, 81, 147
working majority xv–xvi, xvii–xviii

World Bank 92–3, 95
World Social Forums 100

Yahoo 234
young people 20, 31, 154, 217
Yountae, An 197

Zachariah, George 88, 90
Zionism 16, 17, 18–19, 20
Zuboff, Shoshanna 233
Zúñiga, Berta 129

www.ingramcontent.com/pod-product-compliance
Lightning Source LLC
Chambersburg PA
CBHW022041290426
44109CB00014B/933